AF556225

WOMEN IN THE 21st CENTURY

Edited by

Dr. Ram Krishna Mandal

Associate Professor
Dept. of Economics
Dera Natung Govt. College
Itanagar–791 113
Arunachal Pradesh
(INDIA)
Email: rkm_1966@yahoo.co.in

DISCOVERY PUBLISHING HOUSE PVT. LTD.
NEW DELHI-110 002

Published by:
Tilak Wasan

DISCOVERY PUBLISHING HOUSE PVT. LTD.
4383/4B, Ansari Road, Darya Ganj
New Delhi-110 002 (India)
Phone : +91-11-23279245, 43596064-65
Fax : +91-11-23253475
E-mail : parul.wasan@gmail.com
discoverypublishinghouse@gmail.com
web : www.discoverypublishinggroup.com

***First Edition:* 2012**

ISBN: 978-93-5056-147-8

Women in the 21st Century

Printed at:
Shree Balaji Art Press
Delhi

Dedicated

To

Mrs. Archana Mandal

Miss. Anusree Krishna Mandal (Daughter)

Master Avinandan Krishna Mandal (Son)

Acknowledgements

The present study is an attempt at a comprehensive and critical analysis for the role of women in socio-economic development of India with special reference to Education, Entrepreneurship, Micro-finance and Self-Help Groups and overall their entire role in Socio-economic Field.

The present volume is a collection of papers contributed by eminent scholars, academicians, policy makers, bureaucrats and thinkers from different parts of India. The publication of this book would not have been possible without their contributions. Their work is based on diverse source materials which consist of official reports, published journals, books and findings of field work. Most of their writings are based either on the social structural aspects or on the social dynamism and rapid regional socio-economic transformation or on the empowerment of women. I have felt the need to put some of their writings together so as to enable the readers to get an overall idea about the aspect. Some of their writings have been updated, revised and edited for the purpose. I hope that the readers will find it relevant for understanding the four thematic divisions of women in a better way. I hope, this book will benefit immensely the students, researchers, teachers, young scholars, planners and administrators in the area of women study in particular and society of our country in general. I am conscious of the bulk of the work which becomes largely inevitable on account of the intrinsic sweep of the subject. I acknowledge my gratitude to all contributors, whose works are consulted in the preparation of this volume.

I would be falling in my duty if I do not extend my gratitude to my Principal, Shri Tomar Ete, Dera Natung Govt. College, Itanagar, Arunachal Pradesh for generating in me an interest to edit this book.

I also acknowledge the inspiration received from my beloved teacher and guide, Prof. Chandan Kumar Mukhopadyaya, Department of Economics, University of North Bengal, West Bengal. I extend my gratitude to him.

I have received support and cooperation from my colleagues Dr. A.I. Singh and Mrs. Madhuparna Bhattacharjee, I acknowledge a deep sense of gratitude to them.

I am also taking the opportunity to thank profusely to Discovery Publishing House Pvt. Ltd., New Delhi, for publication this book.

Lastly, I am grateful to the members of my family: Mrs. Archana Mandal (wife) and Miss Anusree Krishna Mandal (Daughter) and Master Avinandan Krishna Mandal (son) for their untiring support and patience during the work of this volume.

Dr. Ram Krishna Mandal

Contents

SECTION–II
Women in Micro-finance and Self-Help Groups (SHGs)

SECTION–III
Women Entrepreneurship

SECTION–IV
Women in Education

List of Contributors

Dr. Pavan Mishra, Professor and Director, Rajiv Gandhi Management Institute, Bhopal, (Madhya Pradesh).

Dr. Rambabu Gopisetti, Chairman, Board of Studies in Commerce, Department of Commerce, Telangana University, Dichpally, Nizamabad–503 322. (Andhra Pradesh)

Dr. Meenu Jain, Associate Professor, HOD Dept. of Economics, D.A.V College Yamuna Nagar, Haryana-135001

Ms. Neeru Kang, Associate Professor in Economics, D.A.V College Yamuna Nagar-135 001, (Haryana).

Dr. Ram Krishna Mandal, Associate Professor of Economics, Dera Natung Govt. College, Itanagar–791 113, (Arunachal Pradesh).

Dr. R. Ganapathi, Assistant Professor in Commerce, Directorate of Distance Education, Alagappa University, Karaikudi – 630 003 (Tamil Nadu).

Mr. S. Sannasi, Senior Faculty, Department of Commerce, Park's College (Autonomous), Tirupur–641 605 (Tamil Nadu).

Miss. S.C.Karpagavalle, Assistant Professor Dept of Economics, Bharathiar University, Coimbatore–46.

Dr. A. Sangamithra, Assistant Professor, Department of Economics, Bharathiar University, Coimbatore–641 046, (Tamil Nadu).

Dr. Naagarajan, Assistant Professor, Department of Economics, P.S.G College of Arts and Science, Coimbatore–641 046, (Tamil Nadu).

Mrs. Swati Mathur, Assistant Professor, Rajiv Gandhi Management Institute, Bhopal, (Madhya Pradesh).

Mr. Dulal Ch. Karmakar, Assistant Professor in Economics, P.B.College, Gauripur, Dist. Dhubri, (Assam).

Dr. Mithilesh Kumar Jha, Assistant Professor and Head, Department of Economics, Yingli Government college, Longleng–798 625 (Nagaland).

Mrs. Likha Kiran Kabak, SIRD, Itanagar, P.O.: R. K. Mission–791 113, (Arunachal Pradesh).

Dr. B. Madhura, Assistant Professor, Department of MBA, Vignanabharathi Institute of Technology, H.No. 1-2-342/7/1: Phoolbagh: Domalguda: Hyderabad–500 029 (Andhra Pradesh).

Dr. Preeti Misra, Assistant Professor, Dept. of Human Rights, School for Legal Studies, Babasaheb Bhimrao Ambedkar University, Lucknow–226 025 (Uttar Pradesh).

Dr. Alok Chantia, Assistant Professor, Dept. of Anthropology, Sri Jai Narain Post Graduate College, Lucknow–226 025 (Uttar Pradesh).

Mr. Kaniska Sarkar, Research Scholar of School of Women's Studies, Jadavpur University, 178/A, S.P. Mukherjee Road, Flat No. 1104, Type-III, Kolkata–700 026 (West Bengal).

Dr. K. Usharani, Assistant Professor, Department of Commerce, St Ann's College for Women Medipatnam, Hyderabad–500 028 (Andhra Pradesh).

Dr. Mamoni Sharma, Assistant Professor, Department of Economics, Digboi College, Digboi–786 171 (Assam).

Mr. Sudarshan Prasad Regmi, Research Scholar, Department of Social Science, College of Forestry, Dr. Y.S. Parmar University of Horticulture and Forestry, Nauni (Solan)–173 230, (Himachal Pradesh).

Mr. G.Vanithamani, Ph.D Research Scholar, Department of Economics, Bharathiar University, Coimbatore–641 046, (Tamil Nadu).

Miss. N. Savitha, Research Scholar, Department of Economics, Bharathiar University, Coimbatore – 641 046, (Tamil Nadu).

Mr. Digvijay Singh, Department of MBA, National Institute of Technology.

Introduction

Dr. Ram Krishna Mandal

The status of *women in India* has been subject to many great changes over the past few millennia. From equal status with men in ancient times through the low points of the mediaeval period, to the promotion of equal rights by many reformers, the history of women in India has been eventful. In modern India, women have adorned high offices in India including that of the President, Prime Minister, Speaker of the Lok Sabha, Leader of Opposition, etc. The current President of India is a woman. Scholars believe that in ancient India, the women enjoyed equal status with men in all fields of life. However, some others hold contrasting views. Works by ancient Indian grammarians such as Patanjali and Katyayana suggest that women were educated in the early Vedic period. Rigvedic verses suggest that the women married at a mature age and were probably free to select their husband. Scriptures such as Rig Veda and Upanishads mention several women sages and seers, notably Gargi and Maitreyi. Some kingdoms in the ancient India had traditions such as *nagarvadhu* ('bride of the city'). Women competed to win the coveted title of the *nagarvadhu*. Amrapali is the most famous example of a *nagarvadhu*.

According to studies, women enjoyed equal status and rights during the early Vedic period. However, later (approximately 500 B.C.), the status of women began to decline with the Smritis (esp. Manusmriti) and with the Islamic invasion of Babur and the Mughal empire and later Christianity curtailing women's freedom and rights. Although reformatory movements such as Jainism allowed women to be admitted to the religious order, by and large, the women in India faced confinement and restrictions. The practice of child marriages is believed to have started from around sixth century.

The Indian woman's position in the society further deteriorated during the mediaeval period, when Sati among some communities, child marriages and a ban on widow remarriages became part of social life among some communities in India. The Muslim conquest in the Indian subcontinent brought the purdah practice in the Indian society. Among the Rajputs of Rajasthan, the Jauhar was practised. In some parts of India, the Devadasis or the temple women were sexually exploited. Polygamy was widely practised especially among Hindu Kshatriya rulers. In many Muslim families, women were restricted to Zenana areas.

In spite of these conditions, some women excelled in the fields of politics, literature, education and religion. Razia Sultana became the only woman monarch to have ever ruled Delhi. The Gond queen Durgavati ruled for fifteen years, before she lost her life in a battle with Mughal emperor Akbar's general Asaf Khan in 1564. Chand Bibi defended Ahmednagar against the mighty Mughal forces of Akbar in 1590s. Jehangir's wife Nur Jehan effectively wielded imperial power and was recognized as the real force behind the Mughal throne. The Mughal princesses Jahanara and Zebunnissa were well-known poets, and also influenced the ruling administration Shivaji's mother, Jijabai was deputed as queen regent, because of her ability as a warrior and an administrator. In South India, many women administered villages, towns, divisions and heralded social and religious institutions.

The Bhakti movements tried to restore women's status and questioned some of the forms of oppression. Mirabai, a female saint-poet, was one of the most important Bhakti movement figures. Some other female saint-poets from this period include Akka Mahadevi, Rami Janabai and Lal Ded. Bhakti sects within Hinduism such as the Mahanubhav, Varkari and many others were principle movements within the Hindu fold to openly advocate social justice and equality between men and women.

Shortly after the Bhakti movement, Guru Nanak, the first Guru of Sikhs also preached the message of equality between men and women. He advocated that women be allowed to lead religious assemblies; to perform and lead congregational hymn singing called Kirtan or Bhajan; become members of religious management committees; to lead armies on the battlefield; have equality in marriage, and equality in Amrit (Baptism). Other Sikh Gurus also preached against the discrimination against women.

Women are an integral part in every society. The status of women in society is directly linked with social and cultural traditions, stages of economic development achieved, educational levels, attitude of the society towards women, social and religious taboos, women's own awareness and political attainments for women in society. Such factors affect the national and also regional characteristics of the status of women. The economic status of women is determined by the role played by them in carrying on economic and non-economic activities in society. The nature and type of economic and non-economic role played by women have undergone continued transformation in accordance with the changes in socio-economic factors, education levels and technological developments and with the changing concepts regarding the extent to which women's contribution is desirable and necessary. In the world over it is now recognized that the status of women in society, both in the developed and underdeveloped countries, continues to be inferior to men. Although women's role is crucial in the family and household economy, women have not been given equal rights in social, political as well as economic fields. The necessity of improvement of status of women has been recognized all over the world as an important aspect of national progress and development. It is also felt that the problem of poverty cannot be tackled without providing opportunities of productive employment to women. Productive employment to women would provide necessary economic base and improve their social status. But it is still a fact that women in many countries of the world are facing discriminatory attitude in varying degrees on ground of sex in employment and working conditions.

Women play a vital role in the society. Apart from the matriarchal society, women play a decisive role in most of the patriarchal societies also. The future of children depends, by and large, upon the mothers who generally stay at home and take care of their children's health and education. This is particularly so in countries like India where society and life of people are moulded by traditional and spiritual foundations. Though women are the key factor in the process of change of development, yet in many countries they are underestimated. For example, women in the traditional societies of Asia and Africa take equal part with men in producing foodstuffs, in addition to endless household works, yet their works are not given due weightage. In many parts of rural India women participate equally or even more in some societies with men in various agricultural operations.

According to the International Labour Organization (ILO), there is tendency to under value women's work in rural areas, where they are taken as unpaid family labour, but if it is quantified, the world's Gross National Product (GNP) would increase by 20-30 per cent (ILO, 1981-85). United Nation's Statistics envisaged that women perform 67 per cent of the world's working hours and earn only 10 per cent of the world's income. They have less than 1 per cent of the world's property. Women as human resource in India constitute about 50 per cent of the population and 77 per cent of them belong to rural areas. Majority of them comes from small, marginal and landless families. Their main occupation is agriculture and allied activities, involving them either as cultivator or, agricultural labourers. About 60-70 per cent of labour input is provided by women in production, processing and storage of grain.

In context of Indian women there is a paradoxical picture for the interpreter of Indian Society. Though, the Indian woman is compared to and named as Lakshmi (goddess of wealth), Saraswathi (wisdom) and Durga (Power), yet she is poorest of the poor, less literate than men. She is desolate. In our country where tradition governs, any Indian woman does not stand alone; her identity is defined by her relationship with others, as a daughter, wife or as mother. She is hardly considered as a person in her own right.

In a world where equality is often misunderstood, misinterpreted and exploited for political gains, it is imperative that 'equality' should be redefined. Equality, irrespective of the sex of the individual should promise a life of freedom, choice, opportunities and dignity. The low value for female life is the biggest problem. The desire to have male issues has reduced the chance for girls to be born and thus female infanticide is on the rise. Economic conditions and cultural ethos of India have forged an invisible combination that threatens even the female embryo. Even if a female child is born against such heavy odds, she is not given a chance to survive. She suffers malnutrition, lack of medical attention, early marriage and frequent child births. The crude death rates fostered by abortions and child birth without proper medical care indicate the reduced life span of women. Another major problem is that of illiteracy. Despite a significant increase in the gross enrolment rate of girls in primary schools from 25 per cent in 1950 to 66 per cent in 1980 and 70 per cent in 1982, a large number of girls are still not receiving primary education, while 95 to 100 per cent boys are now enrolled in elementary schools.

Engels, the well-known economist, held that female subordination was the result of the emergence of private property, in particular the private ownership of the forces of production.

Karl Marx had opined that female employment would largely free women from economic dependence on their husbands and so from male dominance within the family.

Sociologists ***Blood*** and ***Hamlin's*** approach was that the employment of the wife outside the home did not appreciable alter power relations within the family: working wives had only marginally more power than whole-time wives.

Viola Klein believed that employment outside the home had some beneficial results; it helped to restore in women their sense of usefulness and renewed their self confidence. Still the mother and housewife role remained primary. There was no evidence from her research data that paid employment produced demands for freedom from traditional female roles.

In our country, the status, role and the various characteristics and problems of women have been culturally much different from the women in the west. In the Post-Independence era, there has been a vast expansion of education and employment opportunities as well as provisions for the protection, welfare and development of our women and many of them are quite modern and advanced like their western counterpart.

Women are the nucleus of our civilization. They have different roles to play in the ever changing social set-up. Women's development is directly related with the nation development. With the dawn of independence our constitution guaranteed gender equality and a large number of schemes and programmes have been initiated for women's development. But the Indian women have to survive in a complex area of socio-cultural, historical, political economic realities.

The International recognition of the status and the problems of women all over the world have resulted in the United Nations declaring 1975 as the international Women's year and the period between 1975 and 1985 as Women's Decade. These are recommendation of the United Nations World Conference (Mexico, 1975) to initiate plans for raising the status of women and for ensuring their full involvement and integration in the process of development at all levels. In India, the appointment of the National Committee on the status of women in 1972 and the publication of its report in 1975 marked the first official attempt to study and recommended changes to improve women's position in society. Declaring 1975 as 'Year of women' by the United Nations, since then there is increased concern of women's sufferings and their empowerment in the society (Medel-Anonuevo: 1995). Very recently the UNDP has brought out its human Development Report 2003, which speaks about the millennium development goals. It lists eight goals out of which the third goal to be achieved is gender equality and empowerment of women. In the budget presented before the parliament for the 2004-05, the Union Finance Minister has spoken about 'gender budgeting'.

Women as an independent target group, account for 495.74 million and represent 48.3 per cent of the country's population, as per the 2001 census. No country can achieve its potential without adequately investing in and developing the capabilities of women. In the interest of long-term development it is necessary to facilitate their empowerment. In many developing countries, including India, women have much less access to education, jobs, income and power than men. Even after five and half decades of planned development Indian women, except a privileged minority, have not achieved expected success in the mainstream of life. If we cannot improve the status and role of women, then our country will be unable to compete over the world.

Women empowerment is a global issue, which has gained momentum in recent decades. In India, besides ratification of international conventions, there are provisions in the constitution and several Legislative Acts have been passed to ensure women empowerment. It however, appears that on this front the situation on ground is far from satisfactory. The position of women and their status in any society is an index of its civilization. Women are to be considered as equal partners in the process of development. But, because of centuries of exploitation and subjugation, Indian women have remained at the receiving end. In this context, in order to provide a big push, Institutional support is necessary to empower Indian women in general and rural women in particular. Women empowerment demands a 'Life-cycle' approach where empowerment is viewed as a process and not as an event, which challenges traditional power equations and relations. Empowerment in its simplest form means redistribution of power that challenges the male dominance. This does not, however, mean that the empowerment process adopts an antagonists approach. It is only to enable women to supplement and coordinate with men. Empowerment is an active process of enabling women to realize their identity, potentiality and power in all spheres of their lives (Sharma: 1992). 'I never define anything', said *Swami Vivekananda* smiling, "Still, it may be described as a development of faculty, not an accumulation of words, or as a training of individuals to will rightly and efficiently. So we shall bring to the need of India great fearless women— women worthy to continue the traditions of Sanghamitta, Lila, Ahala Bai, and Mira Bai — women fit to be mothers of heroes, because they are pure and selfless, strong with the strength that comes of touching the fact of God".

There are several indicators of empowerment. At the individual level, participation in crucial decision-making process, ability to prevent violence, self-confidence and self esteem, improved health and nutrition conditions and at the community level, existence of women's organizations, increased number of women leaders, involvement of women in designing development tools and application of appropriate technology, etc. are very crucial. At national level the indicators are, for example, awareness of her social and political rights, adequate representation in legislative bodies, and integration of women in particular in national development plans, etc.

In India for the first time in 19th century women empowerment movement began under the auspices of Brahma Samaj. Between 1910 and 1920 the number of social organizations for women increased rapidly. Mahila Samities, Women Clubs, Ladies Societies, etc., were formed in different parts of the country linking together women all over India. Activities of these organizations were centred on three fronts namely, health, education and employment. *Swami Vivekananda* summed up the national problems in India in two words: the women and the people. He traced the downfall of India to the continued neglect of our women and of our masses.

Empowerment is a multi-dimensional social process that helps people to gain control over their own lives communities and in their society by acting on issues that they define as important. Empowerment occurs within sociological, psychological, economic spheres and at various levels, such as individual, group, and community and challenges our assumptions about the status quo, asymmetrical power relationships and social dynamics.

Empowerment of women involves many things— economic opportunity, property rights, political representation, social equality, personal rights and so on. The Indian society is a patriarchal system in which women's position within the structure and duties towards the family precede their rights as individuals. Many who argue for empowerment of women do so either with or without a full understanding of the conflicts between the historical and contemporary status of women in the patriarchy and the goals of empowerment. Certainly we may track a great many changes that have occurred in the direction of change in the status of women in India but women have yet to achieve or realize many of the ideal stages of social, psychological, economic and political empowerment. Hence, it is certainly more appropriate to define empowerment as a process rather than an end-point. Empowerment by means of education, literacy or modest income-generating projects is clearly insufficient to ameliorate the prospects for a higher quality of life for women. The process of empowerment is taking place at so many levels that it is quite difficult to gauge the actual nature and extent of empowerment in improving status of women. Certainly the process is entangled in the struggles of civil society against the state, and under the weight of historical practice and ongoing debates over the appropriate role of ideologies. Women constitute 48 per cent of the Indian population, but when we often sermonize human rights, we often forget that women as human beings are also entitled to fundamental human rights. We have denied and continue to deny them basic human rights. Even after 59 years of independence these women continue to live in a state of neglect and exploitation. The concept of women empowerment was introduced at the International Women's Conference at Nairobi in 1985. The term empowerment was defined as "a distribution of social power and control of resources in favour of women". Empowerment is not something which could be made available in the form of a capsule to those whom we think is in need of it. It is not just a concept that could be defined with the help of some universally accepted parameters. Empowerment is a process and includes the following components:

(i) Equal access to opportunities for using society's resources;

(ii) Prohibition of gender discrimination in thought and practice;

(iii) Freedom from violence;

(iv) Economic independence;

(v) Participation in all decision-making bodies;

(vi) Freedom of choice in matters relating to one's life.

Empowerment actually is a process that addresses all sources and structures of power. It is not enough to provide only education to women but they require access to the labour market and employment also. It will however not transform any gender and caste relations. The process has to work on an individual as well as on a collective level. Women have to be organized and acknowledged as a political force also. The process has to challenge both gender and social power relations. It is a process that is much about education, it does not come out of school books. It is a knowledge which has to be expanded. More importantly people should start thinking critically and question it. It generates new notions about power itself. Otherwise when women enter the public structures, given the existing ideology, they operate with the so-called male notions of power which is presented as domination, patronage etc. The question that needs to be answered is that in a society where men control the destiny of women how is it possible to empower women? Before we discuss practical measures and associated difficulties in the process of empowerment of women, let us look at what does the national policy for empowerment of women in India do?

The national policy of empowerment of women has set certain clear cut goals and objectives: The goal of this policy is to bring about the advancement, development and empowerment of women. The policy will be widely disseminated so as to encourage active participation of all stakeholders for achieving its goals. Specifically, the objectives of this policy include:

(i) Creating an environment through positive economic and social policies for full development of women to enable them to realize their full potential;

(ii) The *de-jure* and *de-facto* enjoyment of all human rights and fundamental freedom by women on equal basis with men in all spheres— political, economic, social, cultural and civil;

(iii) Equal access to participation and decision making of women in social, political and economic life of the nation;

(iv) Equal access to women to healthcare, quality education at all levels, career and vocational guidance, employment, equal remuneration, occupational, safety, social security and public office, etc.;

(v) Strengthening legal systems aimed at elimination of all forms of discrimination against women;

(vi) Changing societal attitudes and community practices by active participation and involvement of both men and women;

(vii) Mainstreaming a gender perspective in the development process;

(viii) Elimination of discrimination and all forms of violence against women and the girl child;

(ix) Building and strengthening partnerships with civil society, particularly women's organizations.

The social welfare policies are built on the premise that women lack power, they are denied on basic rights as individuals, limited income and access to resources. It is clear that efforts to improve income and living conditions (the basis of the early social welfare approach) are insufficient in empowering women unless considerations of the basic patriarchal features of society are brought into the equation and the responsibility of states to address its negative effects. Policy makers must also take note of the resistance that women have faced in their entry into public space, and coordinate vigorous efforts to continue legal reform and enhance women's participation in social, economic and political spheres. As we see the discrimination is deep rooted and perpetuated through patriarchy the task to empower women becomes even more challenging. While women in India have the legal right to own land, very few do. For those women who do own land, ownership rarely translates into control of the land or of the assets flowing from the land. The policy prescriptions and legislations assure the equality of right over land for women in India, such as, the Article 25 of the Indian Constitution permits freedom to all. Indian constitution mandates gender equality. The theoretically non-discriminatory nature of law in practice cannot challenge the religious and customary law that guide issues and ideologies on status and treatment of women, property rights related to inheritance, marriage, divorce etc.

The constitutional provisions and amendments to the inheritance laws are not sufficient in themselves to change the patterns of rural land ownership. Increasing women's property rights not just in theory but in practice can positively contribute towards the welfare of poor and would help in bringing about effective change in the nature of current status of poverty as women are more likely to spend income from land on education and meeting the basic needs of children and family. In fact the right over property and land can be an important source of alleviating poverty from rural India. ***Former President A.P.J. Abdul Kalam*** said: *"empowering women was a prerequisite for creating a good nation, when women are empowered, society with stability is assured. Empowerment of women is essential as their thoughts and their value systems lead the development of a good family, good society and ultimately a good nation".*

Education is a milestone for women empowerment because it enables them to respond to opportunities, to challenge their traditional roles and to change their lives. Similar ideas were supported in International Conference—1994. It was said that Education is one of the most important means of empowering women with the knowledge, skills and self-confidence necessary to participate fully in the development process. Educating woman benefits the whole society. It has a more significant impact on poverty and development than men's education. It is also one of the most influential factors in improving child health and reducing infant mortality. At least 60 million girls lack access to primary education and the gender gap in literacy persists till date. Although literacy and school enrolment among both girls and boys have increased dramatically, yet much remains to be done. More and more girls should be enrolled in school, and should complete their schooling. This will become true as the level of education increases. There are signs of progress, as enrolment of boys and girls in primary schools edges closer and closer to parity.

Every year, even at the university level, women are catching up and even surpassing male enrolment in some countries. In Kuwait, Bahrain, the Philippines and Cuba, more women are now enrolling in university than men. Although girls and women's access to education is improving, but they are often channeled into traditionally 'female' fields of study that reinforce their traditional roles in society. As stated in the International Conference on Population Development (ICPD)—1994, countries must recognize: *(i)* The value of ensuring that women begin and complete their education; *(ii)* to eliminate gender bias in all types of educational materials that enforce inequalities between men and women.

Educational programmes for both boys and girls must promote shared responsibilities. As soon as boys begin their education, they need to be taught to take care of their own domestic needs and to share responsibilities at home. Educating both boys and girls in non-stereotyped thinking about male and female roles is critical. Women need to be empowered to become equal to men and thus have equal access to developmental resources and benefits. In order to empower women we need not only to give them more economic power but also bring changes in the entire, social, political and legal systems of the countries because these are responsible for women's lower status in society and the main hindrance in their progress.

Women empowerment came to be associated with social justice and equality. This was real barrier for the feminists and women's movement to grab and thrash the government, law makers, and implementers of laws and point out lacunae in social and political structure which were responsible for women being so powerless. The women groups started evolving strategies to achieve the two goals i.e., equality and social justice. Without further digressing into the issue of empowerment of women whether considered in absolute term or in comparison to men, it is concluded that women's fight is not against men but against the system of patriarchy and all its manifestations. Equality in social systems is a necessary condition for empowerment of women; however it is not sufficient for their development; as development and empowerment are not synonymous. Development refers to "progress of an individual/group in economic, social, political and cultural context" whereas empowerment is defined as "distribution of social power and resources in favour of women".

Education is central to the process of sustainable development. The role of education in empowerment is not only learning of three 'R's (reading, writing and arithmetic) but includes:

- Raising awareness;
- Critical analysis of various structures; and
- Acquiring knowledge for empowerment at all levels.

Education should include not only formal education but also skill training and functional literacy. First and foremost of all is to demystify the myth that girls are not sent to school because they are girls and in view of their primary role as mothers and housewives. Girls and women are not only housewives and mothers but they are also 'workers' in the economic sense. They should be educated to perform an indispensable role in the home and in the household economy, as well as for bringing enlightenment and emancipation. Empowerment of women through education will develop:

- Self-esteem and self-confidence of women;
- A positive image of women by recognizing their contribution to the society, polity and economy;
- Ability to think critically;
- Decision-making abilities and action through collective process;
- Choices in areas like education, employment and health;
- Equal participation in development process;
- Knowledge and skill for economic independence; and
- Access to legal literacy and information relating to their rights.

Participation of women in economic and non-economic activities has been universally recognized as an important element in the adoption of the small family norm, essential for the achievement of the twin goals of economic development and population planning. Such as recognition, however, presupposes not only that existence of a conflict between the economic employment of women and child rearing but also an association between employment of women and their socio-economic status. *Social change is possible only by empowering and educating women. Jawaharlal Nehru once said: "To awaken the people, it is women who is meant to be awakened, once she is on the move, the family moves, village moves and the nation moves". Swami Vivekananda* also once said, "There is no chance for the welfare of the world unless the condition of women is improved. It is not possible for a bird to fly on one wing". Likewise no nation can flourish keeping half of its population in negligence and ignorance, as women constitute half of its human capital. A modern society cannot bring all round development without utilizing the talent of its women.

Until recently, in India as in many other developing countries, the roles of women in the economic activities of the nation were practically ignored. In fact, the preoccupations with specific patterns of economic development often resulted in the relative neglect of women's need and the process of development itself often had some serious negative repercussions on the status of women, thus worsening rather than improving their condition. Today women actively contribute the promotion of economic development in different 'capacities namely as officer, scientist, technician, executive, etc. Now-a-days their work is not confined to family and household chores but has also extended to research fields, factories, offices, administration, science and technology. With the spread of education and training, their mobility has increased and they have come out of their shells to undertake various types of duties and responsibilities. This is mainly to raise the living standard of their families.

Efforts should be made to move beyond land policy and law reform to reforming the laws of succession which continued to disadvantage women even when progressive land and property rights have been enacted. We must also improve land administration and management, secure tenure, and property rights by undertaking practical steps to bring about real benefits to women. In order for legislative amendments to change patterns of inheritance, the social and religious norms that impact inheritance (like bride price practices) must be considered, the public must be educated as to the purpose of the amendments, a plan must be developed for their enforcement, and an effort made to assure that inheritance practices change in accordance with the amendments.

There is a need for an examination of conceptual gaps in linking the formalization agenda more closely to the wider issues of enhancing the rule of law for poor women; a review of existing policies aimed at securing the assets of the poor; a review of existing legal, institutional and financial mechanisms with a view to proposing for the legal empowerment of women;

a review of potential risk factors to be managed proactively in formalization processes, including gender aspects of poverty and development, a programme that could enhance awareness in the media and general public about the benefits that could be gained by formalization approaches, including better legal protection of the assets of the women, and to propose steps that could bring such approaches higher up on the national agenda.

The papers included in this volume are divided under four thematic parts namely: *(i)* Women in Socio-economic Field; *(ii)* Women in Micro-finance and Self-help Groups; *(iii)* Women in Entrepreneurship; and *(iv)* Women in Education. But this division is not exclusive for the volume of *Women in the 21st Century*.

In the First thematic division on "*Women in the 21st Century*", consists of seven papers. Almost all the papers cited about the socio-economic development of women in India and their participation in economic activities.

Dr. Preeti Misra and ***Dr. Alok Chantia in their study,*** "Sexual Harassment with Special Reference to Harassment of Women at Workplace: An Analysis" try to investigate that Women are discriminated even before their birth. One of the severe problems against women is sexual harassment at the workplace. They are subject matter of sexual harassment in each and every society. As the working women go to their workplace regularly they are subjected to chronic sexual harassment by their supervisors, colleagues and other persons.

In his research, "Problems of Family Planning in the Context of Demography: In Some Rural Villages of Bankura District, West Bengal" ***Mr. Kaniska Sarkar*** has seen that weak source of income, lack of education and awareness, superstitions, over all socially degradation is the main signal for the family planning problems in lower caste comparing to general caste. Depending on different nature of problems, the study also analyzes the Government's and N.G.O's activeness and policy for social reform to make a common platform for all; which can be the remedy to solve the problems.

Dr. B. Madhura in her study, "A Study on Employment Conditions of Women in Unorganized Sector in India" has found that the demand for women labour has been increasing consistently as more women entering the workforce by juggling multiple roles (mothers, wives, sisters, daughters) and their by breaking their glass ceilings. Globalize urban Indian women are excelled to become front liners of our times. But unfortunate most of the women workers are engaged in unorganized sector.

In their paper 'SEZs and Women', ***Dr. Meenu Jain*** and ***Ms. Neeru Kang*** have shown that Industrialization has been the forerunner of many social, economic and legal changes in the lives of women. In pre-industrial societies, women remained the domestic helper but in the first half of 19th century, women became the providers, which were traditionally attributed to man. Women contribute significantly in the production. In the industry , women are in great demand due to their cheap labour.

Dr. Meenu Jain in her paper, "Women and 11th Five-year Plan" investigates that women still continue to be discriminated even today in the age of LPG (Liberation, Privatization and Globalization). For growth to be truly inclusive, we have to ensure their protection, well-being, development, empowerment and participation. The vision of 11th Plan is inclusive and integrated economic, social and political empowerment with gender justice.

The Paper, "A Study on Role of Women in the Television Commercials (TVCs)" by ***Dr. K. Usharani*** explains that women are treated as Commodity. Advertising seems to be obsessed with gender and sexuality and continues to represent an arena in which gender display plays a major role. As gender representation is such a dominant feature of modern-day advertising, it is often called the social resource 'used most' by advertisers. The changing role of women in society has created a challenging task for advertisers—how to portray women in advertisements. In this age of liberalization and opening up of our economy to global market forces, women and young girls have became an important target for the media.

Mr. Sudarshan Prasad Regmi in his paper, "Status of Women and Their Role in Socio-economic in Ilam District of Nepal" examines that the involvements of women in saving and credit cooperatives were substantial about 41.33 per cent of which had as high as 53.42 per cent. Similarly, they were attached to other organizations too; of about 14 per cent reported women directly participated to governmental organization, 39.07 per cent and in non-governmental organization, 27.23 per cent. It has been shown that of 41.47 per cent of women reported were fully known about social inclusion and 78.13 per cent stated that all casts' groups and gender should be included without any disparity. It had been observed by analyzing the family planning situation that women had a significant attitude in family planning, average ratio being 10.89: 1 female: male. Use of new technology of information through mobile and get entertained higher by radio or transistor at household level had been advancing their lifestyle.

In the second thematic division on "*Women in the 21st Century*", consists of five papers. Almost all the papers discuss about the empowerment of women through micro finance and self help groups.

In view of ***Dr. Rambabu Gopisetti*** in his paper, "Impact of Self-Help Groups (SHGs), on Women Empowerment: An Emperical Study", Women empowerment is one of the main items to tackle rural poverty and socio-economic issues. The socio-economic impact is examined in terms of the increase in income, savings and assets creation etc. The socio-political impact is examined in terms of entry into politics, change of attitude of husbands towards SHG members and finally, overall improvement in overall status of members of Self-Help Groups.

Mr. Dulal Ch. Karmakar opines in his paper, "A Study of Women Self-Help Groups in the Village of Madaikhali of Dhubri District in Assam" that Self-Help Groups have been playing an important role in reducing poverty of rural people. According to 2001 census, nearly 72 per cent people still live in rural areas. In Indian villages, Self-help Groups, especially women Self-help Groups have undergone revolutionary changes in reducing poverty. Assam is not an exception to that. In the district of Dhubri, total number of SHGs formed is 4139 as on 2003-04 while women SHGs formed 2339 groups.

In the paper "Impact of Micro-finance on Women" by Mr. Digvijay singh it is found that micro-finance is emerging as a powerful instrument for poverty alleviation in the new economy. Micro-finance scene is dominated by Self Help Groups (SHGs) — Banks linkage Programme, aimed at providing a cost effective mechanism for providing financial services to the 'unreached poor'. In the Indian context terms like 'small and marginal farmers', 'rural artisans' and 'economically weaker sections' have been used to broadly define micro-finance customers. Research across the globe has shown that, over time, micro-finance clients increase their income and assets, increase the number of years of schooling their children receive, and improve the health and nutrition of their families. themselves out of poverty. Micro-finance programmes are also acknowledged for having an empowering effect on women.

Dr. Mithilesh Kumar Jha in his study, "Women Empowerment Through Self-Help Groups" investigates that Empowerment is a participatory process of awareness and capacity building which begins at the levels of home and community, adding to greater participation and decision making power and control, and to transformative action enabling individuals or groups to change balances of power in social, economic and political relations in society. Development has social, economic and political dimensions and is incomplete without developing the women who constitute about 50 per cent of the population. Role of women in development is indispensable and community development is unfinished without women's participation and contribution, but women are not always involved in the process of developmental performances which affect their lives. An economically poor individual gains strength as part of a group. Besides, financing through SHGs reduces transaction costs for both lenders and borrowers.

The paper, "Empowerment of Women Through SHG: A Study in Arunachal Pradesh" written by ***Mrs. Likha Kiran Kabak*** and ***Dr. Ram Krishna Mandal*** searches that Women are an integral part in every society. The status of women in society is directly linked with social and cultural traditions, stages of economic development achieved, educational levels, attitude of the society towards women, social and religious taboos, women's own awareness and political attainments for women in society. Although women's role is crucial in the family and household economy, women have not been given equal rights in social, political as well as economic fields. The necessity of improvement of status of women has been recognized all over the world as an important aspect of national progress and development. Women empowerment is a global issue, which has gained momentum in recent decades. In India, besides ratification of international conventions, there are provisions in the constitution and several Legislative Acts have been passed to ensure women empowerment. It however, appears that on this front the situation on ground is far from satisfactory.

In the third thematic division on *"Women in the 21st Century"*, consists of seven papers. All the papers discuss about the entrepreneurship of women and their self- sufficiency.

Dr. R. Ganapathi and ***Mr. S. Sannasi*** seek to find out in their paper, "Women Entrepreneurship and Some Hurdles to Overcome" that the participation of women in economic activities is necessary not only from a human resource point of view but is essential even for the objective of raising the status of women in society. The economic status of women is now accepted as an indicator of a society's stage of development. Therefore, it becomes imperative for the Government to frame policies for the development of entrepreneurship among women. The long-term objectives of the development programmes for women should aim at raising their economic and social status in order to bring them into the mainstream of national life and development. For this, due recognition has to be accorded to the role and contribution of women in the various social, economic, policy and cultural activities.

In their paper, "Women Entrepreneurs: Present Challenges and Future Prospects", ***Dr. A. Sangamithra*** and ***Dr. Naagarajan*** examine that Many women entrepreneurs with home-based and service-related businesses will eventually shift to the information technology industry, making this once male-dominated commerce to be one of equal gender appeal. With progressive changes, the United States economy will refine itself to a financial system that will rely heavily on the internet and e-commerce for their business practices. Enterprises will also focus more on women-related issues and principles. Women entrepreneurs have become a strong driving force in today's corporate world. Not only are they able to equalize their duties of both motherhood and entrepreneurship but they also comprise of almost half of all businesses owned today. Many women entrepreneurs have an average age of 40-60 years old because they have had previous careers in other areas.

Dr. A. Sangamithra and *G. Vanithamani* investigate in their paper, "Women Entrepreneurs in IT Sector: Emerging Opportunities for Developing countries" that India is one of the few developing countries to exploit the opportunities emerged from growth of global IT industry. Participation of women in IT is low in India, but gradually increasing as they constitute 21 per cent of total 650,000 IT workers in the country in 2007 when compared to 15 per cent in 2003. Women business owners are innovators, job creators, and providers of economic security. As owners of small and medium-sized enterprises (SMEs) women can also supply multinational companies with ideas, inventions, technology, raw materials, supplies, components, and business services. Ultimately, female business owners will be recognized for who they are, what they do, and how significantly they impact the global economy.

Again *Dr. A. Sangamithra* and *Miss. N. Savitha* focus in their paper, "Constraints and Prospects of Women Entrepreneurs in IT Sector" that IT sector has brought about changes in the organization of production and labour market situation. The case of India's IT growth is a success story. The gender differential impact of ITs on the labour market is difficult to comprehend as the change is yet to be accomplished and is transitional in nature. In the sphere of ITs production, women are mostly employed at the lower ends, which requires lesser skills. In India, the presence of home based telematic workers has created a lot of debate regarding their informalisation. Younger women who are employed in call centers and software industry, have an edge to acquire skills and prosper in their careers as they are more mobile in comparison to home-based IT workers.

The paper, "Empowerment of Women Through Entrepreneurship" by *Dr. Pavan Mishra* and *Mrs. Swati Mathur* shows that Woman has remained backward owing to many factors though the scriptures laid down an-exalted status for them. In recent years, there has been an increasing awareness and reorganization of the fact women who formed half of the society cannot be ignored. Entrepreneurship of woman will not only enable them to get better jobs and economically self sufficient or independent, but society will also gain. This education must be practically in relation to health nutrition and legal rights.

Dr. Mamoni Sharma in her paper, "Entrepreneurial Career Through Value Addition to Traditional Practices: A Success Story" has explained that The tribal people in the North Eastern Region of India in general have their own life style with distinct production and consumption behaviour. They know how to live with nature and their practices bear high environmental value which was being mostly ignored till few years ago. However, now-a-days the environmental issues become the matter of concern for all over the world and hence the traditional practices have been regaining their weightage. The tribal people of the district in general are very close to nature enjoying an eco friendly life and basically earn their livelihood from agriculture and allied activities. However in recent times they are occupationally diverse. Increasing number of tribal population, lack of job opportunities in their home states, sense of divergence from traditional economic life among the new generation, absence of adequate knowledge about available opportunities and above all, the absence of entrepreneurship zeal among the tribal youths in general are throwing a large number of such youths out of employment. The study is based entirely on primary data collected from direct personal interview with the selected successful entrepreneur.

In the paper, "Entrepreneurial Development: Where is it Heading For?" written by ***Dr. R. Ganapathi*** and ***Mr. S. Sannasi***, it is explained that Entrepreneurial is the risk taker, innovator, facilitator, organizer, employment provider and in shorts the wealth creator. The success of a private economy depends on the blossoming of newer and newer entrepreneurs. In a socialist/ communist economy, the Government may act as an entrepreneur, but admittedly there is a total failure of Government entrepreneurship, as witnessed by the fall of iron curtain economies of former USSR and China. The integration of world economy through globalization has thrown open lot of challenges to entrepreneurs. Of course there are to be taken as opportunities. In this article, the writers have attempted to analyze the role problems and remedial measures for the successful entrepreneurship in India.

In the last thematic division on *"Women in the 21st Century"*, consists of four papers. Almost all the papers have explained about the education of women and their prosperity.

Women are often subjected to the double burden of earning for the family and caring for the children and they are also often excluded from education. Literacy for women may impart knowledge and skills, which enable poor women to improve their earning potential and address their survival needs. The purpose of providing education to women is to make them play a positive role on their own in the development of the nation. It is evident from the empirical research that educational discrimination against women hinders the process of rural development. Expanding educational opportunities for women is desirable for increasing productivity on the farm, greater labour force participation, late marriage, lower fertility, child health and nutrition. Since females constitute a major proportion of the rural labour, it is essential that improved education and skill formation become crucial for better development process. These are investigated by ***Dr. R. Ganapathi*** and ***Mr. S. Sannasi*** in their paper, "Women's Education: A Tool for Rural Development".

Dr. A. Sangamithra and *Miss S.C. Karpagavalle* in their paper, "The Role of Education in Women Entrepreneurship" have tried to find out that Education is seen as "Unique investment" in present and future in reference to Women Empowerment. Access and equality are the two most important components to empower women and to facilitate the delivery of social justice to them. If we want to achieve and sustain a high growth rate must have educate women without any discrimination. Since woman has a prolonged role in procreation, emergency obstetric help must be rendered to all women who experience complications during their pregnancies. "Education is one of the most important means of empowering women with the knowledge, skill and self confidence necessary to participate fully in the development process" says the International Conference on Population and Development (ICPD) Programme of Action. Educated women can recognize the importance of health care and know how to seek help for themselves and their children. Education helps girls and women to know their rights and develop confidence to claim them.

The paper prepared by *Dr. R. Ganapathi* and *Mr. S. Sannasi* on the theme, "Status of Ethics and Values in Educational Institutions" has attempted to sketch that the number of educational institutions in all disciplines has considerably increased in accordance with the growth in population. Due to the introduction of new education policy, the curriculum for all disciplines was changed in a way that it will help the students to understand easily and the examination pattern was also changed to their convenience. This led to the students scoring high marks in all the examinations. Further, due to the entry of private sector in higher education, considerable number of professionals and talented candidates are produced every year by majority of the educational institutions. Nobody can deny this fact. But almost in all institutions, human values are gradually decreasing. We cannot expect good culture from all students. Some students do not give respect to their parents, teachers and elders.

Dr. Ram Krishna Mandal in his paper, "Empowerment of Women Through Education and Some Selected Opinions" has voiced that the Indian woman's position in the society further deteriorated during the medaieval period when Sati among some communities, child marriages and a ban on widow remarriages became part of social life among some communities in India. Still women are fighting hard to get their political justice with limited success in Panchayati Raj Institution where the seats are reserved for 33 per cent of the women. The Women reservation bill is yet to be passed in our parliament which seeks to equalize the advantage of women participation in politics at the national level.

REFERENCES

Aggarwal, J.C.(2004), *"Development and Planning of Modern Education"*, Vikas Publishing House Pvt. Ltd., New Delhi, pp. 273-279.

Alam. K. (1987) *"The Changing Role of Women in the Rural Economy of Assam, Conference Volume of the Indian Economic Association"*. Seventieth Annual Conference, Jaipur.

Anker, Richard (1981), *"Demographic Change and the Role of Women"* in Richard, Anker (ed): Role of Women in Developing Countries, I.L.O. Publications, Geneva, p. 27.

Baruah, S.L. (1992), *"Status of Women in Assam"* Omsons Publications, New Delhi.

Begum, Mustary (2006), *"Women Entrepreneurship in India: Challenges and Strategies"* University News, April 10-16, Vol. 44, No. 15, pp. 13-15.

Bora, M.M. and Bhattacharyya, A. (1996), *"Raising the Status of Plain Tribes Women through Income Generating Training"* in Medhi, K. (ed): Status of Women and Social Change, Women's Studies Research Centre, Gauhati University, Gauhati, pp. 102-03.

Boserup, Ester (1970), "Women's Role in Economic Development, George Allen and Unwin, p. 71.

Chetana, K. (1986), *"Social and Economic Dimensions of Women's Development"*, Discovery Publishing House, New Delhi, pp. 6-9.

Das Lipi, Mishra, S.K. & Nath, N.C. (2006), *"Decent Work and Empowerment of Women in Agriculture"*, Kurukshetra, Vol. 54, No. 7, May, pp. 21-22.

Gulati Leela (1975), *"Female Work Participation: A Study of Inter-state Differences,"* Economic and Political Weekly, January.

Jagdish. P. (1987) *"Women in the Labour Force: A Case Study of Bihar"*, Conference Volume of the Indian Economic Association, Seventieth Annual Conference, Jaipur.

Lah Kar, Bina (1987), *"Development in Women Education"*, Omsons Publications, New Delhi.

Goswami, A.K. (October 1996), *"Women in the Vision of Kalidasa"* in Medhi, K (ed), Status of Women and Social Change", Women's Studies Research Centre, Gauhati University, Guwahati, pp. 54-55.

Mandal, R.K. (2005), *"Socio-economic Transformation of Arunachal Economy"*, Omsons Publication, New Delhi.

Mukherjee, A. and Verma, N. (1984), *"Social-economic Backwardness on Women"*, Ashish Publishing House, New Delhi, p. 24.

Ruhela, S. (1999), *Understanding the Indian Women Today: Problems and Challenges*, Indian Publishers Distributors, Delhi, p. 8.

Singhal. S. (1995) *"Development of Education: Occupation and Employment of Women in India"*, Mittal Publications. Delhi.

Srivastava, Rakesh (2006), *"Role and Importance of Training in Channelising Demand for Participation in Development"*, SIRD-ARUN; Annual Journal of Rural Development, State Institute of Rural development, Itanagar, Arunachal Pradesh, Vol. 1, p. 29.

Sundaram, I. Satya (2006), *"Women Empowerment: Basic Issues"*, Southern Economist, April 1 and 15, Vol. 44, No. 23 & 24, p. 8.

Vashistha, K.C. and Malik, S. (2002), *"Some Strategic Efforts Towards the Empowerment of Women"*, University News, February 4-10, Vol. 40, No. 5, p. 16.

Section–I
Women in Socio-economic Field

Sexual Harassment with Special Reference to Harassment of Women at Workplace *An Analysis*

Dr. Preeti Misra
Dr. Alok Chantia

"Gender equality includes protection from sexual harassment and right to work with dignity, which is a universally recognized basic human right".

In the era of civilization, the old age heinous offences against women are increasing rapidly. Women are discriminated even before their birth. One of the severe problems against women is sexual harassment of women at the workplace. They are subject matter of sexual harassment in each and every society. As the working women go to their workplace regularly they are subjected to chronic sexual harassment by their supervisors, colleagues and other persons. Undoubtedly, sex is a biological need. Every civilized society has some social norms to its citizens to dwell under one roof for the growth and welfare of mankind but the lustful greed for sex is the root cause of sexual harassment, which is a black patch on the face of a civilized society.

Sexual harassment in the form of eve teasing, molestation, sexual assault and rape is a wrong against the honour, dignity and self respect of a woman. It hurts her immensely and throws her in the background. She loses confidence in life and her career is put at stake. There is a strong need for combating this fast growing problem. In a country like India where women are worshipped at par with the Gods, this kind of behaviour against women is unjust, unfair and hippocratic. Sexual harassment at the workplace is a universal problem. Even though the occurrence of sexual harassment at the workplace is widespread in India and elsewhere, this is the first time it has been recognised as an infringement of the fundamental rights of a woman, under Article 19(1)(g) of the Constitution of India "to practice any profession or to carry out any occupation, trade or business". Of late, the problem of sexual harassment at the workplace has assumed serious proportions, with a meteoric rise in the number of cases. Surprisingly, however, in most cases women do not report the matter to the concerned authorities.

In India, Articles 14, 15 and 21 of the Indian Constitution provide safeguards against all forms of discrimination. In recent times, the Supreme Court has given two landmark judgments — Vishakha *vs.* State of Rajasthan, 1997, and Apparel Export Promotion Council *vs.* A .K. Chopra, 1999 — in which it laid down certain guidelines and measures to ensure the prevention of such incidents. Despite these developments, the problem of sexual harassment is assuming alarming proportions and there is a pressing need for domestic laws on the issue. Most developed nations have recognized sexual harassment at the workplace as a serious abuse, resulting from the exertion of power on the victim by the perpetrator. Therefore sexual harassment, in addition to being a violation of the right to safe working conditions, is also a violation of a person's right to bodily integrity. Present paper discusses the meaning of sexual harassment and its growing menace. It also discusses types of harassment and types of sexual harassers along with law dealing with this social malaise.

Meaning of Sexual Harassment

Sexual harassment and rape are two sides of the same coin. Both showcase the power of man to dominate that of women. Both have one victim — 'women'. Both are barbaric in nature; but many people extenuate sexual harassment to rape, just because the victims are not physically harmed. Whereas in rape— the victim is ravished like an animal for the fulfillment of desire and lust of another man. Both have the same object — to undermine the integrity of the victim, physically as well as mentally. Justice Arjit Pasayat has observed that: "while a murderer destroys the physical frame of the victim, a rapist degrades and defiles the soul of a helpless female".

In less graver sense sexual harassment in India is also termed as "Eve teasing" and is described as unwelcome sexual gesture or behaviour whether directly or indirectly as sexually coloured remarks; physical contact and advances; showing pornography; a demand or request for sexual favours; any other unwelcome physical, verbal/non-verbal conduct being sexual in nature. The critical factor is the unwelcomeness of the behaviour, thereby making the impact of such actions on the recipient more relevant rather than intent of the perpetrator. According to India's Constitution, sexual harassment infringes the fundamental right of a woman to gender equality under

Article 14 of the Constitution of India and her right to life and live with dignity under Article 21 of the Constitution. Sexual harassment can occur in a variety of circumstances. Often, but not always, the harasser is in a position of power or authority over the victim (due to differences in age, or social, political, educational or employment relationships). Forms of harassment relationships include:

- The harasser can be anyone, such as a client, a co-worker, a teacher or professor, a student, a friend, or a stranger.
- The victim does not have to be the person directly harassed but can be anyone who finds the behaviour offensive and is affected by it.
- While adverse effects on the victim are common, this does not have to be the case for the behaviour to be unlawful.
- The victim can be of any gender.
- The harasser does not have to be of the opposite sex.
- The harasser may be completely unaware that his or her behaviour is offensive or constitutes sexual harassment or may be completely unaware that his or her actions could be unlawful[1].

For the first time sexual harassment had been explicitly legally defined in India in the case of *Vishaka* vs. *State of Rajasthan and Others*[2], as an unwelcome sexual gesture or behaviour whether directly or indirectly as:

1. Sexually coloured remarks
2. Physical contact and advances
3. Showing pornography
4. A demand or request for sexual favours
5. Any other unwelcome physical, verbal/non-verbal conduct being sexual in nature.

It was in this landmark case that the sexual harassement was identified as a separate illegal behaviour. The critical factor in sexual harassement is the unwelcomeness of the behaviour, making the impact of such actions on the recipient more relevant rather than intent of the perpetrator which is to be considered.

The United Nations General Recommendation 19 to the Convention on the Elimination of all Forms of Discrimination Against Women defines sexual harassment of women to include: "such unwelcome sexually determined behaviour as physical contact and advances, sexually colored remarks, showing pornography and sexual demands, whether by words or actions. Such conduct can be humiliating and may constitute a health and safety problem;

it is discriminatory when the woman has reasonable ground to believe that her objection would disadvantage her in connection with her employment, including recruitment or promotion, or when it creates a hostile working environment".

While such conduct can be harassment of women by men, many laws around the world which prohibit sexual harassment recognize that both men and women may be harassers or victims of sexual harassment. However, most claims of sexual harassment are made by women[3].

Equal Employment Opportunity Commission (EEOC) Definition

In 1980 the Equal Employment Opportunity Commission (in 1984 it was expanded to include educational institutions) defined sexual harassment as:

Unwelcome sexual advances, requests for sexual favours, or other verbal or physical conduct of a sexual nature when:

1. Submission to such conduct was made either explicitly or implicitly a term or condition of an individual's employment.
2. Submission to or rejection of such conduct by an individual was used as the basis for employment decisions affecting such individual.
3. Such conduct has the purpose or effect of unreasonably interfering with an individual's work performance or creating an intimidating, hostile, or offensive working environment.

1 and 2 are called '*quid pro quo*' (Latin for 'this for that' or 'something for something'). They are essentially 'sexual bribery', or promising of benefits, and 'sexual coercion'.

Type 3. known as 'hostile work environment', is by far the most common form. This form is less clear cut and is more subjective.

'*Quid Pro Quo*' Sexual Harassment

'*Quid pro quo*' means 'this for that'. In the workplace, this occurs when a job benefit is directly tied to an employee submitting to unwelcome sexual advances. For example, a supervisor promises an employee a raise if he or she will go out on a date with him or her, or tells an employee he or she will be fired if he or she doesn't sleep with him or her. *Quid pro quo* harassment also occurs when an employee makes an evaluative decision, or provides or withholds professional opportunities based on another employee's submission to verbal, nonverbal or physical conduct of a sexual nature. *Quid pro quo* harassment is equally unlawful whether the victim resists and suffers the threatened harm or submits and thus avoids the threatened harm.

'Hostile Environment' Sexual Harassment

This occurs when an employee is subjected to comments of a sexual nature, unwelcome physical contact, or offensive sexual materials as a regular part of the work environment. For the most part, a single isolated incident will not be enough to prove hostile environment harassment unless it involves extremely outrageous and egregious conduct. The courts will try to decide whether the conduct is both 'serious' and 'frequent'. Supervisors, managers, co-workers and even customers can be responsible for creating a hostile environment.

The line between '*quid pro quo*' and 'hostile environment' harassment is not always clear and the two forms of harassment often occur together. For example, an employee's job conditions are affected when a sexually hostile work environment results in a constructive discharge. At the same time, a supervisor who makes sexual advances toward a subordinate employee may communicate an implicit threat to retaliate against her if she does not comply.

'Hostile environment' harassment may acquire characteristics of '*quid pro quo*' harassment if the offending supervisor abuses his authority over employment decisions to force the victim to endure or participate in the sexual conduct. Sexual harassment may culminate in a retaliatory discharge if a victim tells the harasser or her employer she will no longer submit to the harassment, and is then fired in retaliation for this protest.

Sexualized Environments (Environmental Harassment)

Sexualized environments are environments where obscenities, sexual joking, sexually explicit graffiti, viewing Internet pornography, sexually degrading posters and objects, etc., are common. None of these behaviours or objects may necessarily be directed at anyone in particular or intended as harassment. However, they can create an offensive environment, and one that is consistent with "hostile environment sexual harassment".

Retaliation and Backlash

Retaliation and backlash against a victim are very common, particularly a complainant. Victims who speak out against sexual harassment are often labelled trouble makers who are on their own *power trips*, or who are looking for attention. Similar to cases of rape or sexual assault, *the victim* often becomes *the accused*, with their appearance, private life, and character likely to fall under intrusive scrutiny and attack. They risk hostility and isolation from colleagues, supervisors, teachers, fellow students, and even friends. They may become the targets of mobbing or relational aggression.

Retaliation occurs when an employee suffers a *negative action* after he or she has made a report of sexual harassment, file a grievance, assist someone else with a complaint, or participate in discrimination prevention activities. Negative actions can include being fired, demotion, suspension, denial of promotion, poor evaluation, unfavourable job re-assignment—any adverse employment decision or treatment that would be likely to dissuade a 'reasonable worker' from making or supporting a charge of discrimination. Moreover, a professor or employer accused of sexual harassment, or who is the colleague of a perpetrator, can use their power to see that a victim is never hired again, or never accepted to another school. Retaliation can even involve further sexual harassment, and also stalking and cyber stalking of the victim.

Cost of Sexual Harassment of Working Women

Sexual harassment of women at workplace is likely to have a wide variety of ramifications on the organization, on the employees as well as on the society as whole. It negatively affects morale, motivation and job performance. In order to seek attention to harassment as a social and workplace problem, it is very significant to identify negative/adverse effects of sexual harassment.

Costs on Organization — The concerned organization where the incidents of sexual harassment take place are adversely affected. Sexual harassment leads to workplace tension, which in turn may impede teamwork, collaboration and work performance. Valuable employees can leave the organization which will result in extra monetary load in the form of training, recruiting etc. Financial risks will be increased, when the court action may successfully result in payment of damages and fines. Due to sexual harassment absenteeism rates increase because individual, due to stress reaction, are unable to work.

Lower productivity and organizational commitment are other likely outcomes of sexual harassment which would affect organization adversely. The victims demonstrate poorer work performance in comparison to those who are not harassed. Further, lower job satisfaction and transfer within the organization are other cost on organization. The US Merit Systems Protection Board survey estimates that in 1980 for the 2 years preceding that years survey, sexual harassment cost the federal government $ 189 million for the 2 years preceding the 1987 survey, the cost of sexual harassment was estimated at $267 million further, for the 2 years preceding the 1994 survey (April 1992 to April 1994) the cost of sexual harassment to the government of $ 327 million, the survey of 1994 for preceding 2 years may be summarized as follows[4]:

Job turnover	$ 24.7 million
Sick leave	$ 14.9 million
Individual productivity	$ 93.7 million
Workgroup productivity	$ 193.8 million
Total	**$ 327.1 million**

Costs on Employees — Sexual harassment negatively affects the employee i.e. victim. The consequence of sexual harassment can be devastating in both circumstance while the harassment is occurring and when the employee decides to take action against the harasser…where sexual harassment causes disproportionate numbers of women to feel unwelcome, uncomfortable or threatened in their places of work, or even forced to leave their jobs, it functions as a form of sex discrimination. Allowing it to continue risks many women being reluctant to take traditionally make jobs or jobs in a largely male workforce. Women's equal opportunities are threatened and their position in the labour force undermined when they are dissuaded from applying for higher-status, well-paid, traditionally male jobs. For those reasons sexual harassment has been approached as a form of sex discrimination by emphasizing its discriminatory and prohibiting it in anti-discrimination laws and policies[5].

According to Equaline, the hotline of a women's organization in Korea, many women who seek counseling for sexual harassment feel that for a while they were afraid to meet people and had lost all self-confidence that their mental stress is going to end in mental depression, that they still think about that or that they cannot go outside when it is dark. They also talk about loss of interest in work and feeling ashamed and at a loss of what other people might think. It is too hard for them to stay at the job or they just don't feel like working and have no interest in all anymore in going work[6].

Cost on Society — The incidents of sexual harassment have multidimensional adverse effect on organization, on employee which ultimately negatively affects the society as whole. Sexual harassment impedes the achievement of equality between men and women, it condones sexual violence and has detrimental effects on the efficiency of enterprises and well-being of people, thereby hindering productivity and development. Depending upon the national system for heath case, medical expenses arising form sexual harassment may become a substantial cost to society. As for as physical violence is concerned such expenses are likely to increase in those incidents where an assault leads to injury. The injury may be physical or psychological.

Due to sexual harassment, long-term absenteeism will be carried either in part or in full by society. In addition some workers suffering stress never return to work or become unemployable. For those who do take up work again, fear of the future possibly brought on by new incidents within the workplace may gradually wear the person down psychologically. In both cases, retirement on the grounds of ill health may be a likely outcome. For some, being exposed to violence may lead to welfare dependency preventing individuals from reentering the workplace.

Experience of sexual harassment may represent a potential loss of productivity to targets, witnesses, as well as other people affected by the sexual harassment. This will of course also affect overall productivity levels in a given country especially when premature loss of productive workers and skills are the outcome. Further, the exposure to sexual harassment is likely to affects family and friends. This is particularly the case where a person has become incapacitated by such an event and is in need of both physical care and psychological care in order to deal with the pain and grief. Unfortunately in some cases the experience may lead to a breakdown in relationships and to divorce.

When considering the effects of sexual harassment on society it is worth bearing in mind that people have multiple roles as employees, as customers, as patients, as taxpayers and so forth. Hence the impact of sexual harassment can have multiple costs to society.

Sexual Harassment of Women at Workplace

Sexual harassment of women at the workplace is a fast growing problem in India. The number of cases filed for sexual harassment has risen but women employee are still reluctant to report the matter to concerned authority. Indeed, women suffer it silently and avoid lodging report because she believes that her complaint would disadvantage her in connection with her employment. About half of working women have suffered some kind of sexual harassment at workplace. For the majority of the respondents, mental and physical harassment and gender discrimination have been the most dominant forms of problems relating to sexual harassment. The National Commission for women conducted a survey of working women regarding sexual harassment in 1998-1999 which revealed that 46.58 per cent women who reported facing harassment and discrimination at work, a majority (viz. 68.26%) said that they faced mental harassment caused by acts such as whistling, ogling, winking, passing of level remarks, reciting of obscene songs, abusing, unnecessary, lambasting and sexual gestures.

In India there is a notable gap between the *de jure* and *de facto* situation of women. Flavia Agnes, a noted lawyer and women activist says, "*the power balance is not fair, with the senior harassing you, and even the colleagues do not often lend active support. Women prefer to change jobs for the environment may get hostile*".

A recent case is that of Alka Pande (name changed), ex-director of KPMG — one of the country's leading consultancy firms. She had filed a complaint with the National Commission for Women (NCW) for sexual harassment against two of the firm's senior partners. She has also alleged that once she drew the firm's attention to their misconduct, she was denied, 'avenues of promotion, and her clients were taken away from her'. Alka's case isn't isolated. Sexual harassment at workplace is commonplace.

In *Rupan Deol Bajaj vs. K PS.Gill*[7], a senior IAS officer, Rupan Bajaj was slapped on the posterior by the then Chief of Police, Punjab— Mr. K P S.Gill at a dinner party in July 1988. Rupan Bajaj filed a suit against him, despite the public opinion that she was blowing it out of proportion, along with the attempts by all the senior officials of the state to suppress the matter. The Supreme Court in January, 1998 fined Mr. KPS.Gill Rs. 2.5 lacs in lieu of three months Rigorous Imprisonment under Sections. 294 and 509 of the Indian Penal Code.

In *N Radhabai vs. D. Ramchandran*[8], when Radhabai, Secretary to D Ramchandran, the then social minister for state protested against his abuse of girls in the welfare institutions, he attempted to molest her, which was followed by her dismissal. The Supreme Court in 1995 passed the judgment in her favour, with back pay and perks from the date of dismissal.

In *Vishaka vs. State of Rajasthan and others*[9], the judgement was delivered by J.S.Verma. CJ, on behalf of Sujata Manohar and B.N. Kirpal, JJ., on a writ petition filed by 'Vihska' — a non Governmental organization working for gender equality by way of PIL seeking enforcement of fundamental rights of working women under Article 21 of the Constitution. The immediate cause for filing the petition was the alleged brutal gang rape of a social worker of Rajasthan. The Supreme Court in absence of any enacted law (which still remains absent— save the Supreme Court guidelines as stated hereunder) to provide for effective enforcement of basic human rights of gender equality and guarantee against sexual harassement, laid down the following guidelines:

1. All the employers in charge of work place whether in the public or the private sector, should take appropriate steps to prevent sexual harassement without prejudice to the generality of his obligation, he should take the following steps:

   (a) Express prohibition of sexual harassment which includes physical contact and advances, a demand or request for sexual favours, sexually coloured remarks, showing pornographic or any other unwelcome physical, verbal/non-verbal conduct of sexual nature should be noticed, published and circulated in appropriate ways;

(*b*) The rules and regulations of government and public sector bodies relating to conduct and discipline should include rules prohibiting sexual harassment and provide for appropriate penalties in such rules against the offender;

(*c*) As regards private employers, steps should be taken to include the aforesaid prohibitions in the Standing Orders under the Industrial Employment (Standing Orders) Act, 1946;

(*d*) Appropriate work conditions should be provided in respect of work leisure, health, hygiene— to further ensure that there is no hostile environment towards women and no woman should have reasonable grounds to believe that she is disadvantaged in connection with her employment.

2. Where such conduct amounts to specific offences under the Indian Penal Code or any other law the employer shall initiate appropriate action in accordance with the law, by making a complaint with the appropriate authority.

3. Victims of sexual harassment should have the option to seek transfer of the perpetrator or their own transfer.

As stated by the Supreme Court, these guidelines are applicable to:

(*a*) The employer or other responsible persons or other institutions to prevent sexual harassment and to provide procedures for the resolution of complaints;

(*b*) Women who either draw a regular salary, receive an honorarium, or work in a voluntary capacity- in the government, private or organized sector come under the purview of these guidelines.

Preventive Steps

1. Express prohibition of sexual harassment should be notified and circulated.
2. Inclusion of prohibition of sexual harassment in the rules and regulations of government and public sector.
3. Inclusion of prohibition of sexual harassment in the standing orders under the Industrial Employment (Standing Orders) Act, 1946 by the private employers.
4. Provision should be made for appropriate work conditions for women.

Procedure pertaining to filing of complaints

1. Employers must provide a Complaints Committee which is to be headed by a woman; of which half members should be women.

2. Complaints Committee should also include an NGO or other organization- which is familiar with sexual harassment.
3. Complaints procedure should be time bound.
4. Confidentiality of the complaints procedure has to be maintained.
5. Complainant or witnesses should not be victimized or discriminated against— while dealing with complaints.
6. The Committee should make an annual report to the concerned Government department and also inform of the action (if any) taken so far by them.

Miscellaneous Provisions

1. Guidelines should be prominently notified to create awareness as regards the rights of the female employees.
2. The employers should assist the persons affected, in cases of sexual harassment by outsiders or third parties.
3. Sexual harassment should be discussed at worker's meetings, employer-employee meetings and at other appropriate forums.
4. Both Central and State governments are required to adopt measures including legislations to insure that private employers also observe these guidelines.

The Court emphasized that the guidelines and norms being laid down by it had to be duly observed at all workplaces or other institutions until a legislation is enacted for this purpose and that these should be treated as law under Art 141 of the Constitution. These guidelines are in accordance with the recommendations and conventions of various international organisations like the ILO and the European Communities Commission.

Apparel Export Promotion Council vs. *A.K.Chopra*[10] is the first case in which the Supreme Court applied the law laid down in Vishaka's case and upheld the dismissal of a superior officer of the Delhi based Apparel Export Promotion Council who was found guilty of sexual harassment of a subordinate female employee at the place of work on the ground that it violated her fundamental right guaranteed by Article 21 of the Constitution.

The Supreme Court has held in Apparel Export Promotion Council *vs.* A. K. Chopra, that in any case involving charge of sexual harassment or attempt to sexually molest, the courts are required to examine the broader probabilities of the case and not get swayed by insignificant discrepancies or narrow technicalities or the dictionary meaning of the expression 'molestation'. The Court also held that the statement of the victim must be appreciated in the background of the entire case.

In both cases the Supreme Court observed, that "*In cases involving Human Rights, the Courts must be alive to the International Conventions and Instruments as far as possible to give effect to the principles contained therein- such as the Convention on the Eradication of All forms of Discrimination Against Women, 1979 [CEDAW] and the Beijing Declaration directing all state parties to take appropriate measures to prevent such discrimination*".

These guidelines and judgments have identified sexual harassment as a question of power exerted by the perpetrator on the victim. Therefore sexual harassment in addition to being a violation of the right to safe working conditions, is also a violation of the right to bodily integrity of the woman.

The case of *Vishakha* vs. *State of Rajasthan* led to the formulation of the *Sexual Harassment of Women at Workplace (Prevention) Bill drafted by the National Commission for Women*. It provides for some stern measures to curb the menace of sexual harassment of women at work place. *Recently there was a news that the draft bill on sexual harassment will be passed by the Cabinet in the coming July 2010*. This draft now covers the unorganized sector where women workers have been most vulnerable as well as students[11].

The bill which defines sexual harassment includes any act of verbal or gestural sexual advances, sexually explicit or derogatory remarks or statements, unwelcome sexually determined behaviour such as avoidable physical contact and advances, touching, patting, whistling, pinching, whistling, staring, sexually slanting and obscene jokes, suggestive remarks, compromising invitation, use of pornographic material, demand for sexual favours, threats, innuendoes, physical assault and molestation.

Staring and simple comments on the physical appearance of female colleagues can land a man behind bars for as many as five years and with a fine of Rs. 20 000.

With the enactment of this Act, there will certainly be a decrease in the number of cases of sexual harassment. This Act will prove itself to be a strong weapon in the hands of women to prevent sexual harassment at workplace and combat it.

It may be concluded that sexual harassment is rooted in cultural practices and is exacerbated by power relations at the workplace. Unless there is enough emphasis on sensitization at the workplace, legal changes are hardly likely to be successful. Workplaces need to frame their own comprehensive policies on how they will deal with sexual harassment. Instead of framing committees at the behest of court's intervention, a system and a route of redress should already be in place. The draft bill on sexual harassment attempts to address some of the complexities of this issue, but much more clarity and specificity is needed to avoid the creation of a law that might need another extended campaign of reform.

REFERENCES

1. Heyman, R. (1994). Why Didn't You Say That in the First Place? San Francisco: Jossey-Bass Publishers.
2. AIR 1997 SC 3011.
3. U.S. Equal Employment Opportunity Commission Statistics.
4. A Report by the US Merit Systems Protection Board, *Sexual Harassment in the Federal Workplace Trends, Progress, Continuining Challenges* in Chairmanship of Ben L. Erdreich and Beth S. Slavert at 26.
5. Deirdre McCnn, *Sexual Harassment at Work :National and International Responses.* (Geneva: ILO2005) at 6.
6. Action Against *Sexual Harassment at Work in Asia and Pacific.* (ILO:2001) at 18.
7. 1998 SC.
8. 1995 SC.
9. AIR 1997 SC 3011.
10. AIR 1999 SC 625.
11. *The Hindustan Times* (LKO Edition) Monday 21 June 2010 p. 8.

Problems of Family Planning in the Context of Demography *In Some Rural Villages*

Mr. Kaniska Sarkar

ABSTRACT

The study is based on the population of the three villages namely; Salda, Galia and Hetia in Jaypur Block, Bankura District of West Bengal. The main issue of the study is the problem of population as well as human societies. This problem is very much related with excessive growth of population explosion which must be controlled by proper utilization of family planning. In the study area we see the main problem is family planning. To clarify the reasons, random sample selection is taken for analyzing the socio-economic and cultural pattern and reason for the barrier of family planning in the context of demography of schedule tribe, schedule caste and general caste. Weak source of income, lack of education and awareness, superstitions, over all socially degradation is the main signal for the family planning problems in lower caste comparing to general caste. Different types of socio-economic and cultural groups will be seen by diagrams. Depending on different nature of problems, the study will analyze the Government's and N.G.O's activeness and policy for social reform to make a common platform for all; which can be the remedy to solve the problems.

Introduction

Population characteristics are ever changing. A massive population explosion occurred after the World War II. Coping with this rapid population growth is our primary concern today, as it creates an increasing demand on the already over utilized world resources. This massive increase in population has created problems like housing shortage, rampant hunger, pollution, inflation and unemployment. These problems will further increase as the world's population increases, this call for an understanding society as their patterns of birth, death or migration change.

The word demography is derived from the Greek words, 'demos' means people and 'graphei' means to describe. Thus, demography is the study of the structure of human populations (their distribution by age, sex and marital status etc.) and their dynamic aspects (birth, death, migratory movement etc.). Basically it is a quantitative study of human population. According to Donald Bogue, "Demography is the statistical, empirical, mathematical study of the size, composition and special distribution of human population and changes over time. It involves the operation of the five processes of fertility, mortality, marriage, migration and social mobility. Demography is concerned with virtually everything that influence or can be influenced by population size, distribution of process, structure or characteristics. Fertility, mortality and migration are the dynamic elements of demographic analysis. They are the population processes that lead to change in the social, political and economic structure as well. Population growth occurs as a result of combination of fertility, mortality and migration. At National and International level however, migration is of considerable importance since it relieves population pressure in some places while contributing to growth in other areas—sometimes with beneficial results, sometimes with negative consequences. Apart from these population processes, some other factors are intimately intertwined with population processes. These factors are commonly called population characteristics and they include the distribution of a population by age, sex, race, marital status, education, occupation and income.

Review of Literature

Here we have to say about the previous incident of family planning policy in India which is shown in the article of Dr. A.V. Ramana Kumar's 'India and a one child-policy, Edition in 2003' Here Dr. Ramana Kumar likes to disclose that; the main problem of population explosion in India. In the field of social, economic and culture; the most of the population is bound to face a lot of problems. High growth of population is mainly depending on cheap labour job opportunity and habit of income for family by child labour in India. It means that the poor people is taking the main part to do the population explosion for their existence of life. This economical frame work also weakens the Indian economy as well as nation's development. Dr. Ramana Kumar also showed the bad effect of refugees on socio-economic structure, because the proper strategy could not be accepted to control the population of the poor people as well as refugees by the Government. A lot of policy for poor development has taken by Government but in the field of implementation, all the policies are failure to develop the nation. So it is cleared, the problem of our population explosion and its effect on human society is urgent to prevent.

In the Study of South Asia Research Society, Calcutta and Bureau of Applied Economics and Statistics; 'Population Explosion in West Bengal: A Survey', it is clearly disclosed the account of migration from Bangladesh to India; especially in West Bengal after 1947. In this report we can see the scenario of population explosion and high rate of fertility in West Bengal at that time.

Depending the above two reports the population statistics and circumstances can be observed and as well as the study area is also capable to understand regarding the same subject. But the problem of family planning among different types of castes in the study has not done still now.

Need of the Study

The study area is selected based on a particular social problem; which is family planning problem in different castes. This problem is identified by the different categories of socio-economic and cultural scenario of the society. In the past no such type of job was done particular on the said topic of the human society in the study area. The villages; Salda, Galia and Hetia is suffering for lack of literacy, income, occupation, awareness of good livelihood, awareness of healthy future for next generations in different level in different class of castes. To discuss the problems of the different castes; all the social content of different castes will be analyzed and compared to each other. On another hand the way of remedy and steps to reduce the problem will be also discussed.

Objectives

To study different socio-economic and cultural status of different social community in the study area, we will discuss the literacy rate, income group, level of awareness of family planning, trend of child birth and miss management of abortion process.

1. To enquire the possible reason for the backwardness of knowledge of family planning in different social groups/community, we will also show the level of awareness about the policy.

2. To study the nature of problem of family planning and its difference between castes by comparing in the field of social ingredients.

3. To suggest the possible steps to overcome the problem of family planning, we will also discuss about the remedies.

Conceptual Framework

On this aspect we have to explain about demography and backwardness of family planning. Demography means the scientific study of population in a particular area. It is not only intrinsically valuable in providing data for the statistical estimation of the density of population, sex ratio, fertility and mortality rate and such other information, it is also essential to an understanding of social structure since the organization and other social groups are related to the numerical strength and is modified with the changes in that strength. Data for the study of relation between demographic conditions and social institutions are urgently needed. There fore a census of the village was planned for the elucidation of sociological conditions of the village as the changes of population by knowing in and out-migration civil, moral intellectual condition and so on. In case of statistical data collection we will follow the process of house hold survey and process of data collection from different organizations and related places. The collected data for the study will be analyzed by statistical method to discuss the features of the study area. After having taken the census of the village will come to know; the aspects of relationship pattern, behaviour pattern, education, economy, social awareness, humanity, mentally dimension, culture etc. Demography enriches at the first hand the economic and social features of village prior to conducting intensive field work.

Major Issues and Aspects on the Subject

Lack of education, scarcity of schooling, traditional technique of teaching is the main reason of illiteracy among the poor people. Superstitions among these three groups (Schedule Caste, Schedule Tribe and General Caste) are more or less the main reason for not accepting family planning properly. The study area is very much affected by the wrong interpretation of religious activities and so the communities were affected by the said reasons. Traditional treatment among the Schedule Tribe is not always healthy. These wrong treatments also break up the scientific policy of family planning. Getting political support at grass root level through any kind of policy may harm the technique of family planning specifically among Schedule Tribe and Schedule Caste.

So it is urgent to discuss about the present status of literacy rate, income group, level of family planning awareness, child birth rate and level of dangerous acts due to lack of education and awareness of the people in the study area.

Methodology

The data was derived from A door to door survey was conducted to evaluate the socio-economic back ground and level of knowledge about family planning among the people of study area. Data was also collected from two types of sources: *Primary:* Field work was conducted through questionnaire survey of villagers and interview office staffs; and *Secondary* data got from Literature (reports) from different offices.

The survey covered 60 families which was selected by random process and related to this topic. The demography data were collected from 60 house holds; among which 20 were from the Schedule Caste— 20, Schedule Tribe— 20 and General Caste— 20 house holds from Hetia, Galia and Salda villages of Jaypur Tehsil (Block), Bankura District, W.B. Household and fertility questionnaires/schedule were canvassed and genealogy collected. The house hold schedules were completed with information on age, sex, marital status, place of birth etc. When a member of the household was absent is/her data was obtained from some elder member(s) of the house hold. The fertility schedule was completed with information from married females and the widows on their reproductive performance including wastages. Genealogies were collected by cross checking on fertility data. Information of polygene etc. is also collected. Great difficulties were experienced in the assessment of age as there was no tradition of birth registration and birth days among the Schedule Tribe particularly. Age was therefore estimated by reference to important local events. The same age estimate was used in all analyses. The data on reproductive wastage has not been utilized in view of the possibility that they might be considerable under-reported because of recall lapse. All the demographic data collected were cross checked from several sources where-ever possible.

Family planning among the different caste groups are hampered at study area due to different burning issues like population explosion, weak economic condition/poverty, increasing of no. of illiterate persons, superstitions, increasing of political disturbances, etc.

Study Area

The study area comprises of three villages Salda, Galia and Hetia of Jaypur Tehsil (Block) in Bankura District of State—West Bengal. The district Bankura is situated between 22° 38′ and 23° 38′ north latitude and between 86° 36′ and 87° 46′ east longitude. It has an area of 6,882 square kilometers. On the north and north-east the district is bounded by Bardhaman district. The Damodar River marks the boundary between the two districts. On the south-east it is bounded by Hooghly district, on the south by Paschim Medinipur district and on the west by Purulia district. Bankura district has been described as the "connecting link between the plains of Bengal on the

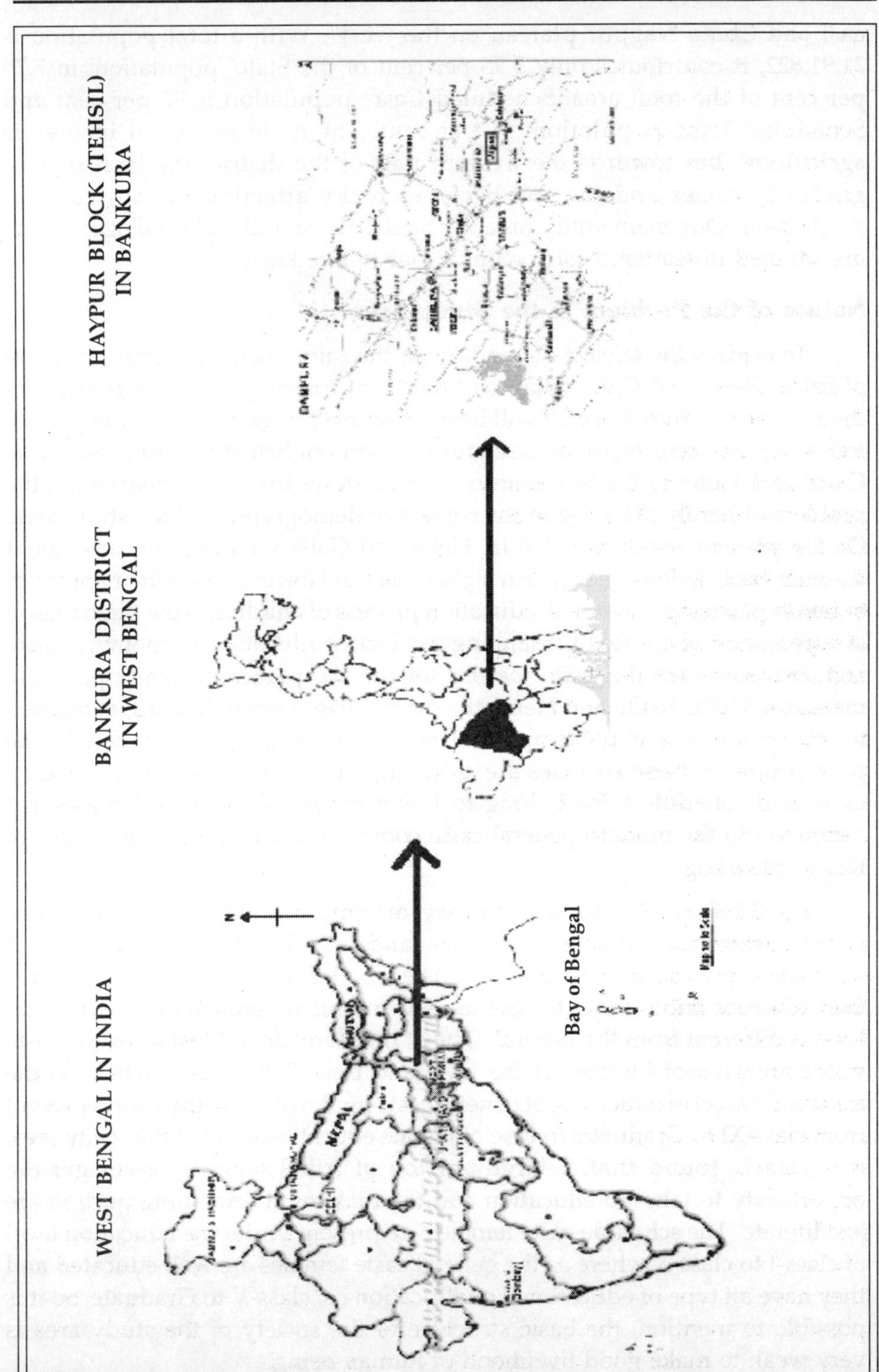
WEST BENGAL IN INDIA
Bay of Bengal
BANKURA DISTRICT IN WEST BENGAL
HAYPUR BLOCK (TEHSIL) IN BANKURA

east and Chota Nagpur plateau on the west". With a total population is 31,91,822, it contributes only 3.98 per cent of the State' population; in 7.75 per cent of the total area. Scheduled Caste population is 32 per cent and Scheduled Tribe population: 11 per cent. The main source of income is agriculture, but towards the western part of the district the land surface gradually raises and the soil becomes rocky affecting the agricultural production. Our main study area i.e. Salda, Hetia and Gelia villages which are situated in scattered form with in four to five km.

Nature of the Problem in the Study Area

To explain the subject depending on the same socio-economic structure of Salda, Hetia and Galia villages of Bankura; some case study reports from the area were selected which will be an example for the present strategy. The following different types of case study reports of Schedule Tribe, Schedule Caste and General Caste community will show the real scenario of "the problem of family planning in the context of demography" of the study area. On the present research in Salda, Hetia and Galia villages; indicates about the main basic difference between higher caste and lower caste in their approach to family planning. The weak education process of children is the main reason of superstition about family planning and lack of education, economy; culture and awareness are the main reasons for the acceptance of family planning measures. Galia, Salda and Hetia; the three villages are backward; compared to other places due to political, social, economic, cultural degradation. So the poor people of these societies are suffering a lot of problems. The schedule caste and schedule tribe belong to lower income groups and backward compared to the modern general caste community particularly in subject of family planning.

Fig. 2.1 shows that for male literacy; maximum of illiteracy rate is present in the community of schedule tribes, and very low level of educational structure is present in the same caste. The schedule caste community is better than schedule tribes though there are fewer male illiterate and its education level is different from the general caste of the study area. Most schedule caste males are present literates at the level and class-V to class-X where as the maximum level of education of general caste (male) of the study area is present from class-XI to Graduate. In case of female education level of the study area, it is clearly found that, a large portion of tribal females never get the opportunity to take up education and the maximum remaining portion are just literate. The schedule caste females are present under the education level of class-I to class-X where as the general caste females are well educated and they have all type of educational qualification i.e. class-V to Graduate. So it is possible to mention, the basic structure of the society of the study area is very weak to make good livelihood of human being.

Table & Fig. 2.1: Literacy Rate (In Percentage) of Three Castes in Study Area

LITERACY RATE OF MALE			
	GEN	SC	ST
ILLITERATE	0	3.33	11.67
LITERATE	0	16.67	11.67
I-IV	0	1.67	1.67
V-X	6.67	10	8.33
XI-XII	8.33	1.67	0
GRADUATE	18.33	0	0

LITERACY RATE OF FEMALE			
	GEN	SC	ST
ILLITERATE	0	5	20
LITERATE	0	3.34	11.67
I-IV	0	10	1.67
V-X	11.67	10	0
XI-XII	10	1.67	0
GRADUATE	11.67	0	0

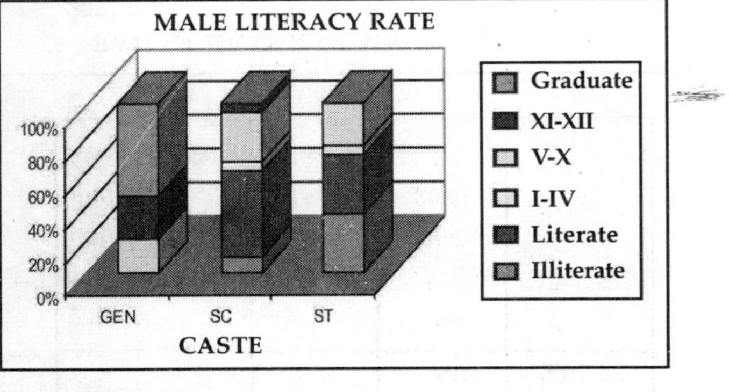

FEMALE LITERACY RATE

100%
80%
60%
40%
20%
0%

GEN SC ST

CASTE

Graduate
XI-XII
V-X
I-IV
Literate
Illiterate

Source: Household survey.

Table & Fig. 2.2: Income Rate (In Percentage) of Three Castes in the Study Area

RATE OF INCOME OF MALE			
	GEN	SC	ST
NIL	0	3.33	0
500-1000	0	0	5
1001-5000	1.67	0	26.67
5001-10000	16.67	26.67	1.67
Above 10000	15	3.33	0

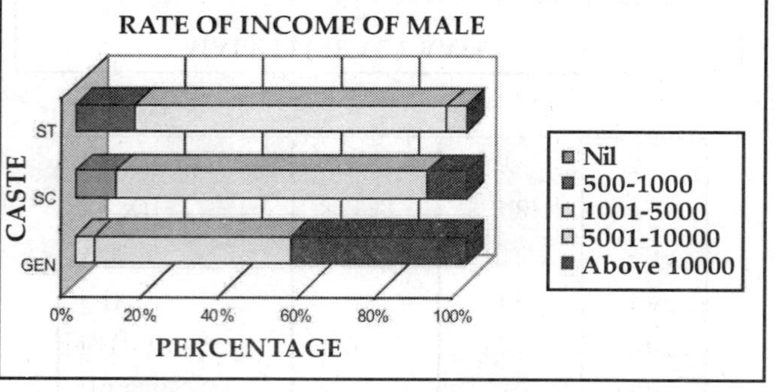

RATE OF INCOME OF FEMALE			
	GEN	SC	ST
NIL	31.67	28.33	25
500-1000	0	3.33	6.67
1001-5000	0	0	1.67
5001-10000	0	1.67	0
Above 10000	1.67	0	0

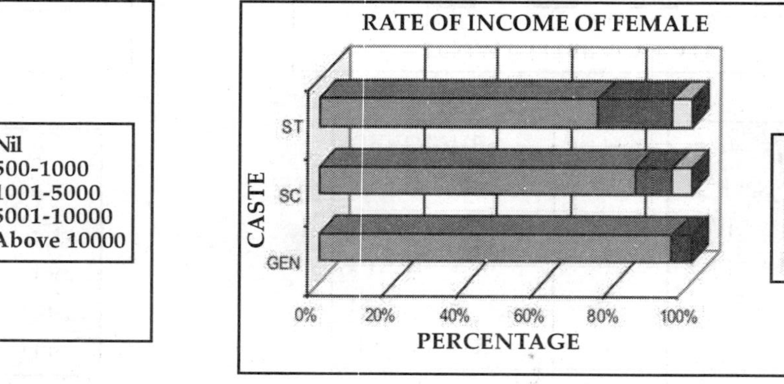

Source: Data from household survey and panchayat office.

To clarify the economic status of these three castes; it clear that maximum of male schedule tribes belong to the income group of Rs. 1000 to 5000, whereas the same population community in schedule caste belong to the income group of Rs. 5000 to 10000. After comparing with these two castes it is also necessary to mention that; maximum of male general caste of the study area belong to the income group of Rs. 5000 to above 10000. On the other hand in case of female economic status; maximum of females do not earn. A few of them in case of general caste is belonging in the group Rs. >10000. In case of schedule caste they belonging to the income group of Rs. 500 to 1000 and in case of schedule tribe is belong in the group of Rs. 500 to 1000 and a little portion is in Rs. 1001 to 5000.

So the economic condition of the study area is very poor. Basically the female income is very low, which is the main obstacle on the way of awareness for family planning.

Table & Fig. 2.3: Awareness of Family Planning Among the Three Castes

AWARENESS LEVEL ABOUT FAMILY PLANNING			
	GEN	SC	ST
HUSBAND	18	6	0
WIFE	19	4	1

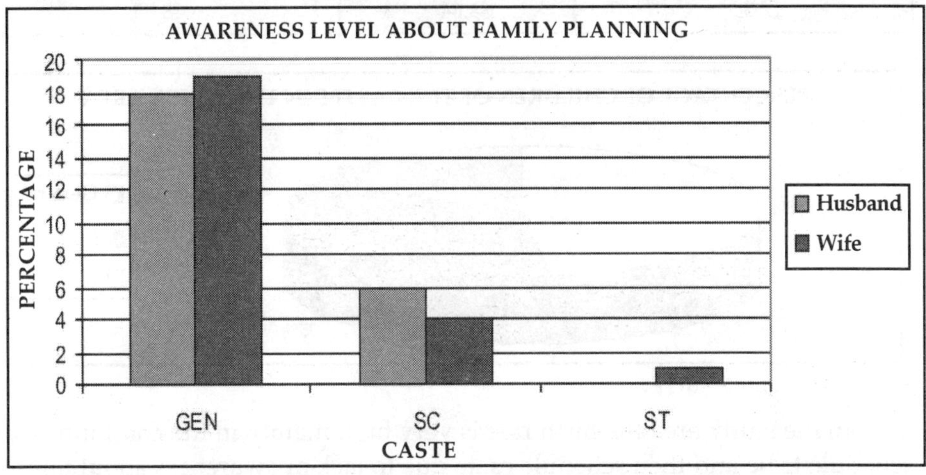

Source: Door to door survey.

After discussing the literacy rate and economic status of the study area; it is possible to interpret the level of awareness of family planning among these three castes. In order to assess the extent of knowledge ability about family planning programme and practices, it was proposed to administer a questionnaire schedule specifically designed for this purpose. Twenty couples were interviewed among the schedule tribe, schedule caste and general caste each. Most information was collected from the females. In very little case I took help from the males. I compare these three groups according to the attitude and reasons for adoption and non-adoption of family planning, live birth's by wife's educational status, source of information regarding family planning, methods choice of respondents, desired family size and actual size and reasons for preferring a male child According to the above given diagram; it is found that; females- 31.67 per cent in general caste is present in the highest position in case of awareness of family planning, where as male of general caste is 30 per cent. In case of schedule caste community only 6.67 per cent of females are concerned about the family planning and 10 per cent male. But no male person in schedule tribe community is concerned about the family planning though 1.67 per cent of females know about the family planning. So it is clear that, the family planning knowledge is not available among the community of schedule caste and schedule tribe compared with general caste.

Table & Fig. 2.4: Trend of Child Birth Among the Three Castes of the Study Area

PERCENTAGE OF CHILDREN AMONG THE THREE CASTES

GEN	SC	ST
17.32	34.64	48.05

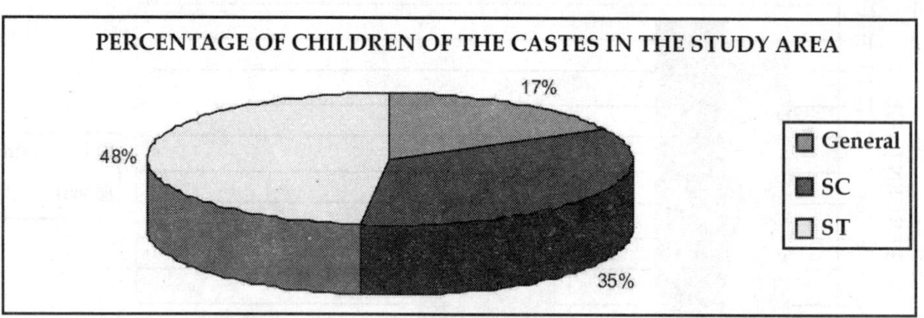

Source: Household survey.

In the study area the birth rate is very high mainly in the community of schedule tribe and then schedule caste due to lack of awareness about family planning which is dependent on education, well source of income, culture, government aid, well communication between all social groups. In my study it is found that, the child birth rate is very high (48.05%) in schedule tribe community; followed by schedule caste- 34.64 per cent. This disturbs the population balance. It is also found that, 17.32 per cent birth rate is present in general caste which proves that; the awareness of family planning in this community works very well. During the survey it was also realized that the schedule tribes and schedule castes are superstitions, this prevents them from accepting of family planning.

Table & Fig. 2.5: Rate of Criminal Abortion Among the Three Castes

GEN	SC	ST
0%	52.17%	47.83%

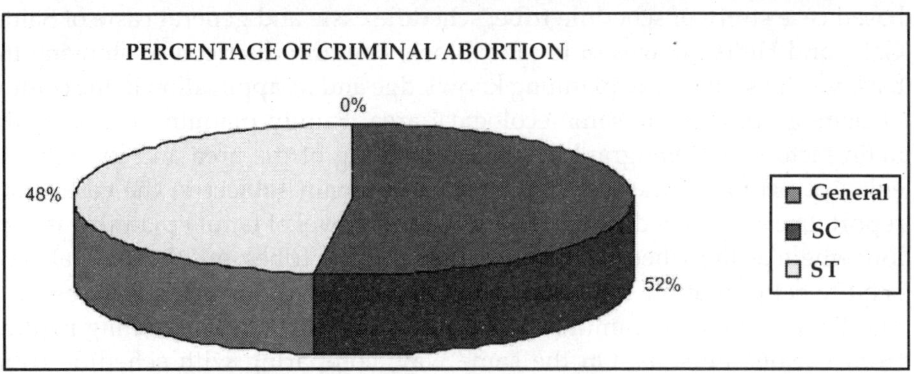

Source: Data from village Dai and clinics.

Backwardness of family planning in the study area is not only the problem in socio-economic factor; it is also a big dangerous problem of human life. The lack of family planning awareness and wrong decision to maintain family planning among the schedule castes and schedule tribes exposes human life to danger. In this circumstances it is found that; the wrong decision about abortion after 20 weeks of pregnancy which called as criminal abortion, may causes death of women. This type of criminal abortion is generally done by rural Dai, illegal clinics, non-register practitioners, etc. In the study area it is also found, 52.17 per cent of schedule tribe women and 47.83 per cent of schedule caste women did the criminal abortion. And the women as well as their husbands or relatives had no proper awareness about the family planning. In case of general caste; not a single case was found for criminal abortion during the study. So it is also mentioned; the awareness of family planning is differed from different castes in the study area.

DISCUSSION

Remarks

The present study is to compare between three genetically distinct ethic groups such as general caste which is placed at the highest rank of the Hindu caste ladder and the schedule tribe which may be placed at the lowest stratum of the same ladder, and schedule caste which may be placed at more or less middle of the same ladder. Both the ethnic groups are studied under same ecological niche i.e. Rarh (plain land) region in Joy Pur Block of the district of Bankura, West Bnegal. They have much socio-economic and cultural relationship in relation to land to each other. Here we observed the similarities and dissimilarities of demographic patterns, family planning practices and its impact of Human Rights on the groups in relation to pregnancy outcomes, family size, number of children and adolescence mortality following essentially International Biological Programme (I.B.P) and Human Adaptability (H.A.) basic design. Socio-economic, educational and cultural based case study of schedule tribe, schedule caste and general caste of Salda, Galia and Hetia villages of Joy Pur Block, Bankura district also showing the backwardness of family planning knowledge and its application in the context of demography in the same ecological area. Family planning is one of the main factors of Demography. Family planning of the area and its rights to enjoy of people of the three villages; is the main subject to the case study report. In case of schedule tribe the awareness level of family planning is very low where as the schedule caste is better that the tribes and the general caste is quite better that the schedule caste. During the study period it is observed that the general caste families adopt any one of the family planning method from various persons. On the same way; comparing with schedule tribe; more schedule caste families adopt any one of the family planning method for various reasons too.

Suggestion and Conclusion

When a teacher puts a tick by a sum, a child knows that; this means that he or she has produced the right answer. When a minister advises us to do what is right, we understand that we are being enjoined to follow the course that is morally correct. Of these conditions, feeling all right, getting it right and acting rightly, it is the last that political and moral philosophers have found the most interesting. But it does not constitute the whole of their subject matter. For there is not only the question of what right conduct is, but also that of what a right is; right is used as a noun as well as adjective; a right as something; one has as well as right as description of a moral act. This idea of a right as a moral possession or as 'normative property' is the stock-in-trade of lawyers and their work has been important in the definition of the concept. A right in this sense can be thought of as consisting of five main elements: a right holder (the subject of a right) has a claim to some substance (the object of a right), which he or she might assert, or demand, or enjoy, or enforce (exercising a right), against some individual or group (the bearer of the correlative duty), citing in support of his or her claim some particular ground (the justification of a right).

Investigating the present scenario and main problem of schedule caste and schedule tribe comparing to general caste in aspect of demographical condition and its social problem i.e. family planning and its proper application to the society; mention must be made of the weak socio-economic condition. The following measures of schedule caste and schedule tribe will remove the barrier of family planning and its utilization on the people of the study area.

Education should be free and mandatory for all. Proper education and its implementation in practical field will develop the society. Female must be educated to boost up the backbone of the society.

Money is one of the main factors to develop the society. So source of income must be oriented for all groups of society.

The study area; Salda, Hetia and Galia villages should be aware in all corners of socio-economic development.

Child exploitation through child labour and other activities. Female exploitation through detachment from education, awareness and early marriage, social domination by males, physical and mental torture by males; should be stopped.

Law should be active and lawful action should be taken very quickly.

To stop all the offences, exploitation, mismanagement; it is the responsibilities of Govt. agencies through the law and its implementation.

Salda, Hetia and Galia villages are mainly affected due to believe on religious unjustified explanations. So the wrong concept of the religious people of the society will be bound the people to do offence on all steps of their life. So it is necessary to make a common platform for all social groups where it will be possible to express scientific explanation before the superstitions.

N.G.O should take part to stop the social offences by helping the law implement agencies and the affected community through the government aid.

All kinds of help from national or international level is very much needed in Salda, Hetia and Galia villages of Bankura district, W.B. to drive out the main problems of family planning and barrier on its application on society.

As the ethnic groups of general caste, schedule caste and schedule tribe are generally distinct and culturally different and are placed in the highest, middle and lowest strata of the stratified ladder, their demographic patterns are similarly very much different from each other following International Jargons of the same type of study. So if we can upgrade the victimized persons or community; the study area will be naturally developed and all the groups will be able to enjoy the same social status.

REFERENCES

Bagchi Jasodhara. Edited (2000): *The Changing Status of Women in West Bengal, 1970-2000*, The Challenge Ahead, Sage Publications, New Delhi/Thousands Oaks/London.

Bakshi S.R. and Kiran Bala. Edited (1999): *Women, Children and Weaker Sections; Social and Economic Development of Schedule Tribes*. Deep and Deep Publications, F-159, Rajouri Garden, New Delhi - 110027 (India).

Census of India (2001): West Bengal—*Special Tables for Schedule Castes and Schedule Tribes. Director of Census Operation*; West Bengal, Abul Hamid Street, Kolkata–700 069.

Dr. A.V. Ramana Kumar. (2003): "*India and a One Child-policy*, Edition in 2003'. http://india_resource.tripod.com/one-child-policy.html

Gupta Ratna. (ed.), (1990): *Profiles of Tribal Women in India in West Bengal—Special Series 34 Bulletin of the Cultural Research Institute, Schedule Caste and Tribes Welfare Department, Government of West Bnegal*, Scheduled Castes & Tribes Welfare Department, Writers' Buildings, Kolkata–700 001.

Ishita Mukhopadhyay. (eds), (2002): *Violence Against Women, A Popular Intervention. Vyas Prokashon*, 40 M.G. Road, Kolkata–700 009.

Krishnaraj Maithreyi. (eds), (1998): *Gender, Population and Development*. Oxford UniversityPress, 2/11 Ansari Road, Daryaganj, P.O. Box 7035, New Delhi, India.

'*Population Explosion in West Bengal: A Survey*', A Study by South Asia Research Society, Calcutta, Statistical Abstract, West Bengal, 1978-89 (Combined Issue), Bureau of Applied Economics and Statistics. http://www.voiceofdharma.org/books/tfst/appii1.htm

Raina B.L. (1990): *Planning Family in India*; Commonwealth Publishers, 4831/24, Prahlad Street, Ansari Road, Darayaganj, New Delhi–110 002, (India).

Srivastava S.K. (2008): *Family Planning and Population Problem in India*; Commonwealth Publishers, 4831/24, Prahlad Street, Ansari Road, Darayaganj, New Delhi–110 002, (India).

3

A Study on Employment Conditions of Women in Unorganized Sector in India

Dr. B. Madhura

> *"Who are you to solve women's problems? Are you the lord God that you should rule over every widow and every woman? Hands off!! They will solve their own problems.*
>
> **—Swami Vivekananda**

Globalization has increased the pace of revolution where majority of women started entering into the employment sector. Today working women constitute nearly 40 per cent of the labour work force. As such the educated women enters into the organized sector whereas the rural women gets engaged into the unorganized sector where women workers are victimized to globalization impact particularly incase of low wages, inequality, discrimination's, unionized jobs, low positions and gender based inequalities. According to the World Bank report, 90 per cent of the women working in the unorganized sector are not included in the official statistics. The present paper aims to bring some of the key issues, problems and challenges of women working in unorganized sector. And in deed to emphasis the institutional changes required for the employment conditions of women in unorganized sector.

> *"You can tell the condition of a nation by looking at the status of its women".*
>
> **—Jawaharlal Nehru**

Internationally one of the most remarkable developments taking place is increase in the country's GDP has been due to the increased growth rate of women workers participation which constitutes the bulk of the labor force in global production. Thousands of working women were organized and women's papers and magazines were published. It was at the second international conference of working women in Copenhagen that Clarka Zetkin, the German communist and famous leader of the international women's movement inspired by the struggle of American women workers moved the resolution to commemorate March 8 as Women's day at International level.

India is the 2nd largest populated country in the world and its female work participation rate in rural areas is 31.0 per cent and in urban areas is 11.6 per cent as per 2001 year. Female main workers constitute 14.65 per cent of the population and men 50.54 per cent, female marginal workers constitute 6.26 per cent of the population and men 0.98 per cent.

The ILO says that women represent:

1. 50 per cent of the population
2. 30 per cent of the labour force
3. Perform 60 per cent of all working hours
4. Receive 10 per cent of the worlds property
5. Own less than 1 per cent of the worlds property

Thus the demand for women labor has been increasing consistently as more women entering the workforce by juggling multiple roles (mothers, wives, sisters, daughters) and their by breaking their glass ceilings. Globalize urban Indian women are excelled to become front liners of our times. But unfortunate most of the women workers are engaged in unorganized sector.

1. Food processing is one of the biggest industry where women absorption is higher
2. 87 per cent of rural women workers are employed in agriculture as laborers and cultivators, harvesters, insecticides, weedicides.
3. 80 per cent of women workers are employed in unorganized sectors like household industries, petty trades and services, building construction.

According to the census of India data about 23 per cent of the female population is identified as workers. In March 2000, employment of women in the organized sector stood at about 5 million constituting about 17.6 per cent of the total organized sector employment in the country.

According to a report of census of India 2001 Tata Services Ltd: statistical outline of India 2001-02 and 2006-07 shows work participation rates of women and men.

	1971	1981	1991	2001
Total labour	30.7	33.5	34.2	30.4
Men	52.6	51.6	51.0	45.1
Women	12.1	14.1	16.0	14.7

Work force participation rate is the proportion of 'working' population to total population.

Thus the female participation rate tends to get underestimated because women work as unpaid family helpers and other family operated economic enterprises as such they are not counted as main workers. Thus segmentation of laborers on the grounds of gender, women workers has become supplementary earners of the family. The following are few reasons as follows:

1. Lack of continuity of jobs
2. Lack of financial aid
3. Absences of medical and accident care
4. Job insecurity and wage discrimination
5. Lack of access to latest technology and modern facilities
6. Lack of vocational and multi skill development programmes
7. Lack of women workers security bill
8. Lack of government support
9. High level of mechanization and automation adversely affecting the village based traditional economics.
10. The structural adjustment programmes (SAP) undertaken to implement the objective of the new economic policy that includes privatization, globalization, modernization, and improving productivity and growth rate has been forcing the working women more into the unorganized sector.
11. Low literacy rate and poor economic condition
12. Market economy, disinvestment, privatization competency and competition, labour reforms growing trends of IT.
13. Employers taking undue advantage of the poverty has found to be impact on the employment of women workers in the unorganized sector.

According to a report of 1999 -2000 of the Ministry of Labour, Government of India, more than 90-95 per cent women are employed in unorganized sectors. Table 3.1 shows the female participation in the unorganized sector.

Table 3.1: Work Participation in Unorganized Labour (*In Thousands*)

	1971	1981	1991	2000
Total labour	17473	22879	26735	27963
Women labour	6.1%	12.2%	14.1%	17.7%

Thus the significant increase in the female employment share in unorganized sector is divided into different industries working under the public and private sector. The statistic of growth rate of employment was relatively more in case of women workers than men but majority of women workers are employed in casual, low paid and insecure jobs which has considerable negative impact on the health and welfare of women. Millions of poor families depend upon the income generated by one/more women in their household as such they do not have welfare benefits like workers in the organized sector. Due to critical financial risks the women undertakes to do low paying jobs such as domestic servants, small traders, artisans, field labourer's, construction centre, tanneries, setting, parting, drying, match making beddi making etc.

Most of the women found to be engaged in agricultural activities, especially the rice transplantations the most arduous job I carried out entirely by women which has an adverse impact on their reproductive health resulting in premature and still births. According to statistics from the year 2006 only 40.4 per cent of women work in agriculture and 42.4 per cent in services as service sector providing more jobs for women.

The unorganized sector women are continued to be at the receiving end of policies often getting victimized in the process of globalization. The basic thrust of government policies towards women labour is to:

1. Remove the handicaps and limitations under which women work.
2. Enhance their bargaining power.
3. Increase their wages and working conditions.
4. Improve their skills.
5. Provide better job opportunities to them.
6. But the unorganized sector workers security bill is unable to give protection to women workers therefore to improve the conditions of employment in unorganized sector, there is need to amen and restrictive the economic and labour policies to suite the Indian context.

7. Micro-finance as the provision of financial services which includes micro lending, micro insurance (refers to the small premium policies to the weaker sections of the society) micro credit (refers to the extension of very small loans to unemployed) savings etc. to the working women to gain access to credit facilities, there are around 800 microfinance intuitions in India.

The Constitution of India has deep concern with regard to the status of women-equality is important and it empowers the state to provide equal opportunities to women along side men the legislative provisions for the protection and welfare of women workers are largely inspired by the International Labor Organization convention on:

1. Maternity Act 1919
2. Night Work 1919
3. Underground Work 1935
4. Equal Remuneration 1951
5. Discrimination Act
6. The Factories Act
7. The Mine Act
8. The Dock Workers Act
9. But no occupational safety and health safeguards. The other legislative measures for women relates to cetin restriction on the lifting of weight, employment in hazardous occupations and provision for separate toilet facilities, rest rooms, and crèches.

Indeed there is a need to emphasis the role to be played by the Government to be conscious about the working women in employment sector and make necessary labour policies and discuss the institutional changes required for the empowerment of the employment of women in unorganized sector.

REFERENCES

1. Datt, Ruddar (2003): *Economic Reforms, Labour and Employment*, Deep and Deep Publications Private Ltd., New Delhi.
2. Datt, Sundaram, K.P.M (2005), *Indian Economy*, S.Chand and Co. New Delhi.
3. George, Abraham: *"Economic References and Female Employment: Issues and Challenges"*, The Indian Journal of Labour Economics.
4. Rajput, Pam Ed, *Globalization and Women*, New Delhi, Ashish Publications, 1994.
5. Women Global March, Women and Employment Insurance, Fact Sheet.
6. Misra and Puri, *Indian Economy*, 2007, Himalaya.
7. Progress of the World's Women, 2000 Report.

SEZs and Women

Dr. Meenu Jain
Ms. Neeru Kang

Introduction

Industrialization has been the forerunner of many social, economic and legal changes in the lives of women. In pre-industrial societies, women remained the domestic helper but in the first half of 19th century, women became the providers, which were traditionally attributed to man. Women contribute significantly in the production. In the industry, women are in great demand due to their cheap labour.

Indian women contribute a significant part of the workforce, Census 2001 has registered 25.60 per cent of female population as workers, 127.22 million, in absolute terms out of a total female population of 496 million. The majority of women workers are employed in rural areas in agriculture as labourers and cultivator. In urban areas, 80 per cent women are employed in unorganized sector, with long hours of work, low wages and without any job security or social security.

WORK-PARTICIPATION RATE IN INDIA 2005			
RURAL		URBAN	
FEMALE	MALE	FEMALE	MALE
32.7%	54.6%	16.6%	54.9%

All over the world the most visible sign of the link between feminization of paid work and export-orientation is still in the EPZs.Their cheap labour forms the basis for the induction of women into export industries such as electronic, garments, sports goods, food processing, toys, agro industries etc.

Starting from an Industrial Park in Puerto Rico in 1947, it was only in 1980s, after the success of Chinese SEZs such as Shenzhers and Pudong that the concept gained. The globalization of production and the increased dependence on export oriented economic growth forced all the countries to create or SEZs—reincarnation of earlier EPZs. They are considered as industrial cluster. Today, there are approximately 3,000 SEZs in 120 countries.SEZs refer to a totally commercial geographical region specially established for the promotion of foreign trade and have more liberal economic laws. They offer numerous privileges to attract foreign invest, create employ opportunities, boosts new technologies and infrastructure.

In India, EPZ started in 1965 in Kandla followed by SEEPZ in 1972 later on all the EPZ were converted into SEZs by legislation – the SEZ act 2005 followed by SEZ rules 2006, there are over 270 notified SEZs as on Dec 2008 . They will be almost tax free – almost 21 tax related legislations and polices have been amended to allow these SEZs to came up in India. The government is contemplating setting up special economic zones exclusively for women as part of the National Mission for Empowerment of Women.The establishment of SEZs has helped women in many ways:

1. More employment opportunities

SEZs have opened up opportunities for wage employment for women in the formal sector. Evidence suggests that women's share to total employment in SEZs is substantially higher than both the economy as a whole as well as the manufacturing sector outside the SEZs. It is found that employers prefer female workers in the belief that manual dexterity, greater discipline and patience make women more suitable for the unskilled and semi-skilled activities carried out in zones.Women dominate the workforce in EPZs in most developing countries. It remains 60-70 per cent in Korea, Sri Lanka, Mexico, Dominican Republic.

The new SEZs are also creating more jobs for semi-skilled workers as compared to the EPZs in India. SEZs employ far more women at 55 per cent of the workforce as compared to the old Export Promotion Zones like Kandla that have been converted to SEZs, where women constitute 30 per cent of the workforce. Currently in India there are 948 units in operation in functional SEZs. These units provide employment is about 1.10 lakh person out of which 40 per cent are females, in absolute term 32185 females out of 100650 persons got employment in SEZs units.

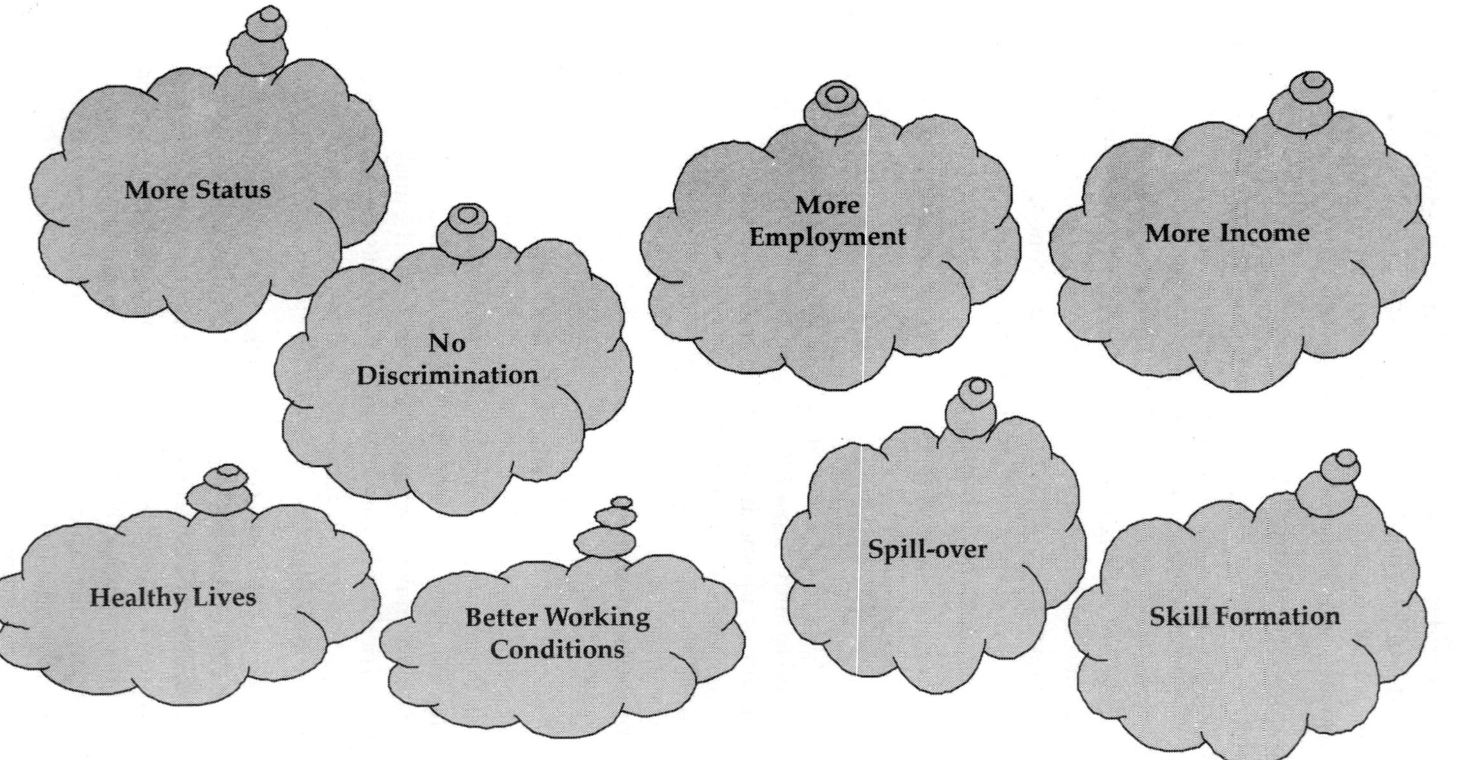

Fig. 4.1: Contribution of SEZs

The Nokia SEZs in Tamil Nadu, where women constitute 50 per cent of the workforce, recruited girls with secondary education and in the 16-21 age groups, after imparting three-month training.

70 per cent of employees in a gems and Jeweller park in Hyderabad are girls, who come from families of landless agriculture labourers.

Apache shoes in Nellore district is employing about 4500 workers, of which majority are women from local villages, who have been imparted training before employing.

The Falta SEZ, in the southernmost part of the South 24 Parganas district, near Diamond Harbour has about 60 per cent of the women workforce.

Infosys, a unit in SEZ in Manimajra, 27.35 per cent females got employment. Thus SEZs are raising hopes amongst women-folk; SEZs could significantly improve women employment in India.

2. Indirect employment

SEZs are township of their own; thereby there is shopping mall restaurants, amusement parks set up around to attract people. Thereby the demand for complementary goods and services generate more indirect employment to women. For every job created inside the SEZ there are two created outside. In this way, women will also be benefited.

3. More increased income

SEZs provide women an opportunity to have increased income. Many are earning cash incomes for the first time — often more than they would elsewhere Madani (1999) report that as 1981 survey in the Dominican republic found that SEZ wages were the main source of working in the zones and that almost half of them were single divorced or widow.ILO(1998) reports that in Guatemala 45 per cent and in Honduras 22 per cent of women report that they were the sole source of income.

Pheeby a female employee in the Nokia SEZ at Sriperumbudur bought a TV, grinder and even a bed at our home for the first time. She says. "The company gifted me a camera phone and I gave my old one to amma". Her colleague K Kavita was able to gift her sister a pair of gold earrings.Earning money has helped her to stand on her own feet.

4. Skilled formation

Units in SEZs directly affect the skill formation as workers are provided additional training on and off the jobs. Everyone knows, improved skill leads to more productivity and income earning capacity of the workers.

5. Higher wages and better condition

Most women work in hazardous, unhygienic and extensive conditions but now women need not to work in oppressive work environment SEZs provide an opportunity to work in healthy conditions. SEZs firms are in general more modern, cleaner, more spacious, better ventilated and better lit and therefore offer better working condition. They are also better in working time, over time payments and sanitary condition. Minimum wages paid in different in these zones are higher than the state level wages and national level minimum wages.

6. No discrimination

There is no discrimination against female workers in these zones. Rather female worker appears to be fetching higher salaries which mean that they are employed in better paying jobs. Satisfaction level is higher for women workers. Female workers get bonus and covered under provident fund. For overtime, they get more wages and compensation. Night shift is not compulsory for female worker.

7. Spill-over to domestic firms

Foreign firms operating in SEZs spread spill- over to domestic firms in SEZs and then to those in the domestic economic. In this way SEZs can play a crucial role in upgrading domestic women entrepreneurial skills.

8. Poverty reduction

Employment creation generated income, creates non pecuniary benefits, improve the quality of life of labour and enhance theirs productivity. These, in turn, have poverty reduction effect. In about 18 months, Sheela s' earnings from SEZs helped the family go from a thatched hut to a house with a roof, and the family has a colour TV and cable.

9. Better status

Moreover, SEZs have made women independent, improved their relative status and bargaining power within households. At present in India 53 per cent SEZs are in the Sunrise sector of IT and ITES. Women employment in this sector, having global bearing has helped to bring about major changes in their lives.

"Earlier we saw girls in trousers only in films and TVs. Now we see it in our neighbourhood", C Chandhrasekhar, the teacher, says. The cutlery, the trousers — these are emblems of the rise of the new Indian middle class in Sular Peta in Andhra Pradesh .Young employees, most of them women, have their lunch in the canteen of a Nokia plant in Sriperumbudur, Tamil Nadu.

They are learning to eat with knives and forks. In Sular Peta, these changes began, after the Appache Special Economic Zone.

No doubt, women are benefited from the SEZs, but behind it, the cost is very high challenges before women force.

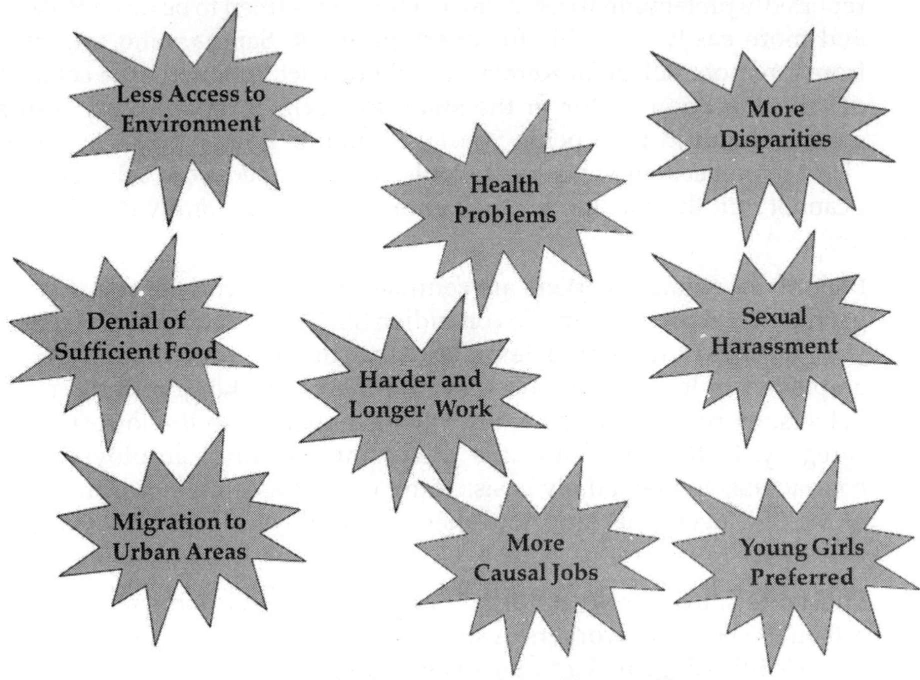

Fig. 4.2: **Challenges Before Women Force**

Shivli lost 12 acres. She is mother of five small kids and is waging a lone battle. She didnt receive any money till now. She was cooking and living in her land under the shade of tamarind tree. Overnight the tree was cut by the land grabbing fellows to push her out from the shade of chinta chettu. They made her a beggar in the Telangana. Anjamma, Chukkamma, Rajamma, Velugulamma. ... So many women are bearing the cost.

(*a*) The data shows that in India SEZs are acquiring large tracts of agriculture lands in the state like Haryana (29221.08ha), Gujarat (25092.09ha), Tamil Nadu (16569.96ha) and Maharashtra (43142.96ha) where agriculture is more advanced. It will lead to large scale displacement of people dependent on agriculture. Compensation is meager, so farmers and their families are unable to sustain themselves. It will lead more and more women to migrate to urban areas and result in swelling the ranks of reserve army of labour. The impact will be extended discrimination of denial of sufficient food, health care, education and dignity. Their access to natural resources is reduced. They have no access to firewood, water sources, no privacy for sanitation.

(b) Since industries in the zones are export-oriented, the emphasis is on minimising production costs so that prices are competitive in the international market. It is the workers, especially women, who bear the brunt of tight competition in the global market. To meet production targets, they are compelled to work harder and longer. Companies reportedly prefer unmarried women who are assumed to be more efficient and more easily available for overtime work. Sajitha, who migrated from a remote village in Kerala's Idukki district, following the collapse of the plantation sector in the state, to Kochi to take up a job in a garments unit in the Cochin Special Economic Zone (CSEZ), explains: "Had there been any way out I would have escaped from this hell. But I cannot quit this job and go back to my village. My family depends on me".

(c) Majority of women workers are contract or casual workers and did not get their legal benefits. Studies on Indian SEZs reveal that the preference was given to unmarried females. Most of the women (85%) were employed in low paying jobs like trimming, checking, packing or as helpers. 64 per cent of the women workers belong to the lowest wage category. In the Falta SEZ ,the dominant system of employment is contractual, and on a daily basis. Many women assemble near the gates of the SEZ every morning, and they are employed if there is work for that day.

(d) Stiff targets, overwork and an unhealthy work environment take their toll on the health of workers. A study on female factory workers, mainly at the MEPZ, done by Padmini Swaminathan, director, Madras Institute of Development Studies, revealed that the women suffered from frequent headaches due to tension and intense concentration at work, acute back pain, joint pains, swelling in the legs, severe abdominal pains, various types of allergies, skin ailments, and piles (the result of sitting in the same position for hours on end).

The majority of women working in the garment units suffered from respiratory disorders such as asthma, persistent cough and breathlessness. Concentrated attention or precision required by some jobs like germs, jewellry etc. produce fatigue. In the modern sector, like IT, automobile industry etc. women workers are forced to work for 12 hours.

(e) Some argue that creation of SEZs does not reduce the local unemployment rate. History tells incentives offered to SEZs compel the already established industries to move in these zones e.g. 'Malquiladorisation' of the Mexican economy where employment in manufacturing industries shifted towards the EPZ sector without increasing the total number of jobs in the economy.

(*f*) In the Falta SEZ, a major industry in the SEZ is waste plastic recycling. Waste plastic is shipped in from all over the world and women are employed to sift through and clean these waste plastics, often contaminated with hazardous chemical and biological waste, with their hands in the horrible working conditions.

(*g*) Sexual harassment is another serious problem faced by working women, not inside but outside the industry.

(*h*) SEZs will divide the women workforce in the two groups: SEZs and non SEZs one group will enjoy all the facilities and incentives and other will definitely suffer. Resources will transfer from domestic sector to SEZs. Therefore disparity and inequalities among women will be widened.

(*i*) SEZs will be given the status of public utility services which will reduce the bargaining power of workers.There are restriction on the right to join a trade union, bans on collective bargaining and the right to strike. Vishakhapatnam SEZ where women working in nightshifts has been permitted. The labour commissioner will be required to take permission from the development commissioner to enter SEZs even for inspection of safety and environmental norms within the factory.

Conclusion

SEZs are expected to have for reaching consequences for the women and environment. Moreover recent recession has reduced economic activity in these zones. These zones should take into consideration the three aspects of the sustainable development. These three aspects are economy, environment and women.

REFERENCES

1. Aggarwal Aradhana; Working Paper (194) on "*Impact of SEZs on Employment, Poverty and Human Development*", May 2007; Indian Council for Research on International Economic Relations", New Delhi.
2. Rao; R. Kavita: "*Impact of SEZs on the Indian Economy — An Initial Evaluation*".
3. Jha; Shankar and Mishra, Sangeeta: "*Special Economic Zones — Boon or Bane*", Papers Presented at the National Seminar on Special Economic Zone, Department of Geography, Delhi School of Economics, University of Delhi, Delhi, 16-17 March, 2007.
4. Yadav Radhika, "*Women at Work — In the Era of Globalization,* Women' link October-December, 2008, pp 3-6.
5. Ghosh Jayanti , "*Globalisation, Export-oriented Employment for Women and Social Policy: A Case Study of India*", Social Scientist, Vol. 30, Nos. 11-12, November-December 2002.

Women and Eleventh Five-year Plan

Dr. Meenu Jain

ABSTRACT

Though India is developing economically and technologically by leaps and bounds, women here still continue to be discriminated. For growth to be truly inclusive, we have to ensure their protection,well-being, development, empowerment and participation. The vision of 11th Plan is inclusive and integrated economic, social and political empowerment with gender justice.

Introduction

Progress and development do not confined to increase in production and income alone but social development is necessary for real development for a country like India. Any development strategy which neglects the need for enhancing the role of women cannot lead to meaningful socio-economic development. Development must benefit women. Nehru said, "Women should be uplifted for the upliftment of the nation, for if a women is uplifted society and nation is uplifted. "According to *Swami Vivekananda,* "there is no chance for the welfare of the world unless the condition of the women is improved. It is not possible for a bird to fly on one wing".

The access of women to development opportunities and the impact of development programmes on women assumes importance as women constitutes half of human resources in all societies. Moreover, the increasing awareness of the existence of significant relationship between the role and status of women and the ultimate economic well-being of the family is reflected in the growing volume of literature on women studies.

Constitutional Provisions

In Independent India 'women's problems were never sought to be treated on gender basis but as a social malaise of a comman society to be cured by the effects of all members of society, men and women alike'.

The importance of women as a important human resource was recognized by the constitution of India. The constitution of India guarantees to all Indian women equality, no discrimination by the state, equality of opportunity, equal pay for equal work. In addition, it allows special provisions to be made by the state in favour of women and children.

The legal system of a country is a primary factor which determines the status and rights of women. State enacted several women-specific and women-related legislations to protect women against social discrimination, violence and atrocities and also to prevent social evils like child marriages, dowry, rape, practice of Sati etc. Prevention of Domestic Violence Act is a landmark law in acting as a deterrent as well as providing legal recourse to the women who are victims of any form of domestic violence. Apart from these, there are a number of laws which may not be gender specific but still have ramifications on women.

Women and Five-year Plans

Women development has remained an integral part of our development plans. In the First Five-year Plan (1951-56), the concept of women's development was mainly 'welfare oriented' The Central School Welfare Board (CSWB) set up in 1953, undertook a number of welfare measures through the voluntary sector. In Second Five Year Plan (1956-61) women were organized into Mahila Mandals to act as focal points at the grass-root levels for the development of women.

During the sixties (Third, Fourth and other interim plans), education received priority along with measures to improve maternal and child health and nutrition services. During seventies (Fifth Five-Year Plan 1974-78), there was a definite shift in the approach from 'Welfare to development which recognized women as participants in development programmes.

In the eighties (Sixth Five-year Plan 1980-85), The Government of India adopted a multi-disciplinary approach with a special thrust on the' three core sectors of education, health and employment. Beneficiary-oriented programmes for women were promoted in Seventh Five Year Plan (1985-90).

Eight Five-Year Plan (1992-97) marked a shift from 'development to empowerment of women'. A further impetus for sectoral contribution to women's programmes was received with the introduction of the concept of Women's Component Plan in the Ninth Plan whereby identified Ministries were required to indicate the flow of funds to the women's programmes and schemes. With the introduction of the National Policy for Empowerment of women, the Government of India had declared year 2001 as women's Empowerment Year.

The Tenth Five-year Plan (2002-07) called for thc three pronged strategy of social empowerment, economic empowerment and providing gender justice to create an enabling environment of positive economic and social policies for women and eliminating all forms of discrimination against them and thus advance gender equality goals.The country amended and enacted women related legislations during Tenth Five-Year Plan. The married women's Property Act (1874), The Hindu Succession Act (1956) were amended and the Protection of women from Domestic Violence Act (2005) was passed.

Though the Constitutional commitments of the nation to women was translated through the planning process, legislation, policies and programmes over the last six decades yet on the eve of the Eleventh plan, a situational analysis of social and economic status of women reflects less than satisfactory achievements in almost all important human development indicators. Economic empowerment as reflected by the work participation rate shows that the percentage of women in the work force increased by only 3 per cent (from 22.5% to 25.7%) between 1991 and 2001. The average wage differential between men and women showed a marked deterioration between 2000 and 2004 for both rural and urban areas.

A study in the Himalayan region tells us that a pair of bullock works 1064 hours ,a man works 1212 hours and a women works 3485 hours on a one hectare farm. But the income they earn is not commensurate with the task they perform. While the literacy rates have shown an improvement from 39.3 per cent to 54.3 per cent of the total female population between 1991 and 2001, yet much more needs to be done especially for socially and economically backward regions and groups.

Still women suffer from womb to tomb in the male dominated society. Poverty and economic dependence are the roots of women's self degradation and crimes against them. Women continue to be victims of violence, neglect and injustice.

Eleventh Five-year Plan

This plan will address these problems by looking at gender as a cross-cutting theme. For the first time in the history of Indian planning there is an attempt to more beyond empowerment and recognize women as agents of sustained socio- economic growth and change in Eleventh Five-year Plan (2007-12).

Table 5.1: Selected Development Indicators Related to Women

	Women	Men	Total
Population (in million 2001)	496.4	532.1	1028.6
Decennial Growth 2001	23.08	22.26	22.67
Sex-Ratio 2001	933		
Expectation of life at birth 2005	66.1	63.8	
Death rate 2005	7.1	8.0	7.6
IMR 2005	61	56	58
Child Morality Rate	18.2	16.4	17.3
Literacy rate	57	77	67.30
Work participation rate 2001	25.7	51.9	–

Source: Annexure 6.1, p. 219, 11th Five-year Plan.

Essence of the Approach

- Recognition of the right of every women and child to develop to her/his full potential
- Recognition of the differential needs of different groups of women and children
- Need for intersectoral convergence as well as focused women and child specific measures through MoWCD
- Partnership with civil society to create permanent institutional mechanisms that incorporate the experiences, capacities and knowledge of Vos and women's groups in the process of development planning.

Six Monitorable Targets

The 11th Plan lays down six monitorable targets:

- Raise the sex-ratio for age group 0-6 from 927 in 2001 to 935 by 2011-12 and to 950 by 2016-17.
- Ensure that at least 33 per cent of the direct and indirect beneficiaries of all government schemes are women and girl children.
- Reduce IMR from 57 to 28 and MMR from 3.01 to one per 1000 live births.
- Reduce malnutrition among children of age group 0-3 to half its present level.

- Reduce anaemia among women and girls by 50 per cent by the end of this plan.
- Reduce dropout rate for primary and secondary schooling by 10 per cent for both girls and boys.

Challenges in the 11th Plan

The challenges can be clubbed under a five-fold agenda:

- Ensuring economic empowerment
- Engineering social empowerment
- Enabling political empowerment
- Effective implementation of women-related legislations
- Creating institutional mechanisms for gender mainstreaming and strengthening delivery mechanisms

Assurances in the 11th Plan

- The plan will ensure increased availability of micro-credit to women in the unorganized sectors
- The plan will ensure effective and independent land rights for women and strengthening women's agricultural capacities
- The plan will ensure the rights of poor, landless and tribal women over forest land ,commons and other resources
- The plan will encourage PPP and corporate social responsibility programmes for women's trainning, capacity building and empowerment
- The plan will make attempts to organize domestic workers and frame regulations with respect to hours of work, holidays etc. for them
- Women in agriculture will be on the top of this plan agenda and a two-pronged strategy will be adopted:
    1. ensuring effective and independent land rights for workers; and
    2. strengthening women's agricultural capacities.
- This plan will ensure that wage works conducive to women and their skills are also included under NREGA.
- Provision of clean drinking water, toilet, and sanitation in urban slums will be an important challenge for ensuring gender justice in this plan.

Eleventh Five-year Plan Schemes

- The objective of gender budgeting scheme is to pave the way for translating gender commitments into budgetary commitments.

- Swayamsiddha, an integrated scheme for women's empowernment through SHGs will be the major scheme to be implemented by the Ministry of WCD in the 11th Plan. Swayamsidha phase II will be launched as a countrywide programme.
- Support to Training and employment programme (STEP), a scheme for skill training of women, will be revamped during 11th Plan. The Rashtriya Mahila kosh will also be integrated with STEP and Swayamsidha for credit linkages.
- The ICDS scheme will have a component of conditional maternity benefits under which pregnant and the lactating mothers will be entitled to cash incentives.
- Ministry of WCD will continue to run its earlier schemes offering support services like Working women's Hostel scheme, Swadhar homes, Short-stay Home Scheme will continue in this plan. In the Eleventh Plan, it is proposed to expand the scope and content of these schemes so as to reach more women and empower them economically and socially.
- The Central Social Welfare Board (CSWB) will continue financing NGOs for implementation of various women and child-related schemes.
- Scheme for Relief and Rehabilitation of Victims of Sexual Assault will be initiated in this plan.

Suggestions

No doubt, Government has started many programmes and policies for women but there is a need to sensitize the women. It is only education that will hasten their economic empowerment. It is the seed that has to be planted in the their minds as it is a route to awareness regarding available opportunities, their rights and responsibilities.

But the attitude of some parents is still biased against the girl child as they do not wish to educate girls. Investment on her education is considered mere wastage of time and resources. Ordinary education to girl child and more advanced educational opportunities are offered to boys in the same family .Such biased attitude of parents should be discouraged so that the girl child is second to none when competing for the opportunities with their male counterparts.

Women entrepreneur still have a long way to go. There is short supply of women entrepreneur in society because of the absence of entrepreneurial element in the education system so entrepreneurial development must be the part of curriculum. Growth of women entreneurship would be supplementary and complementary for women in particular and country in general. Their enthusiasm and skill in constructive performance is met and simultaneously they can earn enough for proper maintenance and improvement of their socio-economic status.

By use of electronic media, field demonstrations ,printed materials and study visits to expose women farmers to the success stories of other women, women can be encouraged for effective participation.

Government started women's vocational training programme. But still no. of female extension workers is not adequate.

Women are not aware of their rights. Those who are aware of it ,find difficult to approach the courts. Fast tracked courts especially dealing in women's rights should be established for speedy justice procedures for redressal of grievances should be made simple and fast. The establishment of courts with judges chosen for their interest in female matters would be an improvement. It will provide more opportunities to female aspirants in the legal profession.

Agrarian reforms should include at least joint ownership of land. Certain states are offering more concessional stamp duties while transferring land in name of female. Such a step would stimulate a chain of changes of relationships and will provide more economic security.

Above all most important is the sensitization of women to become independent. Usually, a lady Sarpanch or a lady minister are a rubber stamp to their male counter part. Here I will recall Fatima Bee, the sarpanch of Kalra village in Andhra Pradesh. Earlier she was a rubber stamp but later on she decided to fight for the cause of women empowerment and got a UNO award on 17th october 1998 in New York for her courage and inspiration to fight against poverty. It is the women who can bring the change in society. Women herself should become brave, courageous and try to develop will power among themselves.

Somewhere, somehow we have to bring back the idealism that will inspire our young to consider women as a full fledged member of a family not as a highly flexible resource of the household. A focused mind and sincere efforts can bring changes. The day is not very far off when women will be economically independent.

REFERENCES

1. Ruby, J.A. and Others, '*Women Empowerment: Meaning, Characteristics and Dimensions*', Southern Economists, May 2009, Vol. 48, No. 1, pp. 41-42.
2. Rajan S. Raja, 'Gender Equality and Empowerment of Women in India', Southern Economists, May 2009, Vol. 48, No. 1, pp. 54-56.

3. Eleventh Five Year Plan 2007-12 Vol. II, Social Sector, Planning Commission, Government of India.

4. Report of the Working Group on Empowerment of Women for 11th Plan, 2006.

5. Census of India, 2001.

A Study on Role of Women in Television Commercials (TVCs)

Dr. K. Usharani

Introduction

The importance of advertising is "steadily on the increase in modern society". Though there has been a visible progress, women's image in the media still remains negative and they are treated as Commodity.

Advertising seems to be obsessed with gender and sexuality and continues to represent an arena in which gender display plays a major role. It has emerged as a world of 'commercial realism' in which we are given 'realistic' images of domestic life and male-female relationships which are not actually real but which provide us with a 'stimulated slice of life'. As gender representation is such a dominant feature of modern-day advertising, it is often called the social resource 'used most' by advertisers. The changing role of women in society has created a challenging task for advertisers-how to portray women in advertisements.

The phase of imperialist globalization is treating women as a commodity. Talk of the commodification of women is very common in the present day world. But why the present day world? In a male dominated society it was prevalent in the precapitalist feudal age also. Unquestionably, in today's period of globalization, where greed for money knows no bounds, the commodification of women has risen to an extreme height. It is now the age of a communication revolution. The electronic media and print media are emerging as an all-pervasive phenomenon. The media now exerts a tremendous influence on society — both positive and negative. However, as regards to women, the media presentation is mostly negative.

In this age of liberalization and opening up of our economy to global market forces, women and young girls have became an important target for the media.

Justification, rather glorification, of eve-testing in an increasing number of ads, all in the name of fun and entertainment, is an area that requires serious probing. This is one aspect that has been a cause of increasing violence against young girls, especially in educational institutions. Look at the whole gamut of images of young boys or girls presented in ads— how comfortable they are passing indecent remarks or exchanging 'sexy' looks.

The projection of the image of a woman as an independent human being, taking her own decisions or making invaluable contributions as a worker, as a citizen, would simply not create a conducive environment for private profit. In India advertisers often treat women with disdain portraying them as if they have been created only to attend to man's creature comforts. They are shown to be exceedingly anxious about their looks, weak, foolish, incapable of looking after themselves and utterly dependent on man.

To top everything else-woman are lesser human beings who can be mocked at, trivialized, cut to size through joke, through gestures, through maxims, through all kinds of devaluing practices- all in the name of 'culture'.

Television has a wide reach and it can be effectively utilized to empower women through innovative programmes. We are aware that the trends in ads in particular and the media at large are to be seen within the broad historical and social context. Further, the audience does not take everything expressed in them verbatim. Yet one should not forget that media has a very significant role to play in shaping social attitudes. Hence it cannot cater to interest of a miniscule section only. It certainly does have a social obligation and responsibility in the development and reinforcement of opinions which leads to a better and more equitable society.

There is nothing intrinsically good intrinsically evil about advertising. It is a tool, an instrument: It can be used well and it can be used badly. If it can have, and sometimes does have, beneficial results such as those defenders described, it also can, and often does, have a negative, harmful impact on individuals and society. Many women and men professionally engaged in advertising do have sensitive consciences, high ethical standards and a strong sense of responsibility. But even for them external pressures —from the clients who commission their work as well as from the competitive internal dynamics of their profession— can create powerful inducement unethical behaviour.

That underlines the need for external structures and systems to support and encourage responsible practice in advertising and to discourage the irresponsible.

The solution can only be a fundamental social change— the change from a profit-based capitalist society to a humanitarian socialist society. We experienced the ushering in of such a society in the former Soviet Union, in which women were given their due place in society, where they were given equal opportunities with men in all spheres- education, health and work, where women were no longer exploited or commodified. We should not forget. Such societies have existed and do exist. It is up to us to make to make the change happen.

Research Methodology

Primary and secondary data were collected for the purpose of the study. Following the observational method, the data was collected and survey research method was employed. The survey research method was used to get the opinion of the people. The research instrument used for the survey was a well structured questionnaire consisting of open and close ended questions. Focus Group interview and observations had also been used to supplement and support the primary data. An on-line survey was also conducted to have a better sample structure so that there would be less bias in drawing of conclusions.

Research Design

The research was mainly focused on primary as well as secondary data.

Survey and Focus Group have been used as the main tools as it enables to get first hand information. The survey and focus group were conducted at Hyderabad. The research describes the attitudes, opinions and views of the people towards portrayal of women in TVCs.

Data Collection

The study is based on both primary and secondary sources of data.

Primary Data

The primary data was collected through survey which was both offline and online. Apart from this a Focus Group interview was conducted. The survey and focus group were conducted at Hyderabad.

Secondary Data

The secondary data has been obtained from various text books, journals, magazines, newspapers and different web sites.

Sample Design

Sample design is a definite plan to obtain a sample from a given population. It refers to the techniques or the procedures the researchers would adopt in selecting items for the sample.

The survey and Focus Group comprised of a cross section of people, of different age groups and professions. Which comprised of, 50 per cent male and 50 per cent female respondents, so that there would be less bias in drawing of conclusions.

The sampling procedure adopted for the study was convenient sampling.

Sample Size

For ascertaining the perceptions of the people towards role of women in TVCs, a sample size consisting of 200 people had been selected.

A Focus Group interview was also conducted comprising of 10 members.

Objectives

1. To study whether TVCs are losing their ethical and moral values.
2. To study the reasons for increased use of women models/actors in TVCs.
3. To study about the impact of negative rolel of women in TVCs on the society.
4. To highlight the points which will help in reduction of portrayal of wrong image of women in TVCs.

Limitations of the Study

- As the study was restricted to the city of Hyderabad, the findings may not be applicable to the entire population.
- The quality of the data collected, entirely relies on the opinion of the respondents (biased or unbiased).
- The respondents were restricted to educated people who watch TVCs.
- Due to resistance from the people for responding the sample size could not be equally divided among different age groups.

Findings and Conclusions

Economic point of view the cost is very low. Even in other sections of the society the women are employed because their salary is very low that is the main reason that the service from women are taken and in turn they are paid less money, when compared to men.

Advertisement or any activity in the society is concerned; there is no difference between men and women. When men can be used in TVCs why not women.

Then, we come to a conclusion that if women are portrayed in a proper way in the TVCs, it is good as they have a good impact on the society. But the TVCs should reflect the values of our society. If they are against our values, it is not good. On the other hand if they are in favour of our values it is good.

I don't believe that TVCs are losing their ethical and moral values 80 per cent of TVCs are alright but may be because of these 20 per cent of TVCs which are wrongly portrayed it looks as if the TVCs are losing their ethical and moral values. Values are there, ethics and morals are there. But such bad TVCs highlight the loss or ethical and moral values and looks as if they are in majority.

There is some kind of misunderstanding. We can't say that there are no values, no ethics, no morals. We can't say that the TVCs don't reflect our culture. There are many ads. Which are good, where the women reflect our culture. We have to mention abut those ads. Also and praise them. But there are some things which our society cannot accept that is to be rectified.

Women are employed because the salaries are low. People are attracted more towards women and the manufacturers can sell their products more easily that is why the women are increasingly used in advertisements.

The main reasons for increased use of women in TVCs are:

1. For commercial purposes.
2. The money power is in younger generations hands that is why the women are used in TVCs to attract them and influence them to buy their products.

Now-a-days women and used a lot in advertisements in a very wrong and bad manner. Their body is being exposed. Our children, young people are getting influenced by such TVCs and they are taking a wrong path such advertisements should be banned. For eg. Amul Macho undergarments.

Advertisements are not only on T.V. but also when we got to cinema to watch movies ads are shown there also. The general public is influenced by these TVCs. So, these two mediums i.e. T.V. and cinema are spoiling the people. The lady is projected in such a way that she is a very good thing without clothes. People are getting attracted and following the wrong path. This is not right and is to be mended.

Just like senior board for movies there should be a sensor board for TVCs which have a bad and negative effect on the society should not be screened at all. The scenes should be censored, improved and then presented on TV for public viewing. So that our children who are the future of our nation don't get spoilt. The government and complain regarding such TVCs people should protest and take out processions.

There 20 per cent of TVCs should also stop. They should turn into TVCs hiving ethical and moral values.

Women these days are more money minded. They want to mint money that is why so men are increasingly used in advertisements.

My opinion is that women and girls when they watch TVCs role of women, they try to copy such TVCs in real life which is having a wrong and bad impact on their lives. It is not practical and reality is different from TVCs.

Women are used as instruments to promote products rather than used as a medium.

Ex: Lux soaps, L.G. Mobile.

According to me the advertisements done on ladies is not correct. It is done for attraction and for money purpose.

TVCs done by women these days is not at all good. Lot of exposing is done. Youngsters, children who are continuously watching TV watch such vulgar ads and get negatively influenced.

Ex. All the TVCs of axe.

We should take steps to improve the TVCs so that the people do not continue to watch such ads. Steps should be taken to reduce skin show; women should not be stereotyped, but shown as a powerful individual contributing to society.

According to me, women should not be employed for vulgar, cheap and filthy advertisements because children who usually watch TV, they also watch advertisements. They get attracted and influenced by these advertisements.

I feel that people get attracted to women that are why women are increasingly used in TVCs. There is nothing wrong in using women in TVCs but they should be properly used.

I think that it does not depend on advertisement but on how we take those TVCs and perceive them. Even if we watch TVCs it depends on use if we follow the good or bad aspects depending on our learnt culture and values. If we are strong then we will not get carried away by TVCs.

How many ads. Can we ban and stop their production. Now a days teenagers, youngsters and also many people in the society enjoy watching modernized and westernized ads. They get attracted to women with less clothes. We can't change people's views and ideas.

The number of women in advertisements has increased because the women have a great impact on society. They play different roles of a mother, sister, daughter and wife. They have a greater influence than men.

The negative role of women in TVCs and its impact on society is not only on children but also on young girls who don't look very good or beautiful. They feel left behind losing their self esteem and confidence. They might end up doing wrong stuff.

Now-a-days we don't find any ad. Where we can say that it has proper ethical and moral values which reflects the Indian society. In Indian society the women don't wear such clothes. Our Indian society is much cleaner than what they show on TVCs.

Culture is totally shifting even those TVCs which were good are following the other TVCs and wrong image of women.

- They are several reasons for increased use of women models or actors. One of the important reasons according to me is the increasing number of working women which includes the acting in TVCs
- Secondly the women have become the prime purchaser in the market.
- Thirdly, the Ad. Agencies by employing women have to bear lower costs.
- Lastly, many women are having good body and acting skills, probably some of them have no other qualification, which directs them towards TVCs.

Yes, TVCs are losing their ethical and moral values due to which people in general and men in particular think that women are no more than sex objects. They think women have to be beautiful with good body rather than thinking about their talents and intelligence.

Recommendation

One thing that I want to remind you all is that from where these ad. Agencies come? From the society. We cannot say that TVCs are having a bad effect on society. The role of women in TVCs are a part of society they do not come from Mars. We cannot put the entire blame on media. The problem is from within the society and we have to correct that. Rather than blaming others we have to correct ourselves. We should find the root of the problem, we watch the TVCs and also blame the media which is not correct, we should rather avoid watching.

Mass Education is necessary for the society. How to watch TVCs i.e. which ones are to be watched and the others avoided is to be taught. Corruption is every where. But not get corrupted ourselves.

As I have already mentioned senior board should be people enough to collect fine from people responsible for making such TVCs. Also the general public should write to the government and complain regarding such TVCs. People should protest and take out processions.

These 20 per cent of TVCs should also stop. They should turn into TVCs having ethical and moral values.

If the TVCs are bad and negative. Women can be used in a proper fashion for Ads of saves, cosmetics do. But not for Ads. Of axe and undergarments.

Every one should feel responsible and try to improve the TVCs portraying wrong image of women. For eg. People should stop watching such Ads. The women should not accept TVCs which portray women in a negative way. The Ad. Agencies should not make such ads. The business people should not pay money. The government should take action.

REFERENCES

Books

- Essentials of Advertising — JS.Chandan/Jagjit Singh, P.N.Malhan.
- Research methodology — C.R. Kothari.
- Statistical Methods — S.P. Gupta.
- Advertising Attractions — Arvind Korba.

Magazines

- 4Ps Business and Marketing

Journals

- Indian Journal of Marketing

Newspapers

- Deccan Chronicle

Websites

- www.monkey survey.com
- www.google search.com
- www.google.com
- www.questia.com

Status of Women and Their Role in Socio-economic

Mr. Sudarshan Prasad Regmi

ABSTRACT

The primary data from 46 and one municipality out of 48 VDCs as well as the secondary data were captured to see the status of women in Ilam district of Eastern Nepal and analyzed. Different aspects of women like involvement in social organizations, income generation activities, perception in social inclusion, domestic violence and household conflicts, time spend in the household works, sources of information and entertainments, role in family planning were analyzed crucially. It was observed that 87.95 per cent women of Ilam earned their income from livestock farming especially small animal and backyard poultry. They spared more of their time/ working hours, about 2 and half, 20 per cent, on animal husbandry works at animal shed and enjoy hardly two hours of leisure, 16 per cent. A 52.58 per cent women observed conflict as beaten by her own husband and were discriminated by family member in her own house. The 60 per cent of women reported that the domestic violence were created due to low education of female as well as polygamy, 43.24 per cent, of their male partner. The involvements of women in saving and credit cooperatives were substantial about 41.33 per cent of which had as high as 53.42 per cent. Similarly, they were attached to other organizations too; of about

14 per cent reported women directly participated to governmental organization, 39.07 per cent and in non-governmental organization, 27.23 per cent. It has been shown that of 41.47 per cent of women reported were fully known about social inclusion and 78.13 per cent stated that all casts' groups and gender should be included without any disparity. It had been observed by analyzing the family planning situation that women had a significant attitude in family planning, average ratio being 10.89: 1 female: male. Use of new technology of information through mobile and get entertained higher by radio or transistor at household level had been advancing their lifestyle. The facts and figures of Nepalese women in relation to the world has been revealed that women of Ilam specially at rural area need specific attention regarding inputs in the field of education, agri-business, conflict resolution for more role in the society. Though they spend more on household work, which if capitalized would help promote livelihood of their family.

Background of the Study

Nepal is a small country having area of 141,181 square kilometer, which is a landlocked between two giant Asian countries viz. China and India. Nepal occupies 0.03 percentage of area of the world and 0.30 percentage of area of Asia. Nepal ecologically has three belts or regions, namely mountain 35 per cent, hill 42 per cent, and terai 23 per cent; and is lengthily distributed from east to west. Administratively, country is divided into five development regions and 75 districts of which Ilam falls to Eastern hill district adjoining to West-Bengal of India.

Nepal has been always an independent and sovereign country with glorious history, culture and tradition which dates back to time immemorial. Nepal is famous in world for its unique features among these the major three important are: the highest peak mountain—Everest (*sagarmatha*); the birth place of Lord Buddha — Lumbini; and Pashupatinath , the Hindu's biggest temple listed under the world heritage lies in Nepal.

Ilam falls under hill ecology and is famous in the region for production of the milk; ginger; the broom grass; the potato. The district experiences temperate in the northern part and sub-tropical climate in the southern part with an average precipitation about 1400 mm to 1500 mm annually and about 85 per cent or more during months of May to September. Basically Ilam is considered as pioneer head in agriculture and livestock husbandry, especially cash crops as mentioned above. In livestock, cattle farming for milk production are highly integrated with agro-forestry and agricultural practice.

Ilam has spread over an area of 171,725 hectare that is only about 12.14 per cent of area of Nepal. The district is divided into three electoral constituencies, nine Ilakas, with households 64435 in 2009, average household size being 6.0. Ilam district ranks to 12th out of 75 districts for its overall composite index with a farm size 0.98 ha and about 5.56 livestocks' density per household (*see the Annex Table 7.1 on page 80*). Demographic trend indicates there is increasing in both population size household size and literacy from 1981 census to the projected till 2011. People are more influenced and affiliated development activities with the neighboring state of India.

Women make up about 40 per cent of world's work force in agriculture, a quarter in industries and a third in services. Women farmers in developing countries grow at least 50 per cent of world's food, for example 80 per cent in some African countries. In addition to income generating activities (in cash and kind), women's household activities include caring for sick, house maintenance, and such vital work as caring for children, prepare food, and fetching water and firewood. Yet women's productivity remains low- both in income generating work and in home production.

According to the population Census 2001, women's contribution in agriculture is 60.5 per cent, but economically they rely on men. Women's ownership of land is 10.83 per cent and house ownership is 5.51 per cent only. Though the women constitute half the population in Nepal, their share in the national economy is insignificant. The population census 2001 shows that only 8.55 per cent women are in government jobs, 26 per cent are involved in the teaching profession, 12 per cent in the media, 10.5 per cent in foreign employment and only 2.05 per cent are judges.

Improving women productivity can contribute to growth, efficiency and poverty reduction, which are the key development goals everywhere.

Gaps and Constrains

The gaps and constrains observed worldwide and related to Nepalese context were reviewed:

- Girls' school enrolment rate lay behind those of boys; dropout rate are higher for girls than for boys.
- Many more women than men are low-paying, low skilled informal activities.
- The combination of poor education and lack of access to services like family planning can be - as prevailing higher maternal mortality rate testify.
- Social and institutional factors such as lack of access to land and information often undermine women's ability to maintain environmental quality and sustainable use of the resources.

- Lack of access to credit for female entrepreneurs' limits the profitability and growth of their enterprises. This relates to the limited education and mobility and, in some cases, cultural barriers restrict women's contact with institutions that offer financial services as do the high transaction cost and collateral requirements associated with making small loans.
- Legal and regulatory barriers that do not apply to men exacerbate the inefficiencies of inequality. Especially, property like — land (the universal collateral) is usually registered in men's name.
- Some country have laws that prevent women registered the land in their own name or from owning or selling it; also restriction prevent women from participating in the labor force on equal term with men.
- The need to balance home and market responsibilities is a major constrains on women's earning, productivity and accumulation of human capital.

Research Methodology

Random sample survey technique was used for collecting the primary data. The primary data were collected from each Village Development Committee (VDC) and Municipality of the district. The format was structured to get information in both closed and open ended questions patterns. Demographic information; use of materials for the family planning by both gender and short term or permanent; involvements to some saving and credit or some other organization; income generating activities for different categories; awareness about household conflicts observed and causes of the conflicts and so on were captured in the primary data collection. All data were analyzed using Microsoft access programme in computer. During data entry two VDCs viz. Chisapani, and Gorkhe were having distorted data, and so were excluded from the analysis.

Review of Literatures

Some Facts and Figures on Status of Women

Followings are some facts and figures found in related publications on the worldwide as well as some country or region specific on the status of women.

A. Health Status of Women and Girls

- More than a half of women die from complications related to pregnancy and child birth every year. Ninety-nine per cent of these deaths occur in developing countries (WHO, 2004).

- Providing basic maternal and new born health service to developing nations would cost an average $3 USD per capita per year. However, once complication developed, saving the life of a mother or infant costs about $230 USD (United Nation Population Fund, 2003).
- There are 50 million abortion worldwide annually, 30 million of them are illegal (Alan Guttmacher Institute, May 1998).
- More adolescent girls than boys are diagnosed with HIV positive, 90 per cent of AIDS cases under age of 20 are girls (US Center for Disease Control, 2002)

B. Access to Education

- Of an estimated 115 million children who currently do not attend school, girls make up 57 per cent (United Nations, 2003).
- Of the world's 979 million illiterate adults, two third are women (UNDP Human Development Report, 2003).
- A recent study shows that increase in women's education made the greatest contribution to reducing the rate of child malnutrition, accounting for 43 per cent of the reduction (UNPF, 2002).
- On an average, by age 18, girls receive 4.4 years less education than boys.

C. Political Power

- In 2003, at least 54 countries had discriminatory laws against women (Amnesty International, 2003).
- Some countries still do not have universal suffrage. Among these are Brunei, Kuwait, Oman, Saudi Arabia, and UAE (Women in Politics, 2003).
- Of more than 180 countries of the world, only 12 are headed by women (Women in Politics, 2003).
- Women hold only 6.4 per cent of seats in Arab States' Parliaments, 14.4 per cent of seats in Sub-Saharan Africa, 17.6 per cent of seats in Europe and 18.5 per cent seats in the Americas (Women's Learning Partnership, 2002).
- In Nepal, under the interim assembly, it is about 33 per cent seats in the parliament occupied by women.

D. Economic Status

- More than $7USD trillion worth of women's work goes unpaid.

- Only one per cent of the world's assets are in the name of women. This percentage may be more in case of Nepalese context only (Women's Learning Partnership, 2003).
- 2.1 billion women live on less than $2 UDS a day, and 330 million women live on less than $1 USD a day (Center for Women Policy Studies, 2003)
- In the Middle East, North Africa and South Asia, only 40 women per 100 men are economically active in the formal economy (US News Center, 2004)

E. Violence Parameters

- During the past 30 years, 30 million women and children have been trafficked for sexual exploitation (United Nations, 2003).
- Gender based violence against women (like female infanticide, sexual trafficking and exploitation, dowry killings and domestic violence) causes more death and disability among women in 15-44 age group than other casualties (like cancer, malaria, traffic accident and war combined) (Center for Women Policy Studies, 2003).
- Up to 47 per cent women reported that their first sexual intercourse was forced (World Health Organization, 2003).
- An estimated 130 million women worldwide have under gone female genital mutilation and 2 million more are mutilated every year and 98 per cent of Somali women have been mutilated.

Nepalese Context

Women Representation

Trade Unions

Trade unions are primarily labor advocacy NGOs often promoting worker's interests and are directly concerned with the workers' well-being and women constitute a substantial proportion among the workers. However, no data are available on the female membership of the trade unions, although of the 3.5 million wage earners, 621 000, about 18 per cent have been reported to be organized (GEFONT, 2001).

Table 7.1 revealed that women constitute about 12 per cent of the central leadership of women in the three largest unions. The Labour Act and Labor Regulations (1993) has provisions of 52 days of paid maternity leave up to two pregnancies, only day time employment, limitation on the loads larger than their own body weight etc.

Table 7.1: Women in Policy-making Bodies in Trade Unions in Nepal

Institutions	National Committee Members		Central Leadership	
	Number	Female %	Number	Female %
GEFONT	35	8.6	206	6.3
NTUC	21	23.8	239	14.6
DECONT	21	9.5	141	15.6
Total	**77**	**14.3**	**586**	**11.95**
Committees under GEFONT affiliates	9203	11.58	–	–

Source: GEFONT, 2001.

Media

There has been much progress in women's participation in media channels, particularly in electronic media, with the democratic changes of 1990 and since opening up of the sector to the private sector. Women constituted 12.3 per cent in 1991 and 12.9 per cent of media personnel in 1991. At that time sole electronic media were Nepal Radio and Nepal TV. With the proliferation of FM radios and private TV channels, women's participation as media workers has increased significantly in 2002 as reflected in the Table 7.2.

Table 7.2: Percentage of Women Involved in Media, Nepal 2002

Media/Year	2002
Print	9.1
Public	4.2
Private	11.2
Radio	29.1
Public	16.5
Private	37.9

Media/Year	2002
TV	30.8
Public	31.8
Private	68.2
Total	**19.4**
Public	4.2
Private	18.6

Source: Asmita Publishing House, 2003

Similarly, there has been a substantial progress in media coverage of women's issues (Asmita Publishing House, 2003). This positive development, nevertheless, has not been accompanied by a changed attitude towards a need for inducting women in this sector by social consciousness for promoting women, but for commercial gains only as accepted by the management in interviews (Asmita, 2003).

Political Status

Women's access to positions of power, political or otherwise has not improved much in the last 10-15 years except at the grass roots level; the 20 per cent reservation by the LSGA-2055 Act has made a difference. One female member in 20-45 ministers has been the rule. Still today women constitute less than 10 per cent in the Central Committees of the major politically parties.

Table 7.3: Access to Positions of Power Per cent Women in Various Positions of Power during Pre-democratic situation, Nepal (1986/87 to 200)

Details	1986/87	1991/92	2000
Parliament/3/	5.70	3.80	6.4
House of Representatives	–	3.4	5.8
Upper House (Rastriya Shava)	–	5.0	15.0
Number of Women in the Cabinet	1	2	2
Executives of the major political parties/2/	–	7.8/2	8.3/3
LSG Structure	0.58	0.54	–
District Councils	na	na	1.5
DDCs	0.74	0.75	6.7
Municipalities	1.13	0.38	19.5
VDCs	0.60	0.58	7.7
Village Councils	na	na	2.1
Ward Committees	na	na	20
Government Administration /1/	2.87	na	7.8
Of which: Officers	3.23	4.39	6.2
High Govt. Position —First and Special Class	1.10	2.46	2.4
Professional and technical human power (All sectors—Censuses, 2001)	16.6	15.1	19.0
Administration and Management (All sectors—Census, 2001)	6.6	9.3	13.8

Source: Acharya 1994; CBS/MGEP, Asmita Publishing House, 2002.

1. Figures relate to 1978, 1993 and 2000.
2. Five nationally recognized parties (NC, UML, RPP, SJN, and NSP)
3. Seven Parties in the Parliament (NC, UML, RPP, SJN, NSP and NPWP)

Only reservation since 1997 has been able to bring out women into politics in significant proportions, 20 per cent at the grass roots level. Compared to 1978, the proportion of women in the government administration has almost trebled. At officer and higher levels it has doubled. Still women constitute less than ten per cent of the government staff.

The proportion of women even among the professional and technical group in the occupational classification had declined in 1991 as compared to

1981 but the trend has fortunately reversed as per the 2001 Census (Table 7.3). The trend of increasing proportion of women in administration and management is more encouraging. During the 1990s, women's awareness and women have been mobilized extensively into groups by various NGOs/ INGOs and the government programmes.

Women's political consciousness is also increasing. The proportion of rural women who knew about women's organizations had more than trebled between 1978 and 1992 (from 4.7% to 14.9%). But still only 15 per cent of rural women know about women's organizations and less than one per cent participated in them. Slightly more than 20 per cent knew about the new constitution, but only 6.2 per cent was aware of its discriminatory features. Awareness in urban was higher (Acharya, 1997) at 29.2 per cent.

In contrast to one per cent women reporting any women's organization membership, a recent survey conducted by GEFONT among women/men workers reports (GEFONT, 2003) that 27 per cent of the women workers interviewed had ever joined one or other woman's organization.

Social Status

Achievements in terms of social development indicators have been significant for both women and men in the last two decades. Access to social services in terms of schools and health posts and hospital beds has increased significantly.

Table 7.4: Social Dimensions of Gender Status, Nepal 2001

Indicators\Census Years	1981	1991	2001
Health			
Sex Ratio (Males per 100 Female)	105.0	99.5	99.8
Mean Age of Marriage (Years)	–	–	–
Male	20.7	21.4	22.9
Female	17.2	18.1	19.5
MMR per 100,000 delivery (Number)	850	539	–
TFR (15-49 ages, 1995-2000 period) (Number)	5.1	5.1	4.1
Life Expectancy at birth (Years)	–	–	–
Male	50.9	55.0	60.8
Female	48.1	53.5	61.0
Education			
Literacy in 6 years+ age group (Per cent)	–	–	–
Male	34.0	54.1	65.1

(Contd...)

Female	12.0	24.7	42.5
Literacy Ratio (Literate female/100 literate Male)	33.8	46.3	65.8
Female in school enrolment (Per cent)	–	–	–
Primary	–	37.2	44.1
Secondary	–	31.5	41.5
Higher Secondary	–	28.7	40.6
Female per cent among full time students	27.2	34.7	43.1
SLC and Above (Females\100 Male) (Number)	21.0	28.2	43.2
Graduates (Females\100 Male) (Number)	18.4	22.5	22.9
HDI Index	0.328	0.416	0.490
GDI Index	–	0.312	0.470

Sources: 1. Population Census, 2001;
2. HDR, 1995 and 2002; and
3. Population Monograph, CBS 1995.

Human development indicators have improved significantly for both men and women. In literacy and education gender disparities are decreasing only slowly. Girl's enrolment has not attended parity even at the primary level. The number of women with SLC and higher degrees still constitute only 43 to 100 men with such qualifications.

Similarly, the numbers of women, with graduate and higher degrees, are still less than 20 to 100 men with such degrees. What is more, this ratio has declined as compared to 1991 figure. The male: female ratio of full time students is still only 43:57. Further, these achievements are very unequally distributed as between the regions, rural and urban areas, among castes and various ethnic groups.

In the health sector the improvement is visible in terms of a substantial improvement in MMR, fertility behaviour and ultimately life expectancy. The mean age of first marriage for both the girls and he boys are increasing. It is well recognized by now that there is a large variation between the Indo-Aryan and the Tibeto-Burman groups and even within each of these groups in terms of social relations governing gender relations. In-spite of this diversity, land is inherited universally in all communities from the father to the son and women lag far behind men in access to knowledge, economic resources and modern avenues of employment.

Marriage is compulsory and seen as a primary means of livelihood for women in all most all communities (Acharya and Bennett, 1981; Gurung, 1999).

Women Violence

Violence against women is also widespread in all communities. Violence, both in the domestic as well as in the public arena is still used extensively by the patriarchy to establish domination over women.

As per the 2001 Census more than five hundred fifty-five thousand women are living in polygyneous marriages. Alcohol and polygyny related violence in the domestic arena is reported high all over Nepal and across all communities (New ERA, 1998).

Dowry related violence was reported to a lesser extent, but it does exist. A large group of young widows, particularly, in the Indo-Aryan community, are subject to covert and overt violence and face both psychological (as forerunners of misfortune) and physical violence, often for her share of property.

Trafficking is widely reported but hard data are impossible to collect. Police estimate trafficking of about 5000-7000 women for commercial sex work annually. In the past, girls and women from the Tibeto-Burman groups, coming from poor rural areas were prone to trafficking.

The patriarchal socialization, which establishes marriage as a respectable livelihood option for the girls, is one of the causes of girls falling to trafficker's traps. The Maoist insurgency has compounded the problem of violence against women and children.

Result and Discussion

Involvement in the local Cooperatives

Data indicated that there were on average 41.33 per cent women involved in different cooperatives of which more that 60 per cent VDCs reported to be more of the average. The highest involvement of women were in cooperative has from Shakhejung, 53.42 per cent; Mahamai, 53.13 per cent; and Fikkal, 52.53VDCs. However, lowest participation was from Smalbung, 8.54 per cent and Banjho, 9.64 per cent.

Domestic Violence and Conflicts at Home

Under the three categories of closed answers to the domestic violence's, women of Ilam responded that only 210, (06.19%) women out of 3394 know well about domestic violence's and 1814, (53.45%) women know only a little of violence's ;whereas 1370 (40.36%) women were not knowing about the domestic violence. Knowing did not at all mean that there were no violence at their house, but they were basically doing not relate about the hostility. It indicates that most of women about 96 per cent were not fully know about the different violence.

Table 7.5: Perception of Domestic Violence by Women of Ilam, 2010

Particulars	No. of Respondents	Percentage
Better known	0210	06.19
Little known	1814	53.45
Not known at all	1370	40.36
Total	**3394**	**100.00**

The cases of violence were also recorded. These were categories under 4 categories of reason of violence and of which highest number of cases were less education of women and polygamy of man and both 620 (43.24%); followed by the reason of drinking habit of husband, 393 (27.41%); and third highest was due to facial beautiful, disease, and disability of women and all together.

Table 7.6: Reason of Domestic Violence of Women of Ilam, 2010

Category	Particular	Number of Respondent	Percentage
I	Dowry (Daijo), birth of female child and both	176	12.27
II	Face beautiful, disease, disability and all	245	17.08
III	Less education, and polygamy and both	620	43.24
IV	Drinking habit of husband	393	27.41
	Total	**1434**	**100.00**

As we interpreting data the reason behind the violence is male born in both highest interrogation goes to male as he is the boss to the house. It is human born reason acceptability and responsibility of male in the society.

Conflict in home environment and condition as women of Ilam reported that only 218 cases of husband beating, 129 cases of family discrimination (hela) and 68 cases of polygamy. Highest conflicts were reported from Mahamai, 26; and Kanyam, 23; whereas no conflict was reported from Barbote, Dhuseni, Fikkal, Sagfara, Januna, Panchkanya, Pashupatinagar. Here again it is male partner of the household has been responsible for conflict.

Table 7.7: Number of Conflict Cases in Household in Ilam, 2010

Particulars	Number of Cases	Per cent
Beaten by Husband	218	52.53
Polygamy	068	16.38
Family Discrimination	129	31.09
Total	**415**	**100.00**

Works and Working Hours of Women

Works under nine categories and rest period were responded and found that women of Ilam district spent about two and half hours working with care and management of animals in the shed. They spare only one third of an hour for care of old members of house. Women spent almost two hours in making food for the family and take similar time for as leisure time. It is observed that about two third of an hour in collection/fetching of water. Women spent about one and quarter hours in children care, home cleaning, cloth washing, and wood collection for the household everyday.

Table 7.8: Time Spent on Different Categories of Household Works by Women of Ilam, 2010

Type of Work	Time Spent (Hr)	Percentage	Type of Work	Time Spent (Hr)	Percentage
Animal care in shed	2.5	20.83	Water Fetching	0.6	05.00
House Cleaning	1.1	09.17	Wood collection	1.2	10.00
Food Preparation	1.8	15.00	Cloth Washing	1.2	10.00
Care of children	1.2	10.00	Care of old persons	0.3	02.50
Leisure period	1.9	15.83	Total	12.0	100.00

Although there were out layers in the data for Lumde and Shantidada VDCs for their externality of data and were excluded. It is also observed that women of Puwamajhuwa and Phakphok VDCs were spending more hours, 14hrs in household works and enjoying a two hours of leisure that was followed by women of Sumbek, Maipokhari, Sangrumba, Lumde, Phuyathappa and Nayabajar, 13 hrs. VDCs. Similarly, women of Danabari, Barebote, Panchkanya, were spending only about 7 hours in work and having only one hour of rest.

Income Generating Activities

Respondents were asked to express their income generating activities in three categories of which poultry, goat keeping and agricultural; retail shop keeping, cottage industries, and doll making; and business, driving and other technical activities were listed. Out of 2921 women respondent expressed their source of income highest from poultry, goat keeping and agriculture activities; 2569 (87.95%) and retailing, cottage industry and doll making as second income generating activities; 234 (08.01%). Women in Ilam are more preferred to raise animals in their household as they are dedicated to have some animals in their house. Now a days, they are diverting their substantial animal husbandry to commercial one along with some NGOs involvement by forming user groups, committees and farming improve breeds and suitable variety of crops.

Table 7.9: Involvement in Income Generating Activities by Women of Ilam — 2010

Sl. No.	Type of Activities	No. of Respondents	Percentage
1.	Goat, poultry raising, and agriculture	2569	87.95
2.	Retailing, Cottage industries and doll making	234	08.01
3.	Business, Driving and other technical jobs	118	04.03
	Total	**2921**	**100.00**

It was observed that activities related to agriculture and livestock were higher in Fikkal (111) and Mahamai (108) whereas, retailing shops and cottage industries were higher in ChulachuliVDCs. Similarly, Business and other technical jobs were highly concentrated to Ilam municipal, but overall the income generating activities were highest in Chulachuli VDC, it may be due to more near to Jhapa. Here it can be related that all short of income activities can be cashed through nearest market, which is Jhapa.

Sources of Information and Entertainment

The information and entertainments are the basic need of any life style in the context of 21st century. These facilities were captured through availability of radio, television, telephone, mobiles and newspapers to the women of Ilam. It was found that radio was the prime source of information and entertainment which accounted, 3862 (95.26%) and the second facility they have mobile, 1858 (45.83%) and the 3rd entertaining facilities was visual television, 1570 (38.73%).

Though newspaper availability were less than 5 per cent but use of mobile had exceeded to 5 times than telephone, which may be due to unavailability of telephone line distribution and cheaper to landline telephone in context to its technology.

Table 7.10: Information and Entertainment Facilities of Women of Ilam-2010

Facilities	No. of Respondents	Percentage
Radio	3862	95.28
Television	1570	38.73
Telephone	347	08.56
Mobile	1858	45.83
Newspaper	196	04.83
Total	**4054**	**100.00**

Although, highest newspapers were read by Pyang, Kolbung and Ilam municipal women but almost all women in Ilam district have radio with them. It seems that facilities of mobiles ranked first by women of Fikkal VDC, 74.3 per cent and Ilammunicipal, 72.12 per cent but women of Jitpur responded zero to mobile facility.

It has observed that 14 VDCs out of 47 i.e. 29.78 recorded were not enjoying reading newspaper, which may be an opportunity to promot newspaper distribution and marketing to those VDCs viz. Danabari, Gajurmukhi, Jirmale, Jitpur, Lumde, Santipur, Sri Antu and so on.

Family Planning

The family planning concept was bifurcated with two categories viz. permanent and temporary family planning and in both the sexes. It is interesting that in both categories female were doing more practice than male. Males were still behind to go forward for uses of contraceptives in family planning. It has drawn attention that females' responsibility to tackle the sensitiveness of reproducing and giving birth to children in that family.

Table 7.11: Use of Temporary and Permanent Means of Family Planning by Both Male and Female of Ilam District — 2010

Sl. No.	Categories	No. of Respondents	Percentage of Total	Female: Male, Ratio
1.	**Temporary**			
	Male	44	00.92	36.4: 1.00
	Female	1600	33.53	
2.	**Permanent**			
	Male	154	03.23	03.6: 1.00
	Female	557	11.70	
	Total	**4772**	**49.38**	**10.89 : 1.00**

Women from Shakhejung, Fikkale, Mahamai and Maipokhari VDCs were reported higher number of female contraceptive users than women of Banjho, Jitpur, Samalbung and Sidhithumka, Similarly, permanent family planning were higher in the women of Ilam, Pasupatinager, Pyang and Sri Antu. Among the males use of condoms has reported as minimal but the permanent family planning was observed in Santipur, Namsaling and Shidhithumka.

It is observed that nearer to capital city or where sub health centers or the highways the use of temporary means as well as permanent means of female family planning are more as it is in the remote villages, which may be due to access of means to the community. Whereas, permanent family planning is more prevalent in the remote area of Ilam as compare to sub-city area.

Social Inclusion

In regards to social inclusion it was asked whether women of Ilam know about the social inclusion and what would be the inclusion of women in the society at three categorical contexts. Although, only 41.47 per cent women were knowing social inclusion the result indicated higher towards covering all casts groups and gender in social inclusion, 1546 (78.12%) whereas minimal responded to work only by women. It is highly appreciable that women are conscious about inclusion and want to significantly cover all casts' groups and gender issues.

Table 7.12: Inclusion of Women in Social Aspects of Women of Ilam — 2010

Sl. No.	Category	No. of Respondents	Percentage of Inclusion
1.	Cover all casts groups and sexes	1546	78.13
2.	Works only by women	108	5.45
3.	Include women in some cases	325	16.42
4.	Knowing the social Inclusion	1979	41.47
5.	Total respondents	4772	100.00

It has been observed that women of Ilam municipality and Sulubung VDC knew higher regarding social inclusion of women and least by Banjho, Jirmale, Jitpur and Santidanda. The least known were the women of remote and rural area of the district.

Involvement of Social Organization

It has been observed that only 13.99 of women were involved and had activist in different organization. The more percentage goes to farmers groups and committees directly handled under different line agencies of government at district level.

It was found that women of Fikkal, Jogmai were highly involved in NGOs, however Panchkanya and Pashupatinagar VDCs' women had shown higher involvement in government organization.

Disabilities

The conditions of disabilities were responded (Table 7.14) and about 56.37 percentage of women recorded only 20.66 per cent of disabilities under seven different types of disabilities. The number of disability found were higher in physical disability, 308 (31.23%) which were followed by listing disability of both ears, 216 (22.00%) of the disability, 986 reported.

Table 7.13: Involvement of Women in Different Organizations at Local Level Institutions of Ilam — 2010

Organizations/Institution	No of Respondent Involved	Percentage of Involved
Non-governmental Organization (NGOs)	182	27.24
Red cross	74	11.07
Governmental Organization (GOs)	261	39.07
Youth Clubs	55	07.99
Children Committee	73	10.93
Labour Committee	20	2.99
Others	3	0.40
Total Involvements	668	14.00 (100)
Total respondents	**4772**	**100.00**

The disability varies from their types. It is observed that females were more prone to vision, 56.73 per cent than male, 43.27 per cent and it is seen also in listening irrespective of age. Though the mental problems rank fourth of the disability but more percentage is observed in youth age than the others age. Listening by single ear and the abandoned problems are less than ten per cent in total.

Table 7.14:Summary of Categorical Disabilities of Ilam — 2010

Type of Disabilities	No. of Observation	Percentage of Observed	(Male and Female) and their Percentage
Physical	308	31.23	
Listening (both ears)	216	22.00	Female: 559
Listening (single ear)	069	07.00	(56.70 %)
Vision (Blindness)	171	17.34	
Mental	102	10.30	
Multi-disability	97	09.80	Male: 427
Abandoned	23	02.33	(43.30 %)
Disabilities	986	20.66	
Respondents	4772	100.00	

Annual Saving and Income

Annual savings as the net income of the household were reported by four ranges of income groups as well as four categories of age distributions for both male and female member of the family. There were 3673 respondents accounting 67.97 per cent of total of which 2081 females reported higher by 19.93 per cent as of 1592 males under different categories.

The actively participation in saving for future indicates some favors towards self help attitude in women of the district. This might be related to saving and credit cooperatives active in the village premier. Although, women exceeded in saving the income both in numbers and amount but the per capita annual saving is lower for women NRs. 8488.70 as compare to men NRs. 9252.51and together average of NRs. 8819.76.

Table 7.15: Annual Savings of Household at Different Range of Income and Age Groups for Both Female and Male, Ilam — 2010

Amount of savings and Age Group	No. of Respondents and Percentage		Total	Average Savings NRs.
	Female	Male		
1. One to five thousand				
– Children	103 (05.1)	032 (01.6)	2020 (54.99)	10100,000
– Youths	820 (40.6)	560 (27.7)		
– Adults	282 (14.0)	166 (08.2)		
– Older	027 (01.3)	030 (00.2)		
2. Six to ten thousand				
– Children	032 (03.8)	005 (00.6)	842 (22.93)	8420,000
– Youths	288 (34.2)	287 (34.4)		
– Adults	105 (12.5)	106 (12.6)		
– Older	009 (10.7)	010 (01.2)		
3. Eleven to Twenty thousand				
– Children	007 (01.5)	004 (01.2)	469 (12.76)	7035,000
– Youths	127 (27.1)	158 (33.7)		
– Adults	085 (18.1)	072 (15.4)		
– Older	006 (01.3)	008 (01.6)		

(Contd...)

4. More than Twenty thousand				
– Children	003 (01.0)	003 (01.0)	342 (09.32)	8640,000
– Youths	129 (37.7)	100 (29.0)		
– Adults	047 (13.7)	042 (12.3)		
– Older	009 (02.6)	009 (02.6)		
Total	**2081 (56.7)**	**1592 (43.3)**	**3673 (100)**	

Note: Figures in the parenthesis indicate percentage in those categories.

Table 7.16: Summary of Total Annual Savings by Gender and Their Per Capita Savings

Gender Category	One to Five Thousand @NRs 5,000	Six to Ten Thousand @NRs 10,000	Eleven to Twenty Thousand @ NRs15,000	More than Twenty Thousand @ NRs 20,000	Total
Female					
– Respondent	1232	434	227	188	2081
– Amount	6160,000	4340,000	3405,000	3760,000	17665,000
Male					
– Respondent	788	408	242	154	1592
– Amount	3940,000	4080,000	3630,000	3080,000	14730,000
Total					
– Respondent	2020	842	469	342	3673
– Amount	10100,000	84200,000	7035,000	6840,000	32395,000
Per capita annual saving	**Male: NRs. 9252.51; Female: NRs. 8488.70; and Average: NRs. 8819.76**				

Recommendations/Conclusion

It is the demand of time to rupture the walls of confinement and set into motion women's talent for equal opportunities and rights. They should demand education and equal rights and opportunity. Women have secured at least 33 per cent seats in the Constituent Assembly, this is positive but changing the traditional patriarchal values prevalent in the society is of outmost. Followings are some of the policy implications which could be done.

1. Educate the half population, that is, women of your society and policy should not forget to maximize this in relation to increase in knowledge and skill so that they could do for their own development in the socio-economic perspectives.

2. Provide soft loan and credit facilities to women, improving women productivity can contribute to growth, efficiency and poverty reduction.
3. Make use of recent technology like mobile and facilitate women to access new technology as well as their right to inform and develop themselves. Government may develop a system to inform them by mobile service about different types of notice and massages for their personal development and any type of agricultural/livestock or entrepreneurial development perspectives.

REFERENCES

Acharya, Meena, (2000) *Labour Market Developments and Poverty: With Focus on Economic Opportunities for Women*, TPMF and Friedrich-Ebert-Stiftung, Kathmandu.

Acharya, Meena and Acharya, Pushpa (1997a) Gender Equality and Empowerment of Women, A Status Report, UNFPA, Kathmandu.

Acharya, Meena and Bennett, Lynn, (1981) An Aggregate Analysis and Summary of 8 Village Studies. *The Status of Women in Nepal*. Vol. II, Part 9. CEDA, Kathmandu.

Central Bureau of Statistics, (1995) Population Monograph of Nepal, Kathmandu.

Central Bureau of Statistics, /NPC/HMG (1996) Nepal Living Standards Survey, 1995/96. Main Findings Vol. I. & II. Kathmandu.

Asmita Publishing House (2002): Patrakarita ma Mahila Prashna (Nepali).

Viktoria Walter (2003): Practicing Gender: The Tool Book, Friedrich-Ebert-Stiftung, Germany.

GDS\FES (1997): Women in Garment Industries, Kathmandu.

GEFONT (2001): Woman Participation in Nepali Labour Movement, Kathmandu.

GEFONT (2003): Search for Alternatives, Kathmandu.

Gurung, Jeannette, D. (1999) (Edit) Searching for Women's Voices in the Hindu Kush Himalayas, ICIMOD, Kathmandu.

HMG\N (1997): Local Self-Governance Act, 1997, Kathmandu.

INSEC (2002): Human Rights Report. Kathmandu.

New ERA (1998) A Situation Analysis of Sex Work and Trafficking in Nepal with Reference to Children, October 1996. Submitted to UNICEF, Nepal.

SAATHI and The Asia Foundation, (1997) A Situation Analysis of Violence Against Women and Girls in Nepal. Kathmandu.

United Nations (1995, 2002): Human Development Report.

UNDP (1998): National Gender Analysis on Elected and Nominated Women Ward Representative, Kathmandu.

National Planning Commission/HMG Sixth Five Year to Tenth Five Year Plans.

National Planning Commission/HMG (1996) Nepal Multiple Indicators Surveillance (NMIS): Primary Education Second Cycle, April-June 1995.

ANNEXES

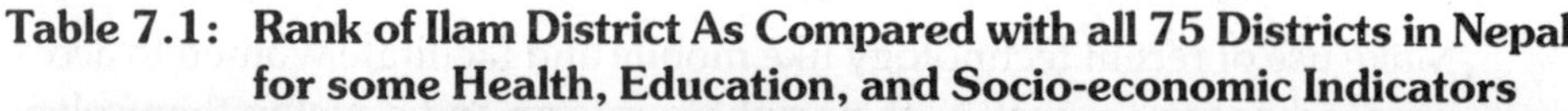

Table 7.1: Rank of Ilam District As Compared with all 75 Districts in Nepal for some Health, Education, and Socio-economic Indicators

Sl. No.	Indicators	Data Value	Rank (Out of 75)
1.	Access to electricity facilities, per cent	43.1	22
2.	Access to having radio facility, percentage	56.8	31
3.	Access to improved toilet facility , percentage	76.4	6
4.	Access to improves source of drinking water	78.3	42
5.	Access to telephone per 1000 population, number	2.92	26
6.	Access to using solid fuels for cooking, percentage	79.5	20
7.	Adult gender imbalance rate in literacy status, per cent	0.71	
8.	Adult gender imbalance rate in non-agriculture Occupation, per cent	0.36	
9.	Agricultural credit, per cent	11.65	
10.	Bank density, in 1000 persons	0.23	56
11.	Child dependency ratio, percentage	66.5	10
12.	Child economic activity rate, per cent	9.4	
13.	Child illiteracy rate, per cent	8.45	
14.	Contraceptive prevalence rate, per cent	52.06	11
15.	Cooperative density, in 1000	7.48	12
16.	Farm size, ha/household	0.98	11
17.	Forest user household, percentage	44.28	46
18.	Health institution density, per 1000 person	2.23	45
19.	Incidence of ARI per 1000 children <5 years	198	38
20.	Incidence of diarrhoea per 1000 children <5 years	209	49
21.	Literacy rate of population 15-24 years, per cent	87.6	4
22.	Livestock per farm household, number	5.57	
23.	Malnourished children <3 years, per' 000	13.6	26
24.	Overall composite index		12
25.	Per capita development budget expenditure, NRS	732	43
26.	Per capita food production	3404	35
27.	Per capita regular budget expenditure, NRS	971	44
28.	Percentage of educationally disadvantaged population	0	1

(Contd…)

Sl. No.	Indicators	Data Value	Rank (Out of 75)
29.	Percentage of Irrigated area	16.27	53
30.	Percentage of marginal farm household	26	18
31.	Percentage share of female in non-agriculture occupations	26.19	18
32.	Post office density, in 100 sq. km	2.34	
33.	Primary School net enrolment ratio, per cent	93.8	15
34.	Proportion of child marriage, per cent	0.17	
35.	Proportion of urban population, per cent	5.7	37
36.	Rank according to child deprivation index		3
37.	Rank according to infrastructure Development		36
38.	Rank according to primary sector development index		26
39.	Rank according to socio-economic and infrastructure deprivation index		11
40.	Rank according to the gender discrimination		3
41.	Rank according to the health development		8
42.	Rank according to women empowerment index		19
43.	Ratio of girls to boys in primary education, per cent	96.8	12
44.	Ratio of literate female to male 15-24 yrs, per cent	92.7	3
45.	Ratio of Student to teachers in secondary education, per cent	34.4	64
46.	Reported death per'000 population	5.102	40
47.	Road density, length/sq. km area	0.22105	18
48.	Simulated mean age at marriage female, years	21.7	6

Table 7.2: Demographic Trend for Ilam District

Particulars	1981 Census	1991 Census	2001 Census	2011 Projected
Population	178356	229214	282806	348066
Male	92031	115377	142434	174933
Female	87325	113837	140372	173133
Sex Ratio			101	101.04
Household	31330	41450	54565	71824
Average Household Size	5.7	5.5	5.18	6.0
Literacy Rate	33.0	52.5	66.23	67.0
Population Density (per sq. km)	104.7	134.6	166	211

Source: CBS, Nepal.

Table 7.3: Religious Population of Ilam during Census 2001

Particulars	Numbers	Percentage
Hindu	133718	47.28
Kirat	102302	36.17
Buddha	44354	15.68
Chritrian	1601	0.57
Sikha	287	0.10
Islam	127	0.04
Jain	27	0.01
Others	390	0.14
Total	**282806**	**100.00**

Source: CBS, Nepal.

Table 7.4: Linguistic Population of Ilam during Census 2001

Mother Tongue	Numbers	Percentage
Nepali	152804	54.03
Bantawa	50048	17.70
Limbu	35868	12.68
Tamang	14145	5.00
Magar	10786	3.81
Sherpa	3766	1.33
Gurung	3407	1.20
Sunuwar	2215	0.78
Others	9767	3.45
Total	**282806**	**100.00**

Source: CBS, Nepal.

Section–II
Women in Micro-finance and Self-Help Groups (SHGs)

8

Impact of Self-Help Groups (SHGs) on Women Empowerment

An Empirical Study

Dr. Rambabu Gopisetti

ABSTRACT

In favour of an accelerated socio-economic development of any community the active participation of women is crucial. In a social set up like India, the participation of women in the development process has to be ensured through tangible measures taken at various levels which result in empowerment of women in the real sense. Women empowerment is one of the main items to tackle rural poverty and socio-economic issues. The socio-economic impact is examined in terms of the increase in income, savings and assets creation etc. The socio-political impact is examined in terms of entry into politics, change of attitude of husbands towards SHG members and finally, overall improvement in overall status of members of Self-Help Groups. Any Nations economic development depends on the people saving habits prevailing in the country. There is a direct relationship between income, savings and investments. The size of savings amount various from group to group based on their surplus amount. On the whole, it is recommended that, the Government should continue the programme with more enthusiastic way to cover, educate, and motivate rural poor women to improve their overall status in the society. The Government should undertake a total development package comprising stimulatory, support and sustaining activities for the development of Self-Help Groups. Government should provide sufficient capital and release loan without any delay. By and large, Self-Help Group movement has brought a lot change in members of the Self-Help Groups.

Introduction

In favour of an accelerated socio-economic development of any community the active participation of women is crucial. In a social set up like India, the participation of women in the development process has to be ensured through tangible measures taken at various levels which result in empowerment of women in the real sense. The women of the country are empowered and they become the active participants in the development process. It can also in the context of the family and in the society at large, including its economy and social system. The present women are in a strategic position covering all the activities like nurturing children to decision makers in economic activities.

Women Empowerment and SHGs

Women empowerment is one of the main items to tackle rural poverty and socio-economic issues. Women have taken up self-help movement through thrift and savings as a mass movement — a path chosen by the women to shape their future destiny. Development agenda of the state in the last few years has been to place the poor, especially women in the forefront have facilitated formation of a large number of self-help groups (SHGs) throughout the length and breadth of the state. The success of any strategy of women empowerment depends upon the following factors:

1. Level of education, hard work
2. Social custom
3. Family planning, small family
4. Health, medical services, cleanliness
5. Environment, tree growing, kitchen gardening.

The process of women empowerment is conceptualized in terms of personal assertions, self-esteem and confidence, ability to project themselves as women attaining socio-political participation and economic independence, ownership of productive assets and provide leadership in both women and community related issues at all levels. For the empowerment of women, several programmes and schemes had been launched in the past few years by Government of India in order to fulfill its vision of expanding women's horizons of autonomous decisions making and control over resources, becoming equal partners to their men folk to achieve "the ultimate goal of complete development".

Hence, the women empowerment can be done through SHGs, which is a voluntarily formed group the member size is 10-20. The group is basically homogeneous in nature. They came together for addressing their common problem. They are encouraged to save in a regular basis. The amount of saving is within the range of Rs. 20-100. They rotate this common pooled resource within the members with a very small rate of interest. Each group has a leader who is called as the president and secretary. They usually maintain records of transaction in daily basis in written format and that has been kept with the president or the secretary. Not only from the internal resources have the members also got loan in bulk amount from mainstream banks, different governmental and non-governmental organizations, donor agencies through MFIs.

Objective of the Paper

In view of the above, the present study has been taken-up with a conscious view to analyse the impact of Self-Help Groups on Women Empowerment through savings, income, asset creation, entry in to politics and overall status of members.

Sample Design

The study is essentially based on primary data. As is evident from the title of the work, it was carried out in Khammam District of Andhra Pradesh. Quota sampling technique was used to arrive at the sample; five mandals were selected from khammam district at first stage. From each mandal two villages were selected, from each village two groups were selected. From each group 10 members were drawn as sample respondents, thus the total sample working out to be 200 members. Thus, the study covered in all five mandals, ten villages and twenty groups are spread over in one district. The details can be seen from Table 8.1 on next page.

Method of Analysis, Data Base and Tools

To accomplish the stated objectives, the study was limited to a select district in Andhra Pradesh. Khammam District was chosen as the researcher has familiarity with villages in the district. A comprehensive questionnaire has been canvassed to the members of SHGs. Through extensive interface and formal and informal interviews, additional information has been gathered and opinion elicited. Primary data has been supplemented by secondary sources of information available from records, brochures, annual reports and other publications wherever required. The data gathered has been processed and tabulated by using MS-Excel software SPSS and in part manually. Two-way tabular form has been used to present processed final data. Simple statistical tools have been used to analyze the data.

Table 8.1: Sample Design

District	Mandals	Villages	No. of. Groups	No. of. Respondents
Khammam	Penubally	1. Yedla Banzar	2	20
		2. Lingagudem	2	20
	Kalluru	1. RK Puram	2	20
		2. Suraiah Banzar	2	20
	Tallada	1. Annarugudem	2	20
		2. Balapeta	2	20
	Sathupally	1. Kistaram	2	20
		2. Ramanagaram	2	20
	Konijerla	1. Gopavaram	2	20
		2. Peddamunagala	2	20
		Total		**200**

Impact of SHGs on Women Empowerment

Impact of Self-Help Groups (SHGs) on women empowerment studied from various dimensions such are Income, Savings, Asset Creation, Family Support, and Involvement in Politics and Improvement in Overall Status. In the present study, the data pertaining to direction of change from the period between before becoming the members of Self-Help Groups and after becoming of the members was obtained in terms of:

1. Increase
2. Decrease
3. No Change categories.

Similar methodology is adopted in analyzing socio-economic and political impact too. The socio-economic impact is examined in terms of the increase in income, savings and assets creation etc. The socio-political impact is examined in terms of entry into politics, change of attitude of husbands towards SHG members and finally, overall improvement in overall status of members of Self-Help Groups.

(a) Impact of SHGs on Income of the SHG members

The economic status of SHG members depend upon the level of income earned by the members. In this context, the present study analyses the change in their income levels. It is very vivid from the Table 8.2 that, increase in income after joining into groups found at 71 per cent, whereas 29 represents that there is no change in their income. Thus, a conclusion is possible here that Self-Help Group movement has a favourable impact on income of the members. This may be due to the efforts made by Government and Non-Governmental Organizations (NGOs) and other Micro-finance Institutions.

Table 8.2: Impact of SHGs on Income of the SHG members

Impact	No. of Respondents	Percentages
Increase	142	71.00
Decrease	Nil	Nil
No Change	58	29.00
Total	**200**	**100.00**

Source: Primary data.

(b) Impact of SHGs on Savings of the SHG members

Any Nations economic development depends on the people saving habits prevailing in the country. There is a direct relationship between income, savings and investments. The size of savings amount various from group to group based on their surplus amount. In the present study, nearly 81 per cent of the respondents reported that their savings amount increased after joining into group and 16 per cent represents that there is no change in saving amount before and after joining into group. It is interesting to note that, 3 per cent of the respondents revealed that their saving amount decreased after joining into group. The reasons beyond that lack of awareness, lack of motivation and illiteracy etc. To improve the saving amount of all the members, there is a need to conduct a campaign programme on Self-Help Group Movement.

Table 8.3: Impact of SHGs on Savings of the SHG Members

Impact	No. of Respondents	Percentages
Increase	162	81.00
Decrease	06	03.00
No Change	32	16.00
Total	**200**	**100.00**

Source: Primary data.

(c) Impact of SHGs on Asset Creation of SHG Members

Improved income levels, if they are managed in an efficient way will result in increased investments in business and asset creation. In the present study, data reveals that, about 49 per cent of the respondents reported that asset creation capabilities increased after becoming member in to SHGs. On the other hand, there is no change in asset creation before and after becoming member into SHG found at 42 per cent. Very astonishing thing is that, there is a decrease in asset creation after becoming member into SHGs stands at 9 per cent. The study finds that, half of the sample respondents are more active in creation of assets. (*See more details in Table 8.4*).

Table 8.4: Impact of SHGs on Asset Creation of SHG Members

Impact	No. of. Respondents	Percentages
Increase	98	49.00
Decrease	18	09.00
No Change	84	42.00
Total	**200**	**100.00**

Source: Primary data.

(d) Impact of SHGs on Change of Attitude of Husbands towards SHG Members

As there is a close nexus between economic and social factors, in the light of the changed economic position an attempt is made to find out as to what extent the members of Self-Help Groups are elevated in their social status. Though there are many indicators of social change in this study, only there aspects have been analyzed:

(*a*) Change of attitude of husbands towards SHG members;

(*b*) Involvement in Politics; and

(*c*) Overall improvement in the social status of SHG members.

In general, in a family male member are dominating in all the activities like legal and property rights etc. They are the decision makers. They do not allow their wives to work in other places. In this context, the present study is a modest attempt to analyze the attitude of family members especially husbands of SHG members. More than half of the members (53.50) reported that there is a tremendous change in attitude of husbands because of the member contributing a share in total family income. About 46.50 per cent of the members stated that there is no change in the attitude of their husbands before and after becoming members into SHGs.

Table 8.5: Impact of SHGs on Change of Attitude of Husbands towards SHG Members

Impact	No. of. Respondents	Percentages
Increase	107	53.50
Decrease	Nil	Nil
No Change	93	46.50
Total	**200**	**100.00**

Source: Primary data.

It can be conclude that, when member became economically strong then only they brought change in attitude of their husbands. It also proved that there is a strong relation between socio-economic and socio-political issues of the members.

(e) Impact of SHGs on Involvement in to Politics by SHG Members

Political space always has been monopolized by men. Representation of women among members of parliament and state legislatures has never exceeded 7 per cent and has typically around 5 per cent over the years despite the increasing visibility of women. However, in the recent past, there is slow and gradual entry of women, particularly those who have been active in Self-Help Group movement being picked up by different parties to different positions such as ZPTC, MPTC, ward members, village sarpanches etc. The level of involvement in politics by Self-Help Group members are shown in Table 8.6.

Involvement in politics by the women are found at 48 per cent after becoming a member into group and 52 per cent reported that there is no change in involvement in politics before and after joining into group. It can be finding from the same table that, nearly half of the members are taken active role politics.

Table 8.6: Impact of SHGs on Involvement in to Politics by SHG Members

Impact	No. of. Respondents	Percentages
Increase	95	47.50
Decrease	Nil	Nil
No Change	105	52.50
Total	**200**	**100.00**

Source: Primary data.

(f) Impact of SHGs on Overall Improvement of SHG Members

The lower status accorded to women in Indian society can be seen from the excessive importance on their roles as wives and mothers rather than as individuals in their own right. The depressed action meted out to widows in hostile jewelry and finery, and even cheap glass bangles to women after the death of their husbands etc. are the few examples. However, there is a social transformation taking place gradually in terms of giving them equal rights in education, property and reservation of seats in political bodies and public offices etc. The overall status of women is a combined indicator of their involvement in decision-making, owning of assets, entry into politics and exposure to public life, leadership and management of Self-Help Groups. By explaining all these indicators to the respondents the data was collected as to whether there was a change in the overall status of women. The overall improvement of Self-Help Group members are presented in the Table 8.7. Nearly two third of the sample respondents are stated that there is a improvement in their lives after becoming as a member into Self-Help Group. Whereas, only 33 per cent revealed that there is no change in their overall status before and after becoming as a member into Self-Help Group. Here, a conclusion thus possible here that, Government should initiate an awareness programme to cover and improve their overall status in their lives.

Table 8.7: Impact of SHGs on Overall Improvement of SHG Members

Impact	No. of. Respondents	Percentages
Increase	135	67.50
Decrease	Nil	Nil
No Change	65	32.50
Total	**200**	**100.00**

Source: Primary data.

Summary of Findings

1. In favour of an accelerated socio-economic development of any community the active participation of women is crucial.
2. Self-Help Group movement has a favourable impact on income of the members. This may be due to the efforts made by Government and Non-Governmental Organizations (NGOs) and other Micro-finance Institutions.
3. To improve the saving amount of all the members, there is a need to conduct a campaign programme on Self-Help Group Movement.
4. The study finds that, half of the sample respondents are more active in creation of assets.
5. When member became economically strong then only they brought change in attitude of their husbands. It also proved that there is a strong relation between socio-economic and socio-political issues of the members.

6. It can be finding from the same table that, nearly half of the members are taken active role politics.
7. Government should initiate an awareness programme to cover and improve their overall status in their lives.

Conclusion

In conclusion, it can be said that the Government should continue the tempo of women empowerment through SHG programme with more enthusiastic way to enable rural poor women to improve their social and educational status in the society. So, the Government should undertake a total development package comprising stimulatory support and sustaining activities for the development of Self-Help Groups by providing sufficient capital and release of loans without any delay. By and large, Self-Help Group movement should be continued to bring a sea change in members of the Self-Help Groups and in turn the rural India.

REFERENCES

Sayulu.K., Sardar.G., Sridevi.B., *Impact of Self-Help Groups on Women Empowrment: An Empirical Study*, Management Researcher, Institute of Management Development and Research, pp. 20-33.

Annual Report 2009-10., Ministry of Rural Development, New Delhi.

Dr. Rambabu Gopisetti., *Working of Self-Help Groups in Andhra Pradesh: An Analysis of Marketing and Finance Aspects*, OU. Hyederabad., Unpublished Ph.D., Thesis.

www.google.com

A Study of Women Self-Help Groups in the Village

Dulal Ch. Karmakar

Introduction

Self-Help Groups have been playing an important role in reducing poverty of rural people. According to 2001 census, nearly 72 per cent people still live in rural areas. We have to consider for the development of these persons. The poor do not have access to financial support from any organized financial institutions. They need only a little amount to undertake their productive activities.

In 1999, Government of India introduced SGSY as a programme for rural development. In this programme an emphasis is made to organize the poor to form Self-help Groups, especially women Self-Help Groups.

A Self-Help group is a group of 10 to 20 members consisting of very poor people contributing equally to the corpus fund. The members of the Self-help Groups have to bear joint responsibilities in taking loans from the banks, in repaying loans, in productive activities.

In Indian villages, Self-help Groups, especially women Self-help Groups have undergone a revolutionary changes in reducing poverty. Assam is not an exception to that. In the district of Dhubri, total number of SHGs formed is 4139 as on 2003-04 while women SHGs formed 2339 groups.

Research Questions

The following are some research questions which are sought to be answered in the study:

- Are the rural poor women improving socio-economic conditions after formation of Self-Help Groups?
- Are they able to borrow funds?
- Are their repayment of loan is 100 per cent?
- Can they save after formation of Self-Help Groups?

Objectives of the Study

The following are the objectives of the study:

- To know the socio-economic characteristics of the female members
- To know their borrowing behaviour
- To know their repayment culture

Methodology

The study is based on both primary data and secondary data. Primary data is collected from 83 members of seven women Self-help Groups of the village of Madaikhali of Dhubri district in Assam. Secondary data are collected from Government report, DRDA Dhubri, Statistical Hand Book-2005, Economic Survey of Assam-2005-06, published research work, books, Kurukshetra journal, Yojana, and articles from newspaper and magazines.

Data Analysis

Madaikhali Village: Madaikhali is one of the villages of the Gram Panchayat, Asharikandi under Debitola Development Block where number of BPL families is 9413. Occupational structure of the people is diversified. They earn their livelihood from occupations of terracotta, fishery, agriculture, business and service. Education scenario of the village is satisfactory. In the village, there are 4 (four) primary schools, 3 M.E. Schools where 1 School meant for girls only. There are 2 High Schools where 1 high school is a Girls' High School. There is also an Art School and a Computer Training Centre. Students of different faculties like technical, engineering, and general higher education are also seen in the village. A number of educated unemployed is found in the village. But the village lacks primary Health Centre to keep the people fit medically. Thus the people, specially the children and mothers face a lot of problems when they are seriously ill. The village people are provided with common tube well and one each to BPL family for drinking water. As for transport and communication facilities, the village is well connected. The road is metalled road. Both traditional and modern transport facilities are available in the village like Thela Carriage (Pushing Carriage), Rickshaw van, Rickshaw, Horse cart, Big Auto Rickshaws (Tempo), Tata Sumo, etc. WLL BSNL service, Airtel service, Aircel service are provided that lead to improvement in the communication system in the village. It is interesting to note that there are 12 PCOs and 1 P.O. in the village. Nearest Gauripur market is only 3 k.m. away from the village where the villagers sell their products and purchase essential products from the market. The village has a nearby river, the Gadadhar. The people of the village spend leisure time in playing card, and enjoying film in the Video hall. The village is very important for its 'Terracotta centre'. Nearly 80 families are engaged in terracotta traditionally for their livelihood. Many researchers and visitors from different places of the country visit the important place. The village is ahead in forming SHGs. Most of the SHGs are women SHGs. SHGs consisting of male persons are also seen in the village.

Socio-economic Characteristics of Women members of the Self-Help Groups

The village contains a number of male as well as female SHGs. Total number of SHGs in the Debitola Development Block is 583 covering 6851 men and 3964 women members. Out of seven SHGs, only three women SHGs are engaged in productive activities — terracotta and sweet production. The women SHGs engaged in borrowing and lending activities do not undertake any productive activity. The SHGs covered under study are shown in Table 9.1.

Age Group of Female Members

The age group of female members in the village who are engaged in SHGs activities is shown in the Table 9.2 (covering 83 members of 7 SHGs).

The Table 9.2 shows that the highest number of women members, i.e., 19, is in the age group (35-45) and the lowest number of the members, i.e., 1, is in the age groups of (65-70) and (70-75). The second highest number of the members, i.e., 18, is in the age group (30-35) which is followed by the age group of (45-50) which has 17 number of female members.

Education

Most of the female members of the group are illiterate. The members who are educated are engaged in discharging the duties of the secretary and the president. They send their children preferably male children to the nearby schools. Education status of the female members of the groups is shown in the Table 9.3.

A total of 83 female members are studied and found that 32 members of different SHGs are illiterate, 26 are in the class group of (I-V), 16 are in (V-X) and 8 are in (X-Graduation) and nil is found in the class group of more than graduation. It is also observed that Binapani SHG which was set up in 2002 has 4 (Four) members who passed Higher Secondary, despite this, they could not take productive activities of the group because of misunderstanding and co-operation of the members.

Table 9.1: The Self-Help Groups

Sl. No.	Name of SHGs (Women)	Year of Establishing	Monthly Contribution (Rs.)	Productive Activities	No. of Members	Regular/Irregular Saving in Groups A/c
1.	Bagurapara Matri Got	2001, December	25	Nil	10	Regular
2.	Madaikhali Women SHG	2000, February	100	Teracotta	13	Regular
3.	Binapani SHG.	2002	50	Nil	13	Regular
4.	Asharikandi Teracotta Mohila SHG	2000, September	60	Teracotta	13	Regular
5.	Barman Para Anusuchita Jati Mohila SHG.	2002, August	30	Nil	14	Regular
6.	Laxmi Women SHG	2002	30	Sweet Production	10	Regular
7.	Matri Unnayan SHG	2000	50	Nil	10	Regular
	Total		**345 approx.**		**83 approx.**	

Source: Field Investigation.

The Secretary, Asharikandi Mahila SHG, in the Terracotta Showroom

Terracotta Park

Table 9.2: Age Group of Female Members

Age group	No. of Women Members
20-25	4
25-30	7
30-35	18
35-40	19
40-45	10
45-50	17
50-55	2
55-60	2
60-65	2
65-70	1
70-75	1
	N=83

Source: Field investigation

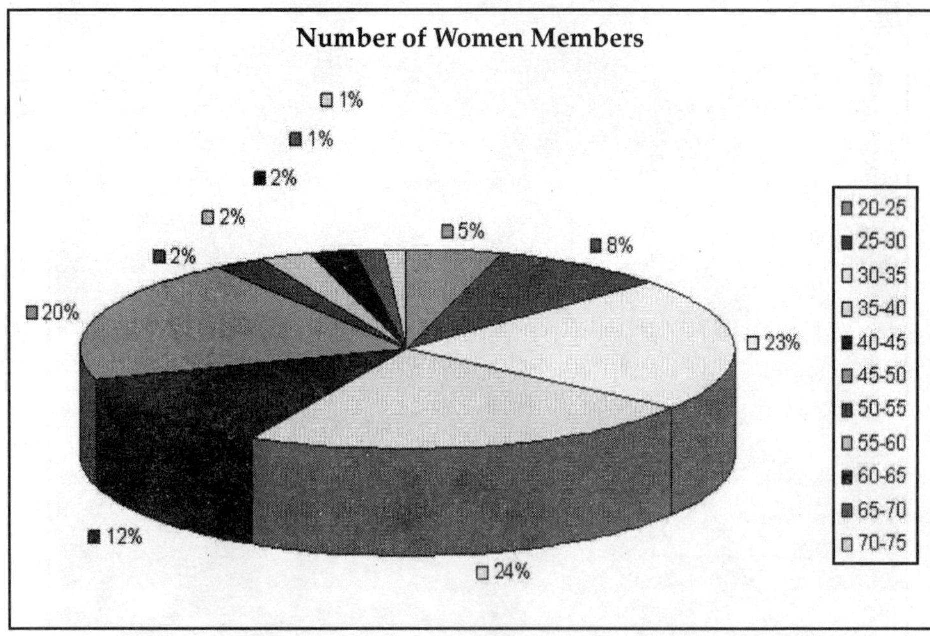

Fig. 9.1: **Age Group of Female Members (Percentage-wise)**

Table 9.3: Education Status

Sl. No.	Education Status (Class-wise)	No. of Members
1.	Illiterate	32
2.	I-V	26
3.	V-X	16
4.	X- Graduation	8
5.	Graduation	Nil

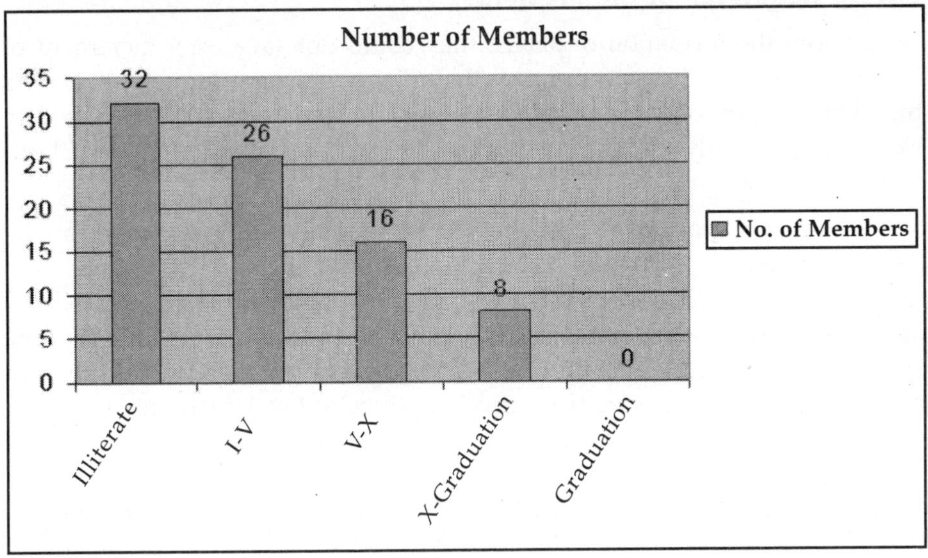

Fig. 9.2

Family Size

Most of the members have big family. Very few of them have one child or two children. Joint family system is found there.

Income Distribution

The poor women members are now able to earn an income monthly through the formation of SHGs. The members take micro credit from the group at 2 per cent or 3 per cent rate of interest p.m. The members are distributed their equal share of groups income earned through lending to the members and to outsiders. Their monthly income gets Rs.1000 p.m. for most of the members.

Borrowing Behaviour of the Members

From the study of 83 female members of 7 SHGs in the village of Madaikhali, the borrowing behaviour was different before the SHGs formed.

Before the formation of SHGs, the members had to go to the village money lenders. The money lenders used to lend money against collateral security at exorbitant rate of interest. As a consequence, they had to sell even their final properties to repay their loan. They became poorer from poor.

After formation of SHGs, They get loan from the group without collateral security at rate of interest ranging from 2 per cent to 3 per cent p.m. The members borrow money from the group when they feel necessary for productive purpose.

Saving Behaviour of the Members

Before the formation of SHGs, they could not save. Any increment of income they earned was fed up by the village mahajan (Money lender).As they belong to poor family, their little income so earned was exhausted in meeting their daily needs. Sometimes they would have to spend without food. They could not send their children to school even.

After formation of SHGs, they have been able to get loan from the concerned group without any collateral security. With the micro finance from the group, the village women members can produce their traditional products and sell in the market and by the process they start getting income supplementing their family income. Moreover, they get share of income from either lending activities or from productive activities which enhance their family income rapidly that leads to raise their standard of living. With it, the women members start saving with the bank. Their saving with the bank ranges from Rs. 20 to more than Rs. 500 monthly depending on progress of SHGs. The saving structure of the female members of the SHGs in the village of Madaikhali in Table 9.4.

Table 9.4: Saving of Members

Saving Group (Rs.)	No. of Women Members
0-30	31
30-60	17
60-100	15
100 and more	20
Total	**83**

Source: Field Investigation.

The Table 9.4 shows that no. of women members in the saving group (0-30) is 31, the highest no. of 83 members under sample study. 20 members are in the saving group (100 and more), and the lowest no. of members are in the saving group (60-100).

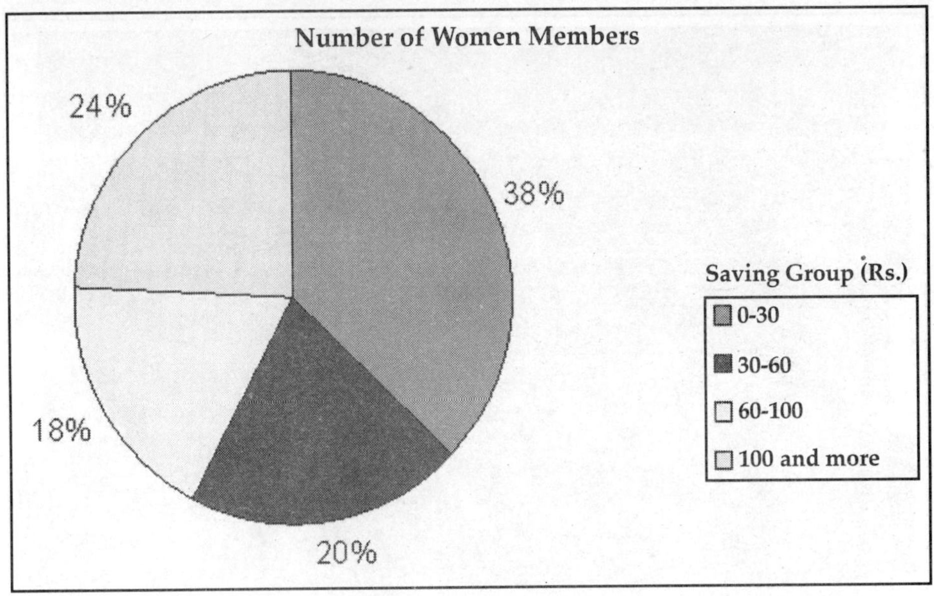

Fig. 9.3: **Saving of Members**

A Success Story

Madaikhali women SHG (SC women group) was established in February 12, 2000. The group is involved in the production of Terracotta. Initially, the group had 16 members and after that it reduced to 13. All are scheduled caste women and 6 of them are illiterate. Initial monthly contribution of the members was Rs. 50 each for first two years and then raised to Rs. 60 and continued for next two years and again, raised to Rs. 80 for another two years and finally, raised to Rs. 100. Thus, small savings is an important concept of the group. After two years of formation they received revolving fund of Rs. 10,000. The corpus Fund is used to lend to its members at 3 per cent rate of interest p.m. They applied for a loan to Asom Grameen Vikash Bank (AGVB), Gauripur and they were granted a loan of Rs. 25,000 in the year 2002. The loan amount of Rs. 25000 is used for the production of terracotta products and a part for lending money to the members. After repayment of loan of Rs. 25000, they again applied for a loan of Rs. 2,50,000 to AGVB, Gauripur and they received this amount of which Rs. 1,25,000 is as subsidy. In March 2007, the working capital of the group has become 3,54,189. Thus, the groups loan liability is Rs. 1,25,000. They repay the loan regularly. Their income has now raised to Rs. 4000 p.m with which they are able to maintain a family of 6 in average. They are maintaining a close link with the banks. They do not depend on village money lenders for loan. Their standard of living has been raised. Now, they send their children to schools, accessing to electric facility at home, installing TV, and telephone even. The members think that the

The Secretary of the Madaikhali Women SHG (Chief of the Success Story)

bankers have become like their family members whom some years back they did not know. Also they think that through the formation of SHGs, their social relationship has developed. They can save money with the bank. The problems the group faced are account keeping and training for improved terracotta productive technique. For their products they do not find local markets. They sell their products in the markets of NE states and other states of India.

Problems Faced by the SHGs

The problems so faced by the SHGs are within the group which stands as constraints in availing the benefits of SHGs formation. Some of them are mentioned below:

(a) Being the conservative society, some guardians do not like women to go outside for marketing purpose and other production related works.

(b) The SHGs face the problem of training. The leader of the group does not have any training for maintaining cash accounts. This is very important problem of the group.

(c) The SHGs face the problem of training.

(d) The products produced by the members sometimes do not find local market.

(e) Most of the SHGs are concentrated in borrowing and lending activities only.

Findings and Recommendations

For a backward district like Dhubri, increasing women's economic productivity is an important strategy for improving the welfare of rural family living BPL. In this context, Self Help Groups (SHGs) emerge as an important strategy in this process of development and empowerment of women. In the district, total number of SHGs formed is 4139 as on 2003-04 while women SHGs formed 2339 groups. That is, a little more than 50 per cent SHGs belong to women SHGs. Most of the SHGs are concentrated in borrowing and activities. Members borrow money from the groups either for consumption purpose or invest a little in the business of head of the family. Thus, tiny resources are accessible to the rural poor people through the SHGs and they are relieved from the hands of village money lenders.

The members of some SHGs could not undertake productive activities because of lack of knowledge of production and marketing information. In this regard they find very little training.

Most of the female members engaged in the SHGs are in the age group of (35-40).

SHGs have come to the rural poor people as a movement developing socially, economically, and culturally. When SHGs were not formed, the poor people borrowed money from village money lenders and they could not repay loan.

After formation of the group, the members develop a repayment culture for their loan. They repay the loan regularly. The BPL category of members is upgraded APL category. The additional income is utilized for sending their children to school, for paying electricity bill, for constructing new house, installing TV and fan. Members are able to save with the banks.

Women members now take part in decision making activities. Also they develop leadership quality with the involvement of the SHGs. Earlier they were preparing foods for the family members and brought up their children. Now they have become economically independent. Women take part in decision making of the family even. They are now aware of their right. They play an important role in controlling family health. The family income of the members has increased from Rs. 360 to 1080 or more.

The findings can be highlighted in the following:

- Rural poor women assist through SHGs in improving socio-economic conditions.
- Through SHGs, the poor women are in a position to borrow funds from the SHGs to undertake productive activities.
- The main concept of the formation of SHGs is 100 per cent repayment of loan. The women members repay their loan almost 97 per cent.
- Now, the women members can solve a little amount.

Suggestions

The following suggestions can be made for the improvement of the problems of the SHGs faced and for the engagement of large no. of poor rural people:

1. An arrangement of training for each and every member for a SHG should be made in relation to marketing information access.
2. Social bindings so existing in the rural areas should be broken with the cultural development of the members.
3. Advancing micro finance to the members is not sufficient; with it denial factor from the family should be abolished.
4. Local markets should be created for selling of the products produced by the female members.
5. 100 per cent repayment of loan culture should be assured by the members of the group.

REFERENCES

Burra, Neera, Deshmukh, Joy and Murthy, Ranjani K (2007): *Microcredit, Poverty and Empowerment*. Sage Publication, New Delhi.

Bhuimali, Anil (2006): *Globalisation and Human Rights*, Serial Publications, New Delhi.

Chandra, Puran (2005): *NGOs in India*, Akansha Publishing House, New Delhi.

Dhar, P.K., (2005): *The Economy of North East*, Kalyani Publisher, New Delhi.

Ganeshmurthy,V.S. (2007): *India: Economic Empowerment of Women*, New Century Publication, Delhi.

Ganeshmurthy,V.S. (2008): *Empowerment of Women in India—Social, Economic and Political*, New Century Publication, Delhi.

Dailies/Weeklies

Begum, Nawajis Ara (1999):Gramanchalar Mohilar Sachetanata, Doinik Agradoot, August 1.

Bose, Devashis and Monimala Devi (2006): Md. Yunus and Approach to 11th Plan. The Assam Tribune, November 1.

Choudhury, Saswati (2004): Experiments in Rural Development. The Assam Tribune, July 7.

Dasgupta, Anupam (2005):Micro and Small Enterprises. Employment News, September 10. Vol. XXX No. 24.

Sharma, Nagendra (2000): Year 2000: Women Remain Where They Were. The North-east Daily, January 1.

The Sentinel (2006): SHGs' Approach most Important Tool to Accelerate Rural Development, June 24.

Journal/Magazine

Agarwal, Sunil (2003): Technology Model for Women's Empowerment: Reaching the Unreached. Kurkshetra May, Vol. 51. No. 7.

Bora, Uttam Kumar (2003): Pub Lohing Gaon Panchayat Elekar Atma Sahayak Got Samuhar Bartaman Sthiti: Samashya Aru Sambhabaniyata, Poyobhara, Assamese Yojana, December Vol. 34, No. 10.

Debroy, Vivek (2006): Khudra Hriner Brihat Padakshep, Desh ABV Pvt. Ltd. Kolkata, November 2

Dhar, Samirendra Nath and Sarkar, Soumitra. (2006): Self-Help Groups: A Microfinancial Approach to Poverty Reduction and Establishment of Human Rights for Rural Women, South Asian journal of Human Right, Serial Publications, New Delhi.

Ghose, Arabinda (2004): Steps to Stimulate Rural Rconomy, (Yojana) Angent, 48.

Hermes, Niels, Lensink, Robert (2007): Impact of Micro-finance: A Critical Survery, Economic and Political Weekly, Fed1 Vol. xiii, No 6. pp. 462-465.

I, BhagyaLakshmi (2004): Women's Empowerment Miles to Go (Yojana) August, Vol. 48.

Joshi, Deepali Pant (2002): Rural Credit. *Yojana,* January.

Kay, Thelma (2002): Empowering Women Through Self-Help Micro-credit Programmes, Emerging Social Issues Division, ESCAP.

Khandeker, S.R. (2005): Micro-finance and Poverty: Evidence Using Panel Data from Bangladesh, *The World Bank Economic Review,* Vol. 19 No. 2. pp. 263-86.

Kour, Amarjeet (2008): Self-Help Group (SHG) and Rural Development, *Kurukshetra,* December, Vol. 57.

Krishna, Anirudh (2003): Falling into Poverty: Other Side of Poverty Reduction, Economic and Political Weekly, February 8.

10

Impact of Micro-finance on Women

Digvijay Singh

ABSTRACT

Micro-finance is emerging as a powerful instrument for poverty alleviation in the new economy. The search for the best way to create opportunity and sustainable development in the less privileged parts of the world has brought about initiatives to overcome poverty and marginalization, and to build more inclusive social, economic and financial systems. In India, micro-finance scene is dominated by Self-Help Groups (SHGs) — Banks linkage Programme, aimed at providing a cost effective mechanism for providing financial services to the 'unreached poor'. In the Indian context terms like "small and marginal farmers", "rural artisans" and "economically weaker sections" have been used to broadly define micro-finance customers. Research across the globe has shown that, over time, micro-finance clients increase their income and assets, increase the number of years of schooling their children receive, and improve the health and nutrition of their families. Micro-finance is generally defined as specialized financial tools — such as small loans, savings accounts and insurance policies — available to poor households and small businesses that do not typically have access to financial services. Inclusive financial services are now recognized as one way to empower individuals and communities to lift themselves out of poverty. Micro-finance programmes are also acknowledged for having an empowering effect on women. In this paper, we are doing critical analysis of:

1. Role of micro-finance in poverty reduction efforts in regard to women.
2. Micro-finance impact on gender conflict and subordination of women.
3. Empowering effect of micro-finance programmes in relation to women.
4. Micro-finance impact on access primary education.

Introduction

"The difficult truth is that the majority of the poor in the world still lack access to sustainable financial services, whether its savings, credit or insurance. The great challenge, then, that awaits us is to face the limitations that impede these persons to fully participate in the financial system. Together we can and we should create inclusive financial sectors that help people to improve their lives".

—Kofi Annan, UN Secretary General, 2003

Since the early national plans, successive governments in independent India have emphasized the link between improving access to finance and reducing poverty, a stance that has had influence globally. The need to improve financial access for India's poor, the overwhelming majority of whom are concentrated in rural areas, motivated the establishment of a vast network of rural cooperative credit banks in the 1950s, followed by a drive to nationalize commercial banks, launched in 1969. This led to thousands of new bank branches in rural areas across the country.

The strategy during the 1970s and 1980s gave the lead role to the nationalized (state-owned) commercial banks, which were charged with loosening the grip of traditional informal sector moneylenders through the use of targeted low-priced loans. The 1990s saw the partial deregulation of interest rates, increased competition in the banking sector, and new micro-finance approaches, most notably, a nationwide attempt, pioneered by non-governmental organizations (NGOs) and now supported by the state, to create links between commercial banks, NGOs, and informal local groups (self-help groups, or SHGs). Better known as 'SHG Bank Linkage', this approach has grown dramatically over the past decade, and while its outreach is still modest in terms of the proportion of poor households served, many believe it is destined to become the country's dominant system of mass-outreach banking for the poor. However, informal sector lenders remain a strong presence in rural India, delivering finance to the poor, the vast majority of whom still do not have access to either formal or semi-formal (micro-finance) sectors. Scaling-up access to finance for India's rural poor, to meet their diverse financial needs (savings, credit, insurance against unexpected events, etc.) through flexible products at competitive prices, presents a formidable challenge in a country as vast and varied as India. But the opportunities, too, are plentiful, and government has an important role to play in creating space and a flexible architecture for innovations.

The organization of rural economic activity in general, and agricultural production in particular, is strongly conditioned by the fact that inputs are transformed into outputs with considerable time lags, and that production and sale outcomes can be highly uncertain because of the vagaries of nature or the swings of volatile commodity markets. In such environments, the ability of agricultural enterprises and rural households to make long term investments, take calculated risks, and create stable consumption streams will be shaped by the set of available financial instruments and strategies to transform one pattern of variable and uncertain resource inflows and outflows into another. If the available set of financial services is very limited, households may have to forego valuable investment and income-generating activities and suffer the consequences of volatile consumption.

Micro-finance is emerging as a powerful instrument for poverty alleviation in the new economy. Although it has been around in its contemporary form since 1974, is a relatively young industry. The recent surge of interest in micro-finance of the past decade has attracted the interest of banks, governments, financial regulators, non-governmental organizations (NGOs), multilaterals, donors, municipalities and foundations, which have at some point held micro-credit to be an almost legendary solution to poverty in the developing world. The United Nations General Assembly designated 2005 as the International Year of Microcredit and the industry gained notable recognition worldwide when Muhammad Yunus won Nobel Prize in Peace in 2006.

In India, micro-Finance scene is dominated by Self Help Groups (SHGs) - Banks linkage Programme, aimed at providing a cost effective mechanism for providing financial services to the 'unreached poor'. In the Indian context terms like 'small and marginal farmers', 'rural artisans' and 'economically weaker sections' have been used to broadly define micro-finance customers. Research across the globe has shown that, over time, micro-finance clients increase their income and assets, increase the number of years of schooling their children receive, and improve the health and nutrition of their families.

Micro-finance is generally defined as specialized financial tools — such as small loans, savings accounts and insurance policies — available to poor households and small businesses that do not typically have access to financial services. Inclusive financial services are now recognized as one way to empower individuals and communities to lift themselves out of poverty. As has been demonstrated since the first experiments with micro-finance, many people living in poverty can improve their livelihoods when given the opportunity to save, invest, and insure.

A more refined model of micro-credit delivery has evolved lately, which emphasizes the combined delivery of financial services along with technical assistance and agricultural business development services. When compared to the wider SHG bank linkage movement in India, private MFIs have had limited outreach. However, we have seen a recent trend of larger micro-finance institutions transforming into Non-Bank Financial Institutions (NBFCs). This changing face of micro-finance in India appears to be positive in terms of the ability of micro-finance to attract more funds and therefore increase outreach. In overall terms an organizational structure will help them achieve more transparency and efficiency.

In India, despite recent economic growth at national level, poverty remains a serious problem for policy-makers because this growth is mainly driven by growth in a few sectors in urban areas, such as industry and service sectors. The incidence of poverty in India is estimated by quinquennial large sample surveys on household consumption and expenditure and, according to the Uniform Recall Period (URP) consumption distribution data in 2004-05, poverty strands at 28.3 per cent in rural areas, 25.7 per cent in urban areas and 27.5 per cent for the country as a whole (Government of India, 2008). Although the proportion of persons below the poverty line has declined from around 36 per cent of the population in 1993-94 to 28 per cent in 2004-05, poverty reduction remains the country's major challenge in the 21st century.

A recent study in Pune district in Maharashtra showed that while the targeting performance of micro-finance through SHGs was unsatisfactory in terms of income, it was satisfactory in terms of caste, landlessness and illiteracy and thus facilitated the empowerment of women (Gaiha and Nandhi 2007). This study also found that loans were used largely for children's health and education and argued against restricting the impact assessment of micro-finance to conventional economic criteria alone.

This sector is home to over 10,000 institutions with an annual turnover of around $12 billion. And this is only the beginning; the demand for micro-credit appears to be growing as more and more nations are faced with the reality of increasing poverty and inequality around the world. In fact, half of the 2.2 billion adults in Africa, Asia and Latin America are not able to save with or borrow from a bank.

So what exactly do we mean by 'micro-finance'? The definition of micro-finance has evolved over time, and still varies between countries and contexts. However, in general micro-finance refers to the provision of financial services to low-income clients, including the self-employed. As defined by the Inter American Development Bank (IADB), micro-finance is "the provision of a broad range of financial services such as deposits, loans, payment services, money transfers and insurance to poor and low-income households and their micro-enterprises".

In this analysis micro-finance will cover any non-traditional financial product to customers whose access to financial services or traditional banking services is hindered by an underprivileged position in the community. Micro-finance encompasses a diverse range of institutional formats, ranging from individual money-lenders to more formal institutions such as village banks, credit unions, financial cooperatives, state-owned banks for small enterprises and social venture capitals funds.

Micro-finance and Poverty Reduction

United Nations Development Programme (UNDP) estimates that of the 3 billion poor worldwide, about half or 1.5 million could be considered working poor or potentially eligible for a micro-credit loan or other types of small-scale financial products. According to the World Bank, there are more than one billion persons worldwide that live on less than two dollars per day, 150 million of which live in Latin America. In the region it is estimated that some 360 million live on the margin of the economy with subsistence-level income and lack basic services such as running water, electricity, medical care and housing. Such poverty is manifested in a wide variety of channels: conditions of minimal survival, lack of education, lack of social integration, lack of access to basic goods and services. In essence, the poor have few alternatives to protect themselves from risk or to manage risks they face daily. According to Amartya Sen., winner of the Nobel Prize in Economics in 1998, the poor continue to be poor because they lack autonomy and power. Sen states, "once empowered, through greater inclusion and access to traditional systems, they become able to change their lives and overcome obstacles that previously were considered insurmountable". However, individuals cannot transform their lives by their efforts alone, or without a society and financial system which allows them the opportunity for development and progress. Sen claims that the first step is to change the way poor are viewed; he explains, "instead of being seen as needy and incapable, society must change paradigm to consider this group as potential architects of their own personal and socioeconomic development". In addressing the challenge of poverty reduction and the impact of access to financial services in this goal, a recent report by FELABAN (Latin American Bank Federation) reveals the important relationship between access to the financial system - defined as the percentage of the population that can freely use financial services - and the reduction of poverty and inequality. Understanding the problem of the lack of access to financial services is particularly important in Latin America, as the levels of poverty continue to be alarmingly high and it is the region with the most income disparity in the world, despite the many reforms that have been implemented in the region over the past half century.

The poverty alleviation paradigm underlies many NGO integrated poverty-targeted community development programmes. Poverty alleviation here is defined in broader terms than market incomes to encompass increasing capacities and choices and decreasing the vulnerability of poor people.

The main focus of programmes as a whole is on developing sustainable livelihoods, community development and social service provision like literacy, healthcare and infrastructure development. There is not only a concern with reaching the poor, but also the poorest.

Policy debates have focussed particularly on the importance of small savings and loan provision for consumption as well as production, group formation and the possible justification for some level of subsidy for programmes working with particular client groups or in particular contexts. Some programmes have developed effective methodologies for poverty targeting and/or operating in remote areas. Such strategies have recently become a focus of interest from some donors and also the Microcredit Summit Campaign.

Here gender lobbies have argued for targeting women because of higher levels of female poverty and women's responsibility for household well-being. However although gender inequality is recognised as an issue, the focus is on assistance to households and there is a tendency to see gender issues as cultural and hence not subject to outside intervention.

Although term 'empowerment' is frequently used in general terms, often synonymous with a multi-dimensional definition of poverty alleviation, the term 'women's empowerment' is often considered best avoided as being too controversial and political. The assumption is that increasing women's access to micro-finance will enable women to make a greater contribution to household income and this, together with other interventions to increase household well-being, will translate into improved well-being for women and enable women to bring about wider changes in gender inequality.

Women's Empowerment

'Micro credit is about much more than access to money. It is about women gaining control over the means to make a living. It is about women lifting themselves out of poverty and vulnerability. It is about women achieving economic and political empowerment within their homes, their villages, their countries'.

In India, the trickle down effects of macroeconomic policies have failed to resolve the problem of gender inequality. Women have been the vulnerable section of society and constitute a sizeable segment of the poverty-struck population. Women face gender specific barriers to access education health, employment etc. Micro-finance deals with women below the poverty line. Micro loans are available solely and entirely to this target group of women. There are several reason for this: Among the poor, the poor women are most disadvantaged — they are characterized by lack of education and access of resources, both of which is required to help them work their way out of poverty and for upward economic and social mobility. The problem is more acute for women in countries like India, despite the fact that women's labour makes a critical contribution to the economy. This is due to the low social status and lack of access to key resources. Evidence shows that groups of women are better customers than men, the better managers of resources. If loans are routed through women benefits of loans are spread wider among the household.

Since women's empowerment is the key to socio-economic development of the community; bringing women into the mainstream of national development has been a major concern of government. The ministry of rural development has special components for women in its programmes. Funds are earmarked as 'Women's component' to ensure flow of adequate resources for the same. Besides Swarnagayanti Grameen Swarazgar Yojona (SGSY), Ministry of Rural Development is implementing other scheme having women's component. They are the Indira Awas Yojona (IAJ), National Social Assistance Programme (NSAP), Restructured Rural Sanitation Programme, Accelerated Rural Water Supply programme (ARWSP) the (erstwhile) Integrated Rural Development Programme (IRDP), the (erstwhile) Development of Women and Children in Rural Areas (DWCRA) and the Jowahar Rozgar Yojana (JRY).

Question is arising that why MFIs should adopt Empowerment approaches?

Given the tension and perceived tradeoffs between different approaches to empowerment in micro-finance mentioned above, many leaders in the micro-finance field become complacent about adopting empowerment strategies in their organizations. Moreover, many assume that providing access to micro-finance services will lead to sufficient empowerment impact and that actively adopting specific empowerment strategies is therefore unnecessary.

However, there are some clear cases for why leaders in micro-finance institutions should consider adopting empowerment approaches in their organizations:

- **Case 1:** Micro-finance practices do not always produce automatic empowerment benefits for women; therefore, empowerment must be strategically planned for in MFIs.
- **Case 2:** Empowerment approaches allow micro-finance institutions to realize their full potential in contributing to a number of critical dimensions of women's empowerment.
- **Case 3:** Empowerment approaches are often compatible with other approaches to micro-finance (e.g. financial sustainability), and can actually enhance the aims of these other approaches in many cases.

Problems and Challenges

Many surveys and reports have conducted in order to find out the difficulty in the way of empowering Surveys have shown that many elements contribute to make it more Difficult for women empowerment through micro businesses. These elements are:

- Lack of knowledge of the market and potential profitability, thus making the choice of business difficult.
- Inadequate book-keeping.
- Employment of too many relatives which increases social pressure to share benefits.
- Setting prices arbitrarily.
- Lack of capital.
- High interest rates.
- Inventory and inflation accounting is never undertaken.
- Credit policies that can gradually ruin their business (many customers cannot pay cash; on the other hand, suppliers are very harsh towards women).

Other shortcomings includes:

1. *Burden of meeting:* Time consuming meetings, in particular in programmes based on group lending, and time consuming income generating activities without reduction of traditional responsibilities increase women's work and time burden.
2. *New pressures:* By using social capital, in-group lending/group collateral programmes, additional stresses and pressures are introduced, which might increase vulnerability and reflect disempowerment.
3. *Reinforcement of traditional gender roles:* Lack of economic empowerment: Micro finance assists women to perform traditional roles better and

women thus remain trapped in low productivity sectors, not moving from the group of survival enterprises to micro-enterprises.There are evidence of men withdrawing their contributions to certain types of household expenditures.

Challenging Economic Empowerment

However impact on incomes is widely variable. Studies which consider income levels find that for the majority of borrowers income increases are small, and in some cases negative. All the evidence suggests that most women invest in existing activities which are low profit and insecure and/or in their husband's activities. In many programmes and contexts it is only in a minority of cases that women can develop lucrative activities of their own through credit and savings alone.

It is clear that women's choices about activity and their ability to increase incomes are seriously constrained by gender inequalities in access to other resources for investment, responsibility for household subsistence expenditure, lack of time because of unpaid domestic work and low levels of mobility, constraints on sexuality and sexual violence which limit access to markets in many cultures.

These gender constraints are in addition to market constraints on expansion of the informal sector and resource and skill constraints on the ability of poor men as well as women to move up from survival activities to expanding businesses. There are signs, particularly in some urban markets like Harare and Lusaka, that the rapid expansion of micro-finance programmes may be contributing to market saturation in 'female' activities and hence declining profits.

Challenging Intra Household Relation

There have undoubtedly been women whose status in the household has improved, particularly where they have become successful entrepreneurs. Even where income impacts have been small, or men have used the loan, the fact that micro-finance programmes have thought women worth targeting and women bring an asset into the household may give some women more negotiating power.

Savings provide women with a means of building up an asset base. Women themselves also often value the opportunity to be seen to be making a greater contribution to household well-being giving them greater confidence and sense of self-worth.

However women's contribution to increased income going into households does not ensure that women necessarily benefit or that there is any challenge to gender inequalities within the household. Women's expenditure patterns may replicate rather than counter gender inequalities and continue to disadvantage girls. Without substitute care for small children, the elderly and disabled, and provision of services to reduce domestic work many programmes reported adverse effects of women's outside work on children and the elderly. Daughters in particular may be withdrawn from school to assist their mothers.

Although in some contexts women may be seeking to increase their influence within joint decision-making processes rather than independent control over income (Kabeer 1998), neither of these outcomes can be assumed. Women's perceptions of value and self-worth are not necessarily translated into actual well-being benefits or change in gender relations in the household (Sen 1990, Kandiyoti 1999). Worryingly, in response to women's increased (but still low) incomes evidence indicates that men may be withdrawing more of their own contribution for their own luxury expenditure. Men are often very enthusiastic about women's credit programmes, and other income generation out programmes, for this reason because their wives no longer 'nag' them for money (Mayoux 1999).

Small increases in access to income and influence may therefore be at the cost of heavier work loads, increased stress and women's health. Although in many cases women's increased contribution to household well-being has improved domestic relations, in other cases it intensifies tensions.

Micro-finance and Basic Education

"Progress in education has 'instrumentally momentous' consequences in relation to the wider 2015 targets" (Sen, 199713). Women's education in particular is among the most powerful determinants of trends in public health and child mortality. Income-poverty reduction is a function of two factors: the rate of growth and the distribution of income. Education generates important benefits in both areas. It is positively associated with the rising productivity and innovation upon which economic growth depends. Equally importantly, improved access to education can help the poor to participate in markets on more equitable terms, improving the distribution of income in the process. Globalization, and the associated emergence of increasingly knowledge-based systems of production, is strengthening the links between education and poverty reduction, both nationally and internationally.

The correlation between parental education and child mortality has been extensively documented. In almost all countries, child-death rates are inversely related to the level of maternal education. The more educated the mother, the healthier she and her child are likely to be. Comparative research focussed on 33 countries during the 1980s found that each additional year of maternal education reduced childhood mortality by about 8 per cent (Caldwell, 198614). For mothers completing five years of primary education, the risk of childhood mortality decreased by around 45/1000 births.

After controlling for socio-economic differences, one survey of 28 countries showed that mothers' education was the single most important influence on child mortality, especially after the first year of life. (World Bank, 199515).... Schools can provide a focal point for community health and nutrition efforts, including pre-natal care, immunization, oral rehydration therapies, control of respiratory infections, and vitamin supplementation..... Educated mothers are not only better able to gain information about health matters and nutrition: they are also far more likely to make use of preventative health care services and to demand timely treatment.iii.... Even within low-income groups, maternal education is positively associated with better nutrition, partially compensating for other aspects of deprivation.

While low income is inevitably associated with deprivation in other areas of human welfare, some countries have achieved far better levels of human development than others that have higher average incomes. For example, comparing performance of Pakistan with that of Vietnam, a country with lower average incomes and higher income-poverty levels. More than half of Vietnam's population lives below the poverty line. What is striking is that, despite this intense deprivation, Vietnam has achieved far higher levels of female literacy, which have in turn contributed to social advances in other areas. However, it cannot be overstated that as important as education is to improved public health, it is not the sole factor. Income-poverty is the primary driver of child malnutrition — and education does not override the structural disadvantages associated with poverty.

Education and Income-poverty

Education is critical to the achievement of the 2015 target of reducing the incidence of extreme poverty by half. At a household level, educational status is one of the strongest influences on income and poverty. The lower the level of educational attainment, the greater the vulnerability to income-poverty.

What is true for households is true also for national economies, with average income levels reflecting levels of access to education. The rate of economic growth and the share of national wealth captured by the poor dictate the rate of poverty reduction. Improvements in both areas depend critically on advances in education.

The benefits of education are equally pronounced in labour markets. Education cannot compensate for disadvantages associated with working in low-wage environments in which the poor are often discriminated against, but it can increase relative earning power. The association between education and income is not automatic. Power relations in local markets, culture, and political decisions shape precise outcomes. Gender is one of the key determinants of the distribution of benefits from education (Herz, 1998; Tzannatos, 1998).

Where women face unequal access to productive resources, services, and sellers' or labour markets, the scope for realizing the potential gains of education is substantially reduced.

Impact on Fertility

Microcredit (increased incomes) and Basic Education both have a significant impact on number of births. The impact of an increased income is less than that of education; however, the impact for education only becomes significant after 6 years of schooling. Thus, a microcredit programme would have an immediate negative impact on births (and would continue to have such an effect) while the impact of an education programme would only start to take effect after a period of 6 years (but the impact would be larger).

"Both income and education have significant negative effects on the number of births, with the impact of education being larger than that of income: the point elasticity's in rural areas are ÿ 0.45 and ÿ 0.15 for education and income, respectively. The influence of education becomes negative only after grade 6, and the simulations show that expanding education beyond grade 9 can have a particularly large effect on fertility, especially for urban women. In addition, the transmission of the education effect appears to occur through raising the value of time for the woman rather than changing tastes or desire for children. There are substantial differences in the estimated impact of education and infant mortality when recent fertility is used as the outcome measure. Education is no longer significant and mortality becomes insignificant among urban women. One possible explanation for this is that the impact of education is long term in Nature and thus more likely to influence lifetime fertility rather than fertility in any given year".

In South Asia, the fertility rate for women with seven or more years of education is 35 per cent lower than for women with no education (Cochrane and Farid, 1984). But changes in fertility reflect a more important change in the ability of women to exercise greater control over their lives. Better- educated women marry later and space births over longer periods, with benefits for maternal and child health.

Better education creates opportunities for employment and income generation, which in turn create incentives for later marriage. Improved access to information and increased self-confidence raise the demand for contraception, and enable women to express that demand. Whatever the precise mechanisms at play, maternal education is one of the keys to achieving the 2015 targets for reducing maternal mortality rates.

Conclusions and Suggestions

During research we found that Micro-finance is emerging as a powerful instrument for poverty alleviation in the new economy. In India, micro-finance scene is dominated by Self Help Groups (SHGs) — Banks linkage Programme, aimed at providing a cost effective mechanism for providing financial services to the 'unreached poor'. The development of the micro-finance sector is based on the concept that the poor possess the capacity to implement income generating activities but are limited by lack of access to, and inadequate provision of, savings, credit and insurance facilities.

Numerous traditional and informal system of credit that were already in existence before micro-finance came into vogue. Viability of micro-finance needs to be understood from a dimension that is far broader- in looking at its long-term aspects too very little attention has been given to empowerment questions or ways in which both empowerment and sustainability aims may be accommodated. Failure to take into account impact on income also has potentially adverse implications for both repayment and outreach, and hence also for financial sustainability. An effort is made here to present some of these aspects to complete the picture.

A conclusion that emerges from this account is that micro-finance can contribute to solving the problems of inadequate housing and urban services as an integral part of poverty alleviation programmes. The challenge lies in finding the level of flexibility in the credit instrument that could make it match the multiple credit requirements of the low income borrower without imposing unbearably high cost of monitoring its end use upon the lenders. A promising solution is to provide multipurpose lone or composite credit for income generation, housing improvement and consumption support. Consumption loan is found to be especially important during the gestation period between commencing a new economic activity and deriving positive income. Careful research on demand

For financing and savings behaviour of the potential borrowers and their participation in determing the mix of multi-purpose loans are essential in making the concept work.

The organizations involved in micro credit initiatives should take account of the fact that:

- Credit is important for development but cannot by itself enable very poor women to overcome their poverty.
- Making credit available to women does not automatically mean they have control over its use and over any income they might generate from micro enterprises.
- In situations of chronic poverty it is more important to provide saving services than to offer credit.
- A useful indicator of the tangible impact of micro credit schemes is the number of additional proposals and demands presented by local villagers to public authorities.

Nevertheless ensuring that the micro-finance sector continues to move forward in relation to gender equality and women's empowerment will require a long-term strategic process of the same order as the one in relation to poverty if gender is not to continue to 'evaporate' in a combination of complacency and resistance within donor agencies and the micro-finance sector. This will involve:

- Ongoing exchange of experience and innovation between practitioners.
- Constant awareness and questioning of 'bad practice'.
- Lobbying donors for sufficient funding for empowerment strategies
- Bringing together the different players in the sector to develop coherent policies and for gender advocacy.

India is the country where a collaborative model between banks, NGOs, MFIs and Women's organizations is furthest advanced. It therefore serves as a good starting point to look at what we know so far about 'Best Practice' in relation to micro-finance for women's empowerment and how different institutions can work together.

It is clear that gender strategies in micro finance need to look beyond just increasing women's access to savings and credit and organizing self help groups to look strategically at how programmes can actively promote gender equality and women's empowerment. Moreover the focus should be on developing a diversified micro-finance sector where different type of organizations, NGO, MFIs and formal sector banks all should have gender policies adapted to the needs of their particular target groups/institutional roles and capacities and collaborate and work together to make a significant contribution to gender equality and pro-poor development.

However, in backward regions, poor people, in addition to micro-finance, need a whole range of Agricultural/Business Development Services (productivity enhancement, risk mitigation, local value addition, and market linkages) need to be provided. To offer these services in a cost-effective manner, it is not possible to work with poor households individually and they need to be organized into groups, informal associations and sometimes cooperatives or producer companies. The formation of such groups and making them function effectively, requires institutional development services.

REFERENCES

Karlan, Dean S., and Zinman, Jonathan. 2005. "Observing Unobservables: Identifying Information Asymmetries with a Consumer Credit Field Experiment". Working Paper 911. Economic Growth Centre, Yale University, New Haven.

Barth, James, Gerard Caprio, Jr., and Ross Levine. 2005. *Rethinking Bank Regulation and Supervision: Till Angels Govern*. New York: World Bank and Cambridge University Press.

Harper, Malcolm, 2002, "Promotion of Self-Help Groups under the SHG Bank Linkage Programme in India", Paper presented at the Seminar on SHG-bank Linkage Programme at New Delhi, November 25-26, 2002.

Barr, Michael. 2005. Micro-finance and Financial Development. *Michigan Journal of International Law* 6(1): 271-96.

Ananth, Bindu, and Nachklet Mor. 2005. "Financial Services Case Study: India". Paper Presented at the Organisation for Economic Co-operation and Development and World Bank's Fifth Services Experts Meeting on Universal Access, February 3-4, Paris.

Mayoux, L. ed (2002b) 'Sustainable Learning for Women's Empowerment: Ways Forward in Micro-finance' Samskriti, New Delhi.

Linda Mayoux, Poverty Elimination and the Empowerment of Women.

Kabeer N (2001), "Conflicts Over Credit: Re-evaluation the Empowerment Potential of Loans to Women in Rural Bangladesh": World Development, Vol. 29, No. 1.

Mayoux, L. 1998a. Women's Empowerment and Micro-finance Programmes: Approaches, Evidence and Ways Forward. The Open University Working Paper No. 41.

Ackerley, B. (1995). Testing the Tools of Development: Credit Programmes, Loan Involvement and Women's Empowerment. World Development, 26(3), 56-68.

Mayoux, L. (1995b). "Beyond Naivety: Women, Gender Inequality and Participatory Development". *Development and Change* 26: 235-258.

Sen, A (1990) 'Gender and Cooperative Conflicts' in I Tinker ed *Persistent Inequalities: Women and World Development,* Oxford University Press.

World Bank (1996). Implementing the World Bank's Gender Policies: Progress Report No. 1. Washington: World Bank.

Almeyda, G. (1996). *Money Matters: Reaching Women Micro-entrepreneurs with Financial Services*. Washington, DC, Inter-American Development Bank/UNIFEM.

Hadjipateras, A. (1996). ACORD Gender Research — Final Report. London: ACORD Journal of Micro-finance, Vol. Three, Number Two Fall 2001.

Lindai Mayoux Sept 2005— Women's Empowement through Sustainable Micro-finance: Rethinking 'Best Practice'.

Hulme, D., & Mosley, P. (1996). Finance Against Poverty, Vols. 1 and 2. London: Routledge.

Ayyagari, Meghana, Asli Demirgüç-Kunt, and Vojislav Maksimovic. 2005. "How Important Are Financing Constraints? The Role of Finance in the Business Environment". Policy Research Working Paper 3820. World Bank, Washington, D.C.

Azariadis, Costas. 2005. "Poverty Traps". In Steven Durlauf and Phillipe Aghion, eds., *Handbook of Economic Growth.* Amsterdam: North-Holland Elsevier Publishers.

Beck, Thorsten, and Augusto de la Torre. 2005. "Broadening Access to Financial Services: Risks and Costs". PowerPoint Presentation. World Bank, Washington, D.C.

Beck, Thorsten, Asli Demirgüç-Kunt, and Ross Levine. 2004. "Finance, Inequality and Poverty: Cross-Country Evidence." Policy Research Working Paper 3338. World Bank, Washington, D.C.

Clarke, George, Lixin Colin Xu, and Heng-fu Zou. 2003. "Finance and Income Inequality: Test of Alternative Theories". Policy Research Working Paper 2984. World Bank, Washington, D.C.

Honohan, Patrick. 2004. "Financial Sector Policy and the Poor: Selected Findings and Issues". World Bank Working Paper 43. Washington, D.C.

Wolfgang, Hannover, Impact of Micro-finance Linkage Banking in India on the Millennium Development Goals (MDG), in NABARD Journal, May 2005.

Mahajan, Vijay and Ramola Gupta, Bharti (2003). "Micro-finance in India: Banyan Tree and Bonsai". Background Paper Prepared for the World Bank. World Bank, Washington DC.

Chakrabarti, Rajesh: The Indian Micro-finance Experience—Accomplishments and Challenges (2004).

Yunus, Muhammad (2002). Grameen Bank II: Designed to Open New Possibilities. Dhaka: Grameen Bank. [Available at www.grameen-info.org/bank/bank2.html.]

World Bank (2004). Scaling-up Access to Finance for India? Rural Poor. Report No. 30740-IN. Washington DC: World Bank.

Government of India, Ministry of Finance, (2001). "Report of the Joint Committee on Revitalization Support to Co-operative Credit Structure" (Patil Committee). New Delhi: Government of India.

Websites

http://www.micro-financegateway.org

www.oneworldaction.org

www.fcem.org

www.oecd.org

www.undp.org/unifem

www.wiego.org

Women Empowerment Through Self-Help Groups

Dr. Mithilesh Kumar Jha

Concept of Empowerment

The term empowerment means the power to make more Concept of the term Women Empowerment: confident or assertive: to give somebody a greater sense of confidence or self-esteem (Oxford Advance Learner 7th ed). When we placed the word women before the said term it becomes Women Empowerment which signifies that women should be attributed more power to be a self confident in all the sphere of life. Empowerment is a process of awareness and capacity building, leading to larger participation, the greater decision-making power and control and transformative action. The empowerment of women covers both an individual and collective transformation. It strengthens their innate ability through acquiring knowledge, power and experience.

Empowerment is defined as the one which facilitates change and enables to do what he or she wants. It is a feeling which activates ones psychological energy to accomplish one's goal.

Empowerment is a process whereby women become able to organise themselves to increase self-reliance and to emphasize their independent right to make choices and control resources, both of which will assist in challenging and culminating their subordination. It is a participatory process of awareness and capacity building which begins at the levels of home and community, adding to greater participation and decision making power and control, and to transformative action enabling individuals or groups to change balances of power in social, economic and political relations in society.

The dictionary definition (Thomas, M. and J. Pierson) links empowerment with self-help groups; "Empowerment can refer to use participation in services and to the self-help movements in which groups take action on their own behalf either in cooperation with or independently of statutory services".

Development has social, economic and political dimensions and is incomplete without developing the women who constitute about 50 per cent of the population. Role of women in development is indispensable and community development is unfinished without women's participation and contribution, but women are not always involved in the process of developmental performances which affect their lives.

Constitution of India and Women Empowerment

India's concern for safeguarding the rights and privileges of women found its best expression in the constitution of India. Giving special attention to the status of women, Article 14 confers equal rights and opportunities on men and women in the economic, political and social spheres. Article 15(3) empowers the state to make affirmative discrimination in favour of women. Besides clause (3) of Articles 15, which permits special provision for women and children, has been widely resorted to and the courts have upheld the validity of special measures in legislation or executive orders favouring women. In particular, provisions in the criminal law, in favour of women, or in the procedural law discriminating in favour of women have been upheld (Kamaluddin Khan). Article 21 also supports it.

Further Article 51 A (e) imposes that duty of every citizen in India to relinquish practices derogatory to the dignity of women.

Section 14 of the Hindu Succession Act, 1956 should be construed harmoniously with the constitutional goals of removing gender based discrimination and effectuating economic empowerment of Hindu women.

The right to elimination of gender based discrimination so as to attain economic empowerment, forms part of Universal Human Rights. Article 2 (f) of CEDAW States are grateful to take all suitable measures; including legislation, to abolish or modify gender based discrimination in the existing laws, regulation, customs and practices that comprise discrimination against women. Article 15(3) of the Constitution of India positively protects such acts or actions.

Moreover the Constitution of India is a basic document which provides for women empowerment within the framework of the plenary provision of Articles 14, 15 (3), 21, 39 (a), 51A (e) and Preamble. The courts always try to interpret the cases which are detriment to women within the area of social justice with these Articles (Kamaluddin Khan).

Concept of Self-Help Groups

"Self-help is the best help and self employment is the best employment". This is the central point of the philosophy of the self-help group. Experiences of the different anti-poverty and other welfare programmes implemented throughout the world in general and India in particular have shown that the key to their success lies in the evolution and participation of community-based organizations at the grass root level. People's participation in credit delivery and linking formal credit institution to borrowers through intermediaries of Self-Help Groups (SHGs) have been recognised as a supplementary mechanism for providing credit support to the rural poor. The structure of rural financial market in developing economy, particularly in India, is dualistic with both formal and informal financial both training and consultancy services to the SHGs and in some cases additionally act as financial intermediaries.

An SHG is defined as a voluntary group valuing personal interactions and mutual aid as a means of altering or ameliorating the problems perceived as alterable, pressing and personal by most of its participants. These groups are voluntary associations of people formed to attain certain collective goals that could be economic, social or both. The policy planners and development planners cherish the myth that poor people do not have the spirit to thrift but recent reports from different parts of the globe confront this.

Self-Help Groups (SHGs) is an association or body of people which is homogeneous, has a common aim and whose members in one way or the other, help one another. It is a micro-cooperative. All or a majority of members of an SHG may be drawn from the low income strata, for instance SHGs have come to encompass a wide range of activities. These range from income generating activities to overcoming problems of addiction and ensuring safe sex. While the SHGs in the developing countries have been dealing with disabilities apart from other activities, the most important job it has taken up is the propagation of microfinance. It has been increasingly realised that lending to a SHG offers unique opportunities, since the recovery rate is between 90 and 100 per cent.

Micro-credit is delivered through self-help groups (SHGs). An SHG is a registered/unregistered group of micro entrepreneurs having homogeneous social and economic background; voluntarily coming together to save small amounts regularly. They mutually agree to contribute to a common fund and to meet their emergency needs on mutual help basis. The group members use collective wisdom and peer pressure to ensure proper use of credit and timely repayment thereof. In fact, peer pressure has been recognised as an effective substitute for collaterals.

An economically poor individual gains strength as part of a group. Besides, financing through SHGs reduces transaction costs for both lenders and borrowers. While lenders have to handle a single SHG account instead of a large number of small sized individual accounts, borrowers as part of an SHG cut down expenses on travel (to and fro from the branch and other places) for completing paper work and on the loss of work days in canvassing for loans.

Self-help-groups (SHGs) are small groups of poor people. The members of an SHG face similar problems. They help other to solve their problems. SHGs promote small savings among their members. The savings are kept with the bank. This is the common fund in the name of the SHG. The SHG gives small loans to the members from its common fund. After six months, if the SHG satisfies the bank as per the check list for quality, bank can give loans to the SHG. Very poor people can save small amounts. Like the little drops of water making an ocean, such savings become lakhs of rupees.

The ideal size of an SHG is 10 to 20 members. The group need not be registered. From one family only one person can become a member of an SHG. The group normally consists of either only men or only women. Mixed groups are generally not preferred. Women's groups are generally found to perform better. Members should have the same social and financial background.

The group should meet regularly. Ideally, the meeting should be weekly or at least monthly. Full attendance in all the group meetings will make it easy for the SHG to stabilise and start working to the satisfaction of all. Membership register, minutes register etc. are to be kept up to date by the group by making the entries regularly.

Due to the flexibility of the micro-credit programme, different SHG models can be experimented with. These different models are:

- Banks deal directly with the SHG, providing financial assistance for on lending to individual members.
- Banks give direct assistance to the SHG while the NGO provides training and guidance to the SHG in effective functioning.
- The NGO can be a financial intermediary between the bank and a member of an SHG, with the NGO accepting the contractual ability for loan repayment to the banks and the linkage between the bank and the SHG is indirect.

Banks give loans directly to individual SHG members on recommendations of the SHG and the NGO. The NGO assists the bank in monitoring, supervising and recovery of loans.

A conservative banker will start with the third model depend on the NGO while a good banker- NGO relationship would start with model two or even model one. However, the general evolutionary process is to move from model three to model two, then to model one, and finally, model four wherein individuals have direct access to the bank.

Self-Help Groups and Empowerment of Women

The credit programmes have ignored women for a long time. Targeting women for credit programmes commenced to receive serious consideration at the International Women Conference at Mexico City in 1975. In India this universal apprehension found recognition in the sixth five year plan (1980-85). Since then a concerted effort has been made in this direction by rural credit institutions to uplift country women. This has led the birth of micro credit scheme.

The statuses of women and related issues have attracted the attention of the academicians, political thinkers and social scientists both in developing as well as developed countries. It has been widely accepted that a society built on the inequality between men and women involves wastage of women resources which no country can afford. Thus the effective management and development of women's resources are of paramount importance for the mobilisation and development of human resources. Poverty and deprivation increase gender inequality which favours a policy for empowerment of women. The goals of poverty eradication and empowerment of women can be effectively achieved if deprived women could organise themselves into groups for community participation and for ascertaining their rights in various services related to their economic and social welfare.

Recently, the individual approach to poverty alleviation programmes has been increasingly replaced by group mode. SHG is expected to be one of the major programmes of poverty alleviation in India. Self-help groups have been instrumental in empowerment by enabling women to work together in collective agency.

Organizations of women in the form of SHGs have laid the seeds for economic and social empowerment of women. The basic strategy adopted to promote empowerment of women through SHGs comprises in organising women SHGs at the village lend around savings and rotational credit programmes using their own resources, facilitating regular interaction and exchange of information, linking SHGs with external credit source like banks, cooperative societies etc, imparting skill training to the members to manage their credit and take decisions, linking SHGs with rural development programmes thus enabling the members to expand their investment capital and develop leadership qualities and self-confidence.

Group dynamic among the women members empower them to fight against social evils in the community like female infanticide, dowry problem, evils of drinking, corruption etc. Formation of clutter level committees also empowers women to form network of group and undertake community-based issues to discuss with government departments. The experience gained in the group-meetings has also emboldened women members to assert their voices not only in the immediate context of their community but also in the larger democratic bodies. The opportunities given to women in the meetings of the federation of the SHGs have also paved way for their participation in the local panchayat elections.

The SGSY is playing the dominant role to enable the women. Its progress is depicted in the Table 11.1.

Table 11.1: Physical Progress of Women Swarozgaries under SGSY (1999-00 to 2005-06)

Year	Women Swarozgaries Assisted	Percentage of Women Swarzgaries Assisted
1999-2000	1,16,690	44.62
2000-2001	4,09,842	40.73
2001-02	3,85,891	41.16
2002-03	3,82,613	46.84
2003-04	4,69,824	52.41
2004-05	5,00,751	58.38
2005-06	4,95,954	58.39
Total	**3,064,765**	**48.63**

Source: Calculated on the basis of Annual Report (2005-06) of Government of India, Published by Ministry of Rural Development.

The number of the women SHGs formed so far constitutes 90 per cent or more of the total number of SHGs. In 1999-2000, 1,16,690 women swarozgaris were assisted which constituted 44.62 per cent of the women swarozgaris. In 2005-06, the number of women swarozgaris swelled to 4,99,154, registering a growth of about 11 per cent during the period 1999-00 to 2005-06. The total number of women swarozgaris assisted was 30,64,765, its 48.63 per cent swarozgaris was assisted during the period under consideration (Table 11.1).

The assessment of the performance of women self-help groups has brought results with significant implications for policy makers (Nagrajan,B.S and Lalitha). The assessment highlights the facts that:

(a) Poor women can save if adequately motivated

(b) Rural poor women need credit

(c) Rural poor women are bankable

(d) SHGs are people's institutions and with their support the women can march towards empowerment

(e) Credit delivery system through SHGs is a cost-effective approach to improve the outreach of banking services

(f) SHGs can promote individual/group ventures of income generating programmes under the effective guidance of NGOs

Swarnajayanti Gram Swarozgar Yojana (SGSY) has economically boosted the women's status. Now they are depositing their savings in bank through SHGs and gradually its share grows well except in the year 2009-10. Its progress, outstanding, etc. are depicted in Economic Survey 2010-11 as "The share under the SGSY in total savings accounts was 16,93,910 SHGs forming 24.3 per cent of the total SHGs having savings accounts in the banks. During the year under review, the average savings per SHG with all banks marginally decreased from 9060 as on 31 March 2009 to 8915 as on 31 March 2010. They ranged from a high of 11,352 per SHG with cooperative banks to a low of 7136 per SHG with RRBs. As on 31 March 2010, the share of women SHGs in total SHGs with savings bank accounts was 53.10 lakh, i.e.76.4 per cent as compared to last year's share of 79.5 per cent. 5.22 As on 31 March 2010, 48.51 lakh SHGs had outstanding bank loans of 28,038 crore as against 42.24 lakh SHGs with bank loans of 22,680 crore as on 31 March 2009 registering a growth of 14.8 per cent in the number of SHGs and 23.6 per cent in bank loans outstanding to SHGs. These figures included 12.45 lakh SHGs (25.7%) with outstanding bank loans of 6251 crore (22.3%) under the SGSY as against 9.77 lakh SHGs with outstanding bank loan of 5862 crore as on 31 March 2009. Commercial banks had the maximum share of outstanding bank loans to SHGs with a share of 66.7 per cent followed by RRBs with a share of 22.8 per cent and cooperative banks with a share of 10.5 per cent. As on 31 March 2010, average bank loan outstanding per SHG was 57,795 as against 53,689 as on 31 March 2009. It varied from a high of 62,289 per SHG in the case of commercial banks to a low of 33,894 in the case of cooperative banks 5.23. On the basis of the data received from banks by the National Bank for Agriculture and Rural Development (NABARD), the gross non-performing assets (NPAs) in respect of bank loans to SHGs were 2.94 per cent of the bank loans outstanding to SHGs, as on 31March 2010".

The analysis of SHGs in terms of outreach and sustainability has revealed mixed results. Outreach has several dimensions like breadth of outreach, depth of outreach and quality of outreach. Breadth of outreach is illustrated by number of members covered and depth of outreach cannot success in covering the difficulties of supplying financial services to the poor. Quality of outreach is reflected in the range of financial services offered, transaction cost incurred by the members and the extent of member satisfaction regarding the conditions of loan and fulfilment of demand for financial services.

Women Empowerment in Bihar

Mass poverty is one of the major critical problems confronting planners in Bihar. There is no denying the fact that the soul of India resides in villages. More than 72 per cent of population of the country lives in villages whereas in Bihar the corresponding figure is 89.5 per cent.

Bihar is the second largest and one of the most populated states in India. It has a geographical area of 94,163 sq. km. with a population density of about 880 per sq. km. The total population of Bihar is 8.29 crore as per the 2001 population census. Out of the total population of the state about 188 lakh (23 per cent) are the total main workers. Some relevant statistics about the economy of Bihar are given in the Table 11.2.

Table 11.2: Statistics on Bihar Economy

Sl. No.	Items	Figures
	1	2
1.	Area	94,163 sq. k.m.
2.	Population	8.29 crore
3.	Main Workers	1.88 crore
4.	Population Density	888 persons per sq. km.
5.	Female literacy rate	33.57 per cent
6.	Female literacy in rural area	30.03 per cent
7.	Literacy rate in scheduled caste women in rural area	5.40 per cent
8.	Sex ratio in rural area	927 female per 1000 women
9.	Population density in rural area	803 person per sq. km.
10.	Average Annual Exponential growth rate (1991-2001)	2.49 per cent
11.	Population growth rate (1991-2001)	28.33 per cent
12.	Rural population	74,199,596

(Contd...)

	1	2
13.	Rural area of Bihar	92,358.40 sq. km.
14.	Child population (0-6) in rural area:	
	Male	19.93 per cent
	Female	20.20 per cent
15.	Number of Panchayats	1,138,00
16.	Number of Districts	38
17.	Death Rate	79 per thousand
18.	Infant Mortality Rate	62 per thousand
19.	Infant Mortality Rate (Boys)	59 per thousand
20.	Per capita income (2003-04)	Rs. 5780

Source: Singh, Indrabhushan and Usha Kumari., (2007) "Jeevika Mega Project: Empowerment of Rural Poor in Bihar", Kurukshetra December, pp. 14-15.

Table 11.3: Workers in Bihar (2001)

	Particulars	Number of Workes (in '000)
1.	Total main workers	18795
	(a) Cultivators	7719
	(b) Agricultural Labourers	8114
	(c) Livestock, forestry & others	64
	(d) Mining and Quarrying	12
	(e) Manufacturing, Processing, Servicing and Repairs	
	(i) Household industry	292
	(ii) Others	276
	(f) Construction	89
	(g) Trade and Commerce	708
	(h) Transport and Storage	188
	(i) Other services	1339
2.	Marginal Workers	941
3.	Non-Workers	44790

Source: Same as Tables 11.1 and 11.2.

The focus of rural development in Bihar has mostly been along the same lines as followed by the central government. So the state of Bihar, too, has focussed on generation of employment opportunities, upliftment of underprivileged sections by enhancing beneficiary oriented quality of life, apart from providing several basic amenities, improving rural infrastructure and emphasis on agricultural development. Actually, poverty does not simply mean lack of adequate income, it must be viewed as a state of deprivation spanning the social, economic and needs context of people which presents their effective participation, as opportunities for the poor has remained as one of the important components of poverty alleviation and rural development for which a number of programmes have been initiated in India since the 1970s. The final link of this series of employment oriented programmes (viz. IRDP, TRYSEM, SITRA, FWP, NREP, RLEGP,JRY,JGSY etc.) is a self-employment programme. Swarnajayanti Gram Swarozgar Yojna (SGSY) is conceived as a holistic scheme of micro-enterprises covering various aspects of self-employment, viz. organisation of rural poor in self-help groups, capacity building, training and skill upgradation, credit and marketing.

Hence the Government of India and also the Government of Bihar adopted various strategies and programmes for rural development and employment generation in the last five decades to meet out these challenges. Poverty is a curse to humanity and the persons suffering from it are not only economically deprived of but are also socially dejected ones, hence, the focus of government policies and plans shifted towards poverty alleviation through area specific and target oriented programmes from 4th plan onward. The yard brought new programmes to cover the failure of earlier ones, but the administrative setup remained almost the same with minor changes. However, the actual position of beneficiaries (weaker sections like SC, ST, women, handicapped, agricultural labourers, rural artisans, marginal and small farmers living below poverty line) could not improve accordingly and most of them are still not in a position to meet their needs properly. The reasons are the large size of family, illiteracy, ignorance and lack of spirit to work, besides, most of them have no future planning and are mingled with present needs. Moreover, the bureaucratic attitude of the concerned officials, misappropriation in utilisation of assistance and poor involvement of the prospective beneficiaries checked their performance. Thus the earlier programmes could not attain the desired goal successively and became a politically motivated programmes hence modification was urgently required.

Providing rural households access to financial services, particularly credit, has been a priority agenda for the central government since Independence. It was considered an effective tool to earn a sustainable living. As a part of this strategy, several subsidy linked credit programmes were initiated. Within this policy context, the development of India's financial sector inevitably resulted in substantial achievements in enhancing access to credit in rural areas. Though the organised banking has largely undermined the role of the money lender regarding the provision of credit, yet it is also realised to the credit needs of the formal sector, even though this sector accounted for the bulk of the total employment generated. So the rural poor in the unorganised sector have not yet been able to come out of the clutches of moneylenders charging usurious interest rates. The rural poor generally need finances for mixed purposes (i.e. a mix of production and consumption needs), which are mutually affected by each other. They are poor, so they cannot meet the contingencies of life on their own. In certain circumstances they have to sell or pledge their productive assets (whatever they have) to meet their needs, in the absence of any outside help. This pushes them into the vicious cycle of debt and impoverishment. The formal credit system generally excludes them for want of a collateral. Conversely, borrowing from an informal source is very convenient, though the terms are very hard. As a result, the credit needs of the rural poor are only partially met by formal credit agencies. Presently, the overall share of the organised sector in credit flow to the rural poor is only around 16 per cent. Hence, a system would have to be put in place, which is flexible and responsive to the financial needs of the poor and is capable of supplying timely and adequate credit. Banking policies and procedures need to be reviewed to enable banks to adopt a more proactive approach to lending to economically viable activities in the informal sector. For this generally the services of cooperatives and non-banking financial intermediaries are dependent upon for on-lending to finance informal sector activity. Another important mechanism through which banks can meet the credit needs of the informal sector is the self-help groups which provide micro credit for informal sector activities.

Dr. Azad undertook a study of SHGs in Sabour Block of Bhagalpur district (Bihar). On the basis of random sampling method four villages-Farka, Khankita, Chanderie and Sabour were selected. From each village one SHG, altogether four SHGs were selected. From each SHG 10 women members, altogether 40.

Respondents and 40 Non-SHG members were selected for measuring the impact of SHGs regarding socio-economic aspects. The data were collected through schedule and questionnaire.

Table 11.4 reveals that the majority of groups (84%) were organising two meetings in a month for effective working of groups. Most of the groups (45%) were saving Rs. 25-30 per month per member. About 42 per cent members were taking loan for agricultural activities, besides goat (9%), cow/ buffalo (16%), poultry (8%), Bidi making and others (7%). In the case of loan recovery, 71 per cent members have exerted group pressure if loan were not paid timely.

Table 11.4: Operational Mechanism of SHGs in Sabaur Block, District Bhagalpur (Bihar)

Sl. No.	Operational Mechanism	Variable	Per cent
1.	Number of meeting of SHGs	Once in a month	16
		Twice in a month	84
2.	Per month saving of SHGs (in rupees)	10-25	20
		25-30	45
		30-35	20
		35 & above	15
3.	Members initial deposits for opening bank accounts	Rs. 500 & above	100
4.	Internal loan towards different activities	Goat	09
		Cow/ buffalo	16
		Poultry	08
		Bidi Making	18
		Agriculture activities	42
		Others	07
5.	Loan not paid in time	*(a)* Group pressure of late payment	71
		(b) Low level	29

Source: Azad, Chandra Prakesh, (2006), "Empowerment of Women through Self-Help Groups: A Study of Sabour Block of Bhagalpur District", *Journal of Regional Studies*, Vol. 16-17, No. 31-34, January 2005, December 2006, p. 59.

The result of impact on socio-economic status through SHGs shows that the total number of SHGs were not having positive result as compared to the total non-member of SHGs. Only 9 per cent of the total numbers has their annual income. Expenditure patterns also shows that the status of women were found insignificant on education, housing facilities, consumption and size of holding.

The SHGs in Sabour have not produced any positive result. Efforts are made on this line. The problems of SHGs in Sabour block of Bhagalpur district are multifarious and multi-dimensional. These problems can be solved by changing the attitude of society, family and nation towards the weaker sections of the society, poor men and women.

Empowerment of Women in Nagaland

Feat of Likuphy SHG

"Anitoli was once one of the helpless housewives solely depending upon her husband's income. Many other women inhabitants of her colony — the

Agricultural Colony, Kohima were still worse off. Their husbands scanty daily wage income forced them to hand to mouth existence. Only pastime of these helpless housewives was to gather at one place after finishing their daily chores and gossip. They very much wanted to do something, to be able to earn but fell very helpless".

The story of their lives would have continued this way but for the concern shown by the Project Officer of Cooperative Education Project of the National Cooperative Union of India (NCUI). A beginning was made by organising a motivational meeting in their colony and inviting them all to come and listen to how they too can start earning something on their own by forming a self-help group.

This actually provided them the opportunity they were looking for and soon ten of their group responded to form their own self-help group, which was registered on the 20th April 2006. Shortly their group became active. They started holding meetings at least once in two weeks. They would all attend these meetings as the absentee would have to pay a fine of five rupees. Cooperatives Education Project officials helped them to learn more about income generating activities that they could undertake. They were also invited to participate in various seminars conducted by National Cooperative Union of India-Cooperative Education Field Project (NCUI-CEFP) Kohima. This training programme was conducted in collaboration with the Nagaland State Industries Department.

The group then not only started making woollen shoes and earn a steady income but also to go beyond. One of their group members Ms. Hekali was invited by the Land Resource Development Council as a Master Trainer to train a group of women SHG Tsunoyn village for a week. For this she earned a handsome amount of Rs. 500 per day.

Later, the group was also trained in woollen carpet making. The other achievements of this SHG is in making of banana chips, potato chips, preparing papads/rotis from sticky rice and making pickles. They have mastered the art of stitching jute bags and are skilled in other handicrafts besides their traditional handloom items.

This SHG now has a steady income of their self. They have no difficulty in contributing Rs. 50 per month to their fund as each member's monthly income at present ranges from Rs. 500 to 600. Their total savings have accumulated to over Rs. 40,000 not a mean feat considering that these very women at one time were in awe of talking any official for help. At that time they felt terribly shy to sell the things made by them. No more now, they not only participate enthusiastically in various exhibition-cum-sales conducted by NCUI-CEFP, but also conduct sale of pickles, other processed foods, woollen items etc once in a week at their premises. Products made by their SHG get sale as hot cakes.

This group also has another advantage. Being urban based, the educational status of members is from seventh to tenth standard. This plus point has also been a contributing factor to the fast growth of the SHG. Two of the group members have also honed skills in piggery. Two piglets purchased from the group fund are being reared by these two members. These would fetch a price of Rs. 15,000 per pig. Half of the sale amount will go the group fund.

Thus each member of the group has to participate in one activity or the other to earn some money of their own from which they also pay their monthly contribution of Rs. 20 to the SHG fund. They have opened their bank accounts, learnt office maintenance, budget making etc. They have participated in various skill development programmes conducted by the NCUI-CEFP. The project personnel make arrangements to organise such programmes in collaboration with various other Department of the Nagaland State Government like Land Resources Development, Industries, Horticulture and Agriculture Departments. The leadership development programmes are mobilised by the lady mobiliser of the CEFP. The success of this SHG speaks in terms of their chairman having been chosen to represent the State Department of Cooperatives to give a demonstration on jute bag making at the Farmer's conference. The conference held in June 7-8, 2006 was graced by the chief minister of Nagaland as a chief guest, where Ms Anitoli, the chairman of this Likuphy SHG proudly held the demonstration. Thus the group has gained confidence in attending functions with prominent presence of high level state officials and VIPs. Not only that, Ms Anitoli has also participated and gave a talk about her SHG on the International Women's Day on March 8, 2007 to motivate many more to follow her footsteps.

The story of this tribal women's self-help group from a small colony of Kohima town is truly a motivating story for other groups of women. How insecure and helpless they felt when they were unable to earn even a single paise. Once determined and with help from NCUI-CEFP, they quickly mastered various skills to produce items having demand in the market and also picked up the nuances of financial matters. And with regular upgradation of skills they became conscious about education of their children. They are also more aware about healthcare of their own-selves and of the family and want to conduct healthcare programmes for the community. They have learnt the lesson maybe a bit late. The lesson they want to pass on to other women is that early to learn and early to work together makes one healthy, wealthy and wise.

The aforesaid description shows that Self-Help Groups (SHGs) play a dominant role to empower the women especially rural women. They are playing the significant role to shape the economic status of women, enhance the equality of status of women as participants, decision makers and beneficiaries in democratic economic and social sphere of life. They train the women to take active part in socio-economic development of the nation. They are also heading for remove the social limitations of women such as false notion and latent role in decision making. Women are now more confident, self-sustaind and prudent in all aspects. Once again this empowerment process definitely will shape the environment in favour of women which will force the all to proclaim as in ancient India was proclaiming "Yatr naryastu pujynte ramanteh tatr Debtah". It meant that the place where women are respected, worshiped God resides their means that is the God's abode. Inglorious and infringed condition of women is going to be removed very soon due to this SHGs movement.

REFERENCES

Azad, Chandra Prakash., (2006), "Empowerment of Women Through Self-Help Groups: A Study of Sabour Block of Bhagalpur District", *Journal of Regional Studies*, Vol. 16-17, Nos., 31-34, January 2005, December 2006, pp. 58-59.

Brouman, F.J.A., (1984), "*Informal Savings and Credit Arrangements in Developing Countries: Observations from Sri Lanka*" in Dale W. Adams, G.H. Graham and J.D. Von Pischke, (Eds), *Undermining Rural Development with Cheap Credit*, Westview Press, London.

Encarta® *World English Dictionary* © & (P) 1998-2005 Microsoft Corporation.

Government of India, 2011, *Economic Survey* 2010-11.

Harper, M., (1998), *Profit for the Poor*, Oxford & IBH, Publishing Co., Delhi.

Hoff, K. and J.E. Stigtiz., (1990), "Introduction: Imperfect Information and Perspectives", *The World Bank Economic Review*, Vol. 4, No. 3.

Jha, Mithilesh Kumar, (2010), *Micro-finance and Rural Development in India: A Study of Role of Self-Help Groups in Rural Development*, Ph.D., Thesis, BRA Bihar University, Muzaffarpur, Bihar.

Mehendale, Leena, 2000, National Commission for Women — An Appraisal, *Yojana*,Vol. 44: No. 11, November.

Mosley, P. and R.P. Dahal, (1985), "Lending to the Poorest: Early Lessons from the Small Farmers Development Programme, Nepal", *Development Policy Review*, Vol. 3, No. 2.

NABARD. (1995), *Report of the Working Group on Non-Governmental Organizations and Self-Help Groups*, Mumbai.

Nagrajan, B.S. and N. Lalitha, (1999), A Critical Study of Women Self-Help Groups in Selected Districts of Tamil Nadu (A Report), Project funded by ICSSR, New Delhi, Gandhi Gram Rural Institute (Deemed University), Gandhigram University, Tamil Nadu.

Owusu, K. Opuku and William Tetteh., (1982), "An Experiment in Agricultural Credit: The Small Farmer Group Lending in Ghana", *Savings and Development*, Vol. 6, No. 1.

Pattanaik, B.K., 2000. Women Welfare and Social Development, *Yojana,* Vol. 44: No. 11, November.

Rajasekhar, D., (1996), "Problems and Prospects of Group Lending in NGO Credit Programme in India", *Savings and Development,* Vol. 20, No. 1.

Singh, Indrabhushan and Usha Kumari, (2007) "Jeevika Mega Project: Empowerment of Rural Poor in Bihar", *Kurukshetra,* December, pp.14-15.

Smith, D.H. and K. Pillhiemer., (1983), "Self-Help Groups as Social Movement Organisations: Social Structure and Social Change", *Research in Social Movements, Conflicts and Change,* Vol. 5, No. 2.

Sood, Archna., (2007), "March of A Women's SHG in Kohima" *Kurukshetra,* Vol. 56, No. 1, November. p. 43.

Stiglitz, J.F. ,(1990), "Peer Monitoring Credit Markets", *The World Bank Economic Review,* Vol. 4, No. 3.

Thomas, M. and J. Pierson, (1995), *Dictionary of Social Work,* Collin Educational Publishers, London.

Wehmeier, Sally and *et al,* 2010, New Oxford Advanced Learner's Dictionary, Oxford University Press, Oxford, 7th Edition.

Yaron, J., (1992), "Successsful Rural Finance Institutions" *World Bank Discussion Paper 150,* Washington, D.C. USA.

12

Empowerment of Women Through Self-Help Groups

Mrs. Likha Kiran Kabak
Dr. Ram Krishna Mandal

Introduction

Women are an integral part in every society. The status of women in society is directly linked with social and cultural traditions, stages of economic development achieved, educational levels, attitude of the society towards women, social and religious taboos, women's own awareness and political attainments for women in society. Such factors affect the national and also regional characteristics of the status of women. The economic status of women is determined by the role played by them in carrying on economic and non-economic activities in society. The nature and type of economic and non-economic role played by women have undergone continued transformation in accordance with the changes in socio-economic factors, education levels and technological developments and with the changing concepts regarding the extent to which women's contribution is desirable and necessary. In the world over it is now recognized that the status of women in society, both in the developed and underdeveloped countries, continues to be inferior to men. Although women's role is crucial in the family and household economy, women have not been given equal rights in social, political as well as economic fields. The necessity of improvement of status of women has been recognized all over the world as an important aspect of national progress and development. It is also felt that the problem of poverty cannot be tackled without providing opportunities of productive employment to women. Productive employment to women would provide necessary economic base and improve their social status. But it is still a fact that women in many countries of the world are facing discriminatory attitude in varying degrees on ground of sex in employment and working conditions.

Women empowerment is a global issue, which has gained momentum in recent decades. In India, besides ratification of international conventions, there are provisions in the constitution and several Legislative Acts have been passed to ensure women empowerment. It however, appears that on this front the situation on ground is far from satisfactory. The position of women and their status in any society is an index of its civilization. Women are to be considered as equal partners in the process of development. But, because of centuries of exploitation and subjugation, Indian women have remained at the receiving end. In this context, in order to provide a big push, Institutional support is necessary to empower Indian women in general and rural women in particular. Women empowerment demands a 'Life-cycle' approach where empowerment is viewed as a process and not as an event, which challenges traditional power equations and relations. Empowerment in its simplest form means redistribution of power that challenges the male dominance. This does not, however, mean that the empowerment process adopts an antagonists approach. It is only to enable women to supplement and coordinate with men. Empowerment is an active process of enabling women to realize their identity, potentiality and power in all spheres of their lives.

There are several indicators of empowerment. At the individual level, participation in crucial decision-making process, ability to prevent violence, self-confidence and self esteem, improved health and nutrition conditions and at the community level, existence of women's organizations, increased number of women leaders, involvement of women in designing development tools and application of appropriate technology, etc. are very crucial. At national level the indicators are, for example, awareness of her social and political rights, adequate representation in legislative bodies, and integration of women in particular in national development plans, etc.

President A.P.J. Abdul Kalam, said empowering women was a prerequisite for creating a good nation, "when women are empowered, society with stability is assured. Empowerment of women is essential as their thoughts and their value systems lead the development of a good family, good society and ultimately a good nation".

Social change is possible only by empowering and educating women. *Jawaharlal Nehru* once said, "To awaken the people, it is women who is meant to be awakened, once she is on the move, the family moves, village moves and the nation moves".

India lives in her villages where 72 per cent (as per 2001 Census) of her people live in. Development of India is possible only when rural India is developed. Despite massive development efforts undertaken by the Centre Government and State Governments in different five year plan periods through different schemes such as IRDP, DWCRA, ICDP and TRYSEM, the problem of mass poverty, malignant growth of unemployed youth and large scale migration of people to urban areas persist in rural areas. Unless we improve the rural economy, we neither lessen the burden of poverty nor solve the problem of unemployment. Development of India's rural economy is vital for growth than urban economy. Micro-finance has come to mean the provision of credit and other financial services to the poor so that they can reduce their poverty and raise their living standards through the proper utilization of credit. Micro-finance, micro enterprises and Self-help Groups are the solution of poverty alleviation problem of rural poor to bring them to enter the main stream of economic development. Microfinance is an upcoming sector. Pegged at just a few million dollars in the early 1990s, this sector has grown into a $20 billion global industry by 2007, reporting close to 100 per cent growth year-to-year over the previous decade. Apart from growing in size, microfinance is today seen by most governments as a useful tool for poverty alleviation. Such favourable attention has led to the creation of an enabling policy environment in many countries. It is estimated that presently this sector employs more than half-a-million people globally. All of this has also led to a growing interest of the global capital markets in microfinance institutions (MFIs). Given the remote locations serviced by them, MFIs have used many rapidly developing information and communication technologies (ICTs), which has allowed many large ICT firms to also start making serious inroads in this sector. The early breakthroughs in the sector came in Bangladesh, but today India has become a major player in this sector in the world. Given the size of the population needing microfinance services in this diverse country, India has also been the right setting for development of several different models of making these services available. On top of that, the rapid changes in the economic arena have also brought in significant changes in this sector in recent years. Given these complexities and the diversities of size, clients served, models and players capturing the state of such a sector is surely a difficult task.

It shows that about a thousand microfinance institutions have reached about 14.1 million people, with an outstanding loan portfolio of Rs. 59.5 billion. On the other hand, cumulatively 3.48 million SHGs, with a membership of 58 million, have been linked to banks with an estimated loan portfolio of Rs. 80 billion. These groups have also accumulated a savings of Rs. 35.1 billion with the banks. It, however, needs to be noted that the report uses different basis of reporting for these two forms. While for MFIs it reports outstanding amounts and number of current borrowers, for the SBLP it has used the cumulative lending figures as reported in the NABARD reports and the web site. Therefore, these data are strictly not comparable. But it does indicate that the SBLP has emerged as a large microfinance model in the country (Datta, Sankar, 2009). Micro-finance for micro enterprises development through self-help group for poverty alleviation vis-à-vis socio-economic empowerment of women is considered as one of the effective strategy in the globe in the present context. It has proved effective in many parts of the world including India. Rural scenarios are changing through the SHGs. Lives of women in Andhra Pradesh, Tamil Nadu, Kerala and many corners of the country have improved considerably through SHG revolution in India. Self-help Group is a group of persons who have voluntarily become the member of the group to achieve common goal by collective efforts. Goal would be different as per the status of the groups. Suppose for BPL group the goal would be to come above poverty line by venturing into income generating activities with the help of credit facilities from banks and group itself.

Now-a-days empowerment especially women empowerment has become a buzz word especially in the context of development of rural poor and women. Empowering the poor for their development is one of the topmost prioritized agenda in development paradigm of every developing and underdeveloped country. What is this empowerment after all? We can say in laymen language that the Empowerment is about power, and about changing the balance of power. Exercising this power within and being able to take and give decision as and when required that matters or influence her or his life and exercising this power for common development of the society. In every society, there are powerful and powerless groups. Power is exercised socially, economically and politically by one person to other person or to group of persons. In nutshell, any person who have power or have enough confidence to give and take decision and influence other in a particular matter may call as empowered person. Therefore, women empowerment is a holistic concept. It is a multidimensional in its approach and involves a basic realization and awareness of women powers, potentialities, capabilities and competences, rights and opportunities of all round development in all spheres of life. Women empowerment is a process which enables women to have access and control over various factors necessary for their economic independence, political participation and social development. One cannot be empowered in one day. It is a process oriented. In the process changes are generated in individual ideas and perception abd create awareness about one's rights and opportunities for self development in all important spheres of life. Empowerment of women may normally mean equal access to and control over important productive resources. Women empowerment, therefore, may normally describe as a process by which women would be able to develop their confidence level and increase their inner strength and self reliance to decide and determine their important choices in life.

In Arunachal Pradesh "Micro-finance Vision—2011" has been set to implement it in a mission mode. Under this mission, the objective is to promote 5000 Women Self-help Groups and link it with credit by 2011. The Department of women and child development has been made as Nodal department to implement the mission. SHG movements have entered in the Arunachal Pradesh also due to some NGOs even though it is in nascent stage in comparisons to other successful State. DRDA and Blocks has also formed some groups in these remote areas subject to the availability of fund for subsidy grant. The dawn of entrepreneurship has already entered in the remote of Arunachal Pradesh. Notable factor here is that support services are very poor in supplementing these movements such as skill training, providing raw materials, marketing of products, transportations, connectivity, etc. In absence of these support services the SHGs are limited in thrift and micro credit activities. Economic activities are limited to their inherent talent i.e. handloom and handicrafts and farm based activities. Due to these reasons the SHG movement could not pick up its momentum in the state. SGSY could not also yield expected result owing to various constraints and lack of support from Government Departments and PRIs, etc. Due to these factors SHGs formed under SGSY are not able to sustain for longer duration and fails to bring desired social impacts.

The objective of the paper is to investigate the role of SHGs in promoting income generating activities and poverty alleviation in order to achieve socio-economic empowerment of the women and also to search the problems preventing the SHGs to sustain in the society. This paper is divided into VI Sections. Section-I deals with introduction of Subject studied, state, district and study area. Review of Literature is also included in this 1st Section. Section-II tells us about the location and short description of the study area. Section-III illustrates the methodology, data source and collection, processing, analysis, interpretation of data and also profile of sample SHGs. Section-IV examines the socio-economic empowerment of the women generating from SHGs. Section-V seeks to find out the problems preventing the SHGs. and Lastly Section-VI draws the conclusions and suggestions.

SECTION - II

Location and Short Description of the Study Area

Brief Profile of the District: The study shall be conducted only under Papum Pare District. Itanagar, the capital of the state, is also located in this district. As per the 2001 census, the district has a population of 1, 22,003 of whom

64,184 are males and 57,819 are females. The Nyishi tribe is the main inhabitants of the District. As on date, the district have one sub-division with District Administration at Yupia and Itanagar and one Additional Deputy Commissioner Office at Sagalee, five CD Blocks namely Doimukh, Kimin, Balijan, Sagalee and Mengio and ten administrative circles. There is a 750 KW hydel power plant at Itanagar and a 5623 KW Diesel Generating installed plant. 80.74 per cent of the villages are electrified. As on March, 2007 there are 23 branches of 8 nationalized banks, 1 rural, 1 state cooperative bank and 1 private bank operating in the district. The literacy rate is around 69.3 per cent. The Rajiv Gandhi University, a Central University is located at Doimukh in this district. The North East Regional Institute of Science and Technology, a Deemed University is located at Nirjuli near Itanagar. There are two colleges, one Polytechnic institute, 12 higher secondary, 17 secondary 54 middle and 93 primary schools located in the district. Handloom weaving and cane and bamboo works are the major traditional activities amongst the tribe of the district. Maximum SHGs are engaged in these traditional activities in district.

The proposed study was conducted in the month of August, 2008 specifically in Doimukh Block which is nearest to the Capital City, Itanagar amongst these five blocks and Sagalee CD Block located at 95 km away from Itanagar connected with pucca and half kutcha roads.

Study Area

1. *Chimpu village* located at a distance of 7 kilometer from capital city, Itanagar is still living in fully rural setting. Actually maximum inhabitants of village are migrants from Kurung Kumey District, most backward District in the State with 98 per cent poverty rate as per 2002 BPL Rural Development census. Due to poor connectivity and lacking in other basic amenities in Kurung Kumey, people are flowing into Capital city mainly for treatment of various diseases mostly water & sanitation and alcoholism borne diseases. They are settling in and around capital complex to access the medical facilities. Chimpu village has expanded in a short span of 2-3 years because of these migrations. So to say new village has created. Among these migrants some has got job in government sector, some are engaged in petty trade and contracts works. Maximum are practicing jhum cultivation (shifting cultivation) following conventional method of agriculture under the deep hilly forest as they do in their original place. The literacy level of the villagers are also very low only few can just read and write. In these circumstances, they are struggling for their both ends and to access the basic amenities viz; education for their children, medical facilities, drinking water, credit facilities, etc.
2. *Sagalee* a small town about 95 kilometers far from the capital town Itanagar has witnessed the increasing number of SHGs because of the

efforts of many development stakeholders' departments and organizations. The entrepreneurships zeal has already entered in that area especially amongst the women which contributes in formation and stabilization of groups besides the efforts of development stakeholders department and organization. Women are basically engaged in permanent as well as jhum cultivation. People are practicing the jhum as well as permanent cultivation. But level of literacy amongst the women is generally very low.

SECTION - III

Methodology and Data Source

Since the proposed study was adopted in limited geographical area, only few groups were selected as sample for study. In the present study it was felt that any single method of data collection and its analysis were bound to have a limited relevance in meeting the overall objectives of the project; hence different tools were used to collect the data. To carry out the research in addition to primary data, collection of secondary data was attempted from the Rural Development Department for the status of SHGs in Papum Pare District. The main tool of data collection was the pre-structured Questionnaire and Interview method to achieve the objective of the study. The members of the sample SHGs were interviewed to drive the primary data. The questions were structured keeping in mind about the objectives and hypotheses of the study. The interview schedule contained mostly close-ended questions, though some open ended questions were also included.

Simple random sampling method was adopted for selection of sample for the study. Only two CD Block were chosen for the study i.e. Doimukh CD Block and Sagalee CD Block under Papum Pare District. From Doimukh CD Block, two SHGs viz. Nit and Aryum SHGs and from Doimukh CD Block, three SHGs viz; Poum Poyi, Karupu and Numum were selected for in-depth study to understand the level of empowerment of each group. Thus, total five SHGs were randomly selected for this study. The groups of Chimpu village under Doimukh CD Block were promoted by NGO and three groups of Laptap village, Khamlee village and Pech Hoj village under Sagalee CD Block were promoted by DRDA and Block. From each group, few members (available on the day of meeting) were selected for in-depth interview and discussion. The total respondents of the questionnaire were 40 out of 58 members from five SHGs. The following sample groups of SHGs from two CD Blocks are shown below in Table 12.1.

Data Collection and Processing: Both primary and secondary data were collected using a combination of methods such as formal and informal discussions, structured interviews questionnaire, focus group discussion and

Table 12.1: Study Areas and Profile of Sample SHGs

Sl. No.	Name of CD Block	Name of Village	Name of SHG	Date of Formation	Caste of Members	No. of SHG Members	Marital Status
1.	Doimukh	Chimpu	Aryum	January, 2004	Nyishi	8	All married
2.	-do-	-do-	Nit	March, 2004	Nyishi	8	All married
3.	Sagalee	Laptap	Poum Poyi	6th January, 2003	Nyishi	15	All married
4.	-do-	Khamlee	Numum	January, 2006.	Nyishi	15	All married
5.	-do-	Pech Hoj	Karupu	6th January, 2003	Nyishi	12	All married
Total	–	–	**5**			**58**	**All married**

Source: Field Survey.

Study area in the block was selected based on the following criteria:

- Presence of active groups promoted by DRDA and NGO.
- Groups by different agency
- Group functioning for 2-3 years
- Groups linked with bank credit for taking up income generating activities.
- Nearer to Itanagar.

personal interviews with the SHG members, promoting institutions such as NGO, Block officials, etc. The data thus collected from all the 40 set of questionnaire of the members of five samples SHGs were analyzed. The socio-economic profiles of each member were covered in the individual questionnaire and group profiles were covered in the questionnaire set for group.

SECTION - IV

Socio-economic Empowerment of Rural Women through Self-help Groups

Success Story: SHG has changed the lives of some members significantly such as, Smti Yura Yaro, SHG has played vital role in improving the quality of her life. She was illiterate, ignorant and innocent women prior to the joining of SHG. On one fine day her Journey started from Lodo Kure village under Tali Circle, the remotest area of Kurung Kumey District, with her husband Shri Yura Nyelo to see the hustle bustle of little Itanagar Town for the first time during 2002 (Itanagar was little town by then). She never saw the vehicle, roads and markets before that time. Her husband held her tightly in a bus with the fear of falling down, as they traveled for the first time. Finally they landed at Chimpu village and became able to manage to have a small home for themselves. During her staying for few months with relatives, she narrated how she was so innocent, unaware of every thing going around before her joining in the evening class of total literacy campaign run by SARRA, an local NGO. She behaved very roughly during the initial period. She could speak only Nyishi language (her mother tongue). She couldn't speak and understand the Hindi or Assamese languages, the common language spoken in the State. So there was a lot of communication problem while trying to say something with other non Nyishi people specially the shopkeepers. Moreover, she could not differentiate between Rs. 10 and Rs. 100 notes. As a result she could not bargain and pay the price of the commodities as per the cost. She used to give all the money she had to the shopkeepers while purchasing something without knowing the value of money. Finally she was convinced by the SARRA (Society for Advancement and Recreation in Rural Areas) to continue the class in the evening after a day long work in agriculture field. Evening batches of SARRA adult school were used to turn themselves into Arium SHG (the name of SHG) formed in January, 2004 which eventually changed her life now. She learned to talk little Hindi and Assamese to communicate with non-Nyishi besides learning the calculation of numbers, writing at least her own name. She learned how to dress herself while going to attend group meeting and other places. She has now knowledge about some government Programmes such as Total Literacy campaign, SGSY, etc. She saves Rs.100 every month in group account by realizing the importance of saving. SHG has changed her attitude towards life she told. Today she is sustaining with agriculture produce that she can brought from her home after day long toiling in the mountain i.e., jhum cultivation. She needs more training to build her capacity and skill to reduce her drudgery as well as increase her income through some income generating activities that can yield more than her jhum field.

Likewise, there are many members benefited from the process of SHGs. In Aryum SHG where Smti Yaro belongs, maximum of the members are engaged in agricultural activities. Basically they cultivate for their own consumption only. But vegetables and sweet potatoes they grow in the jhum paddy field are for business purpose also. In this way they can meet the cash requirement. Some members are engaged in petty trade and piggery. They took loan from the group and run the petty trade such as poultry, piggery, shop and petty contractual works. Though their lives have improved significantly, moved from worse to better but not moving towards the best because they are not earning enough income to cross the poverty line. As per the cost of living prevalent in Itanagar, at least Rs.5000 to 6000 income per month per family of 5 to 6 members is required to lead the life above poverty line.

In Nit SHG formed in March, 2004, there are five members who are involved in income generating activities. Two members are doing vegetable marketing, two members are having grocery shop and one is having wine shop. These members have taken a loan from the group corpus and ventured into these income generating activities. They are earning minimum net profit of Rs.1500 per month. Though it is not enough to cross the poverty line, they are at least trying to live a minimum decent life. To cross the poverty line, each members should earn at least Rs. 5000 to 10000 per month. It may be possible by upgrading their skill of management and quantum of loan. It is noticed that skill and quantum of loan are interrelated. The group members are not competent enough to venture into income generating activities. Therefore, they took small dose of credit from their own group for their immediate family needs and for petty trades. They are bound to continue in the traditional sector due to lower skill because majority of them are illiterate. The few who are literate have only primary education or have studied up to middle school level. This makes them incompetent to deal with the banking agencies and other development agencies. Over a period of time, to increase the quantum of loan per member is possible from their increasing corpus through saving and interest earned if their knowledge and skill are increased. However, upgradation of skill is depending on the institutions and if any government programme comes to impart them the skill specific to the activities, then they will be able to embark on skill based income generating activity.

Poum Poyi SHG, a group of 15 women from Laptap and nearby villages formed on 6th January, 2003 is one of the best SHG in the Sagalee in terms of its age, economic activities and functioning of group. This group is found for doing the highest economic activities which are:

1. Agri-Horti production
2. An approximately 2½ hectares orange garden at Poum hill in Laptap village with above 2000 plants nursery
3. Crafts making and Handloom production
4. Seasonal cash crops garden
5. Fixed wage work, treated as social services amongst the group
6. Participation in occasional exhibition/fairs for marketing of their products
7. Food catering as and when opportunity comes
8. Community development work etc.

The above activities are in addition to their main activities i.e,. cultivation. Out of 15 members, 8 members are engaged in Handicrafts production, 6 members in weaving and 1 member is having a grocery. They are maintaining separate directory for these each production.

It is elicited from the information provided by the group and through observation that this SHG can be rated as best performing SHG under SGSY. Over the years of working experience with lots of economic activities besides their agriculture field, their empowerment level in terms of economic and social aspects have increased significantly. In an interview they are found to be quite confident of taking up any economic activities that benefits the group and thereby its members. They are also found to be confident to intervene the cases of gender discrimination as they have already solved many such problems in their village i.e., child marriage, domestic and polygamy, the social issues in Nyishi society. Though the Nishi men want to uphold the practice of polygamy as a custom but the Nyishi women oppose it. It causes lots of problems in the family particularly because of injustice, discrimination, mental and physical torture to women and female child.

From the observation of their activities of Poum Poyi SHG, the way they perform and with data support given by them, the level of education, confidence, awareness on gender discrimination, etc. have improved tremendously. The members of Poum Poyi SHG are empowered economically, socially and politically to a great extent.

In the same way, Numum SHG and Karupu SHG from Sagalee are also equally advanced. They understood the importance of collective power and therefore work together for the benefits of each member in all spheres i.e., economic and social activities. Members are getting the micro loan from group @ 3 to 5 per cent per month. Members of the group are doing their economic activities such as agriculture, horticulture, handloom and handicrafts and grocery shops individually.

Status of SHGs in the study area: As mentioned earlier, 5 sample SHGs selected for the study are promoted by SARRA (NGO) and BDO & CDPO, Sagalee. Initially, women were suspicious in joining the SHGs. Gradually they understand the benefits of thrift and credit and other benefits of SHGs and they have formed into a group. When we asked about reasons for joining SHG, members cited as many as 7 to 8 reasons viz. to avail credit, developing saving habit, to meet unexpected demand for cash, motivated by NGOs/ government officials, solidarity, exchange of ideas/experiences, attend adult education classes and empowerment. Among all the reasons mentioned, 'to avail credit', to meet unexpected demand for cash and to save money and earn interest are the prime factors to join the SHGs.

Regular meetings, compulsory attendance and savings are the main features of the SHGs. These meetings are conducted at the group's leader's house either fortnightly or monthly depending on the convenience of the members. There is a penalty for late attendance and absentee. Thus, there is 70 to 100 per cent attendance always. Usually, in the meeting saving, flow of credit, income generating activities, recovery, social issues, etc. are kept as agenda.

Other than Karupu SHG, all other sample SHG saved Rs.100 per month uniformly. The total savings of these 5 SHGs is around Rs. 1003460 as on August, 2008. The group wise saving are presented below in Table 12.2.

Table 12.2: Savings of SHGs

Name of the Group	No. of Members	Rate of Saving per Month	Total Corpus Fund	Credit taken from Bank
Aryum SHG	8	100	190000	–
Nit	8	100	180000	150000
Poum Poyi	15	100	317460	63000
Numum	15	100	100000	–
Karupu	12	2000 (one time deposit)	216000	–
Total	**58**	–	**1003460**	**213000**

Source: Field Survey.

Generally, the above saving is used for internal as well as some external lending. Availability of loan is depending on the availability of cash balance in the group account. Loans are given at 3 to 10 per cent interest. For internal lending they keep 3 to 5 per cent and for external i.e. non-member lending they charged at 5 to 10 per cent interest per month. Women are realizing that they have not only access to but control over an amount which they cannot do individually in the situation. They opened bank accounts in the name of group to ensure safety of money saved and to access more mainstream credit.

The study reveals that Credit for consumption and medical, education fees for children, purchase of inputs for agriculture and petty trades are the reason for which loans are borrowed by all the respondents. Two groups are also linked with banks to undertake income generating activities through which women could achieve economic independence and self confidence to some extent. They are actively participating in training and fairs wherever they are given a chance. Except Poum Poyi SHG, remaining other four SHG has not taken up any major income generating activities. When we enquired on this, they explained that they felt need loan from bank to start micro enterprises. However, this does not seem to main reason. The main reason is that they are lacking in skill and confidence to plan and manage a micro enterprise.

Savings Habits: SHGs promote thrift mobilization by considering it as an entry point of any activity. In the first or second meeting, the groups unanimously decide the rate of saving per month or per week collectively. The entire sample groups undertaken for study are saving monthly. Thrift and credit are the main activities of the group which is also the basis of group formation and its sustenance for longer duration. Rural poor women are formed into a group mainly to access credit whenever required from pooled savings. SHG plays tremendous role in creating saving habits amongst the women of Arunachal Pradesh. Here the indigenous people do not have the saving habits earlier. In emergency situation, community people come forward and share the crisis of that family. There was no banks in rural areas, therefore the question of saving habits do not arise. With the opening of banks in the rural areas and opening of bank account by the SHGs, saving habits are inculcating. As an individual, it is quite difficult for them to open account and save regularly but as group they are doing. Keeping of money in the banks for unforeseen happening or reaping its benefits after certain period of time was not in their mind before joining the group. SHGs are effectively playing the role of mini micro-finance institutions for the group. From the record of saving amount it is reflected that saving habits are already inculcated amongst the group members of the entire sample group.

Improvement of Status of Women: The attempts of SHG approach are making its impact on the society especially among the women. The focus of the micro-finance projects such as SGSY and other bank linkage loans are actually not successful in development of micro enterprises in the state, but successful in developing sustainable household livelihoods, decreasing household vulnerability and community development up to great extent. The micro-finance has enabled women to make a greater contribution to household income, either through their own economic activity or equally becoming a channel for loans to household activity. This contribution is recognized and valued by other household members and lead not only to increased household well-being, but women's increased role in decision-making and improved well-being for women themselves. This increased status in the household in itself in turn gives women the support they need to enable them together with men to bring about wider changes in gender inequality in the community.

In addition to the economic empowerment, social and political empowerment too has been attained. The group activities have given them a chance to come out to the mainstream, to realize the potentialities within themselves. This has lead to a change in their outlook towards society. The status of being a woman is no more considered as a curse. All these, in fact, are looked upon as boon to bring them closer, to bind them closer and as a mean to lay the foundation of a new gender equity society.

SHG has become an instrument to bridge the gap that exists in the society — the gender gap and the social gap between the rich and poor. By contributing economically, women have gained a pivotal role in the decision making of the family. The inequality between the rich and the poor are slowly decreasing. The days are not far when these differences will be the minimum.

The transformation of any society has to begin from women, because women are the centre of a family - the foundation stone on which the family is built. When a woman is changed, the family is changed and a change in the family brings changes in the society. The impact of past fifty years of efforts by the state and the central government to eradicate poverty from the society, in spite of the better educational, economic, political, cultural and social environment is not minimal mainly because almost all the programmes failed to include women in it. It is in this decade the women empowerment policy has been introduced and become integral part of the development strategy. Therefore, SHG is a silent revolution - a revolution which has all the potentiality of bridging the gender gap and building a world where poverty and gender discrimination with its all evils will be uprooted.

In the study area also, as mentioned earlier, the status of women have improved though upto not that stage where it should be. The SHGs in Chimpu village have changed the socio economic status of the entire members including their family. They are no more prone to economic vulnerability.

Attitudinal Change: To bring about gender equity society it is important that any move to enforce laws must be accompanied by a movement to bring about an attitudinal change in our society. The existing laws and rights for women need to be strengthened and more vigorously implemented. Where policies and programmes do not serve the special needs of women, they need to be amended or recast. Where benefits do not reach our women in general and rural women in particular, there is need for special intervention to enhance accessibility.

Though women have contributed significantly in every sphere of life, yet for various historical, social, religious and cultural reasons and in spite of many constitutional guarantees and legislative measures, women still remain backward for their rightful place in society. The findings of the National Status for Women Committee have revealed that the status of women has been declining steadily. This observation has indicated that the initial recognition of women's rights, which emerged during the freedom struggle and was expressed in the Constitution, is actually not considered seriously. It is just there for knowledge sake not to be implemented. Our menfolk are failing to consider women as equal partner and place them in the same level. They want to continue to rule and dominate like the British over women. Though our country got independence in 1947 i.e,. 63 years before but poverty still being the crux of the problem. It will be there till the attitude doesn't change particularly of men.

Therefore, it is not enough to amend laws and rights. Changes of attitude within each individual towards gender equality are must for empowerment of women in a silent move without creating any chaotic situations. To bring attitudinal changes amongst the women under sample SHGs undertaken for the study it is found that SHG approaches are playing tremendous role because of its process oriented approach, member of the SHG are automatically becoming assertive after joining into the SHGs. In the process, awareness is created on rights and many other welfare aspects in the group. Their confidence level increases. Banks have also encouraged them to venture into economic activities which have reduced their economic vulnerability.

SECTION - V

Problems Faced by SHGs

Indeed, for bringing our womenfolk into the mainstream of our national life it is crucial that a major change in the social value system becomes the need of the day so that evil practices towards women like polygamy, force marriages, child marriage, etc. may then be given a decent burial. The problem is tough involving as it does getting rid of a custom which plagued in our society being introduced and practiced by ancestors. We are failing to understand the suitability and convenient in continuing this practice with the passage of time from primitive agriculture and barter to cash economy. Righteous indignation by some women organization is understandable but the flight against social evils should begin in the minds of men. In fact, there should be a public outcry against such case. For obvious reasons, legislation cannot prevent, much less eradicate, the evil of keeping more than one wife and subsequent family restlessness. The real and more effective deterrent could therefore be the social distaste or disapproval of such practitioners. Such a milieu has to be created so that even the mention of the word 'polygamy or polyandry' is considered vulgar and is condemned outright.

The main drawbacks in women's development have been mainly pre-occupation with repeated pregnancies without respite in physical workload, lack of education in formal and non-formal and a predominance of social prejudices along with the lack of independent economic generation activity or independent assets, particularly the rural women are concerned.

With the above social background, working in a group is not easy. Male resistance against women SHG is prevalent. But it does not last long. Economic benefits though in a small way from the group have encouraged men to allow women or wife to participate in the group over the time. However, still in some parts of the village resistance is prevalent. As more of the awareness on benefits of SHGs is spreading, the numbers of SHG are increasing in many districts. The SHG plants have already developed its roots. Therefore, it needs water, manure and proper care to grow into big tree and become independent in yielding fruits and green leaves. These water, manure and care in terms of training, credit, infrastructure and marketing support are the main constraint in nurturing and strengthening the SHGs in the state. Very poor road connectivity due to hilly terrain, poor telecommunication and primitive method of agriculture are the main characteristics of the state.

In the context of SHG growth, the serious problem is that of marketing of the SHG products and denial of the state to provide safety net to the SHG producers in the face of the big business houses and the transnational corporations. Advertising, branding, selling and marketing by the latter overpowers the micro enterprise of the SHG members. The shift of policy towards power loom discouraging handloom for which many SHGs are facing serious problem for their existence. In such a context, self-employment jargon appears to be a distant dream that would ultimately make the poor responsible for their own fate as micro-finance philosophy throws the onus of poverty to the poor. This is the greatest hypocrisy of the micro-finance philosophy. In a country like India issue of poverty are diverse. For the landless poor are issue can be addressed largely through redistribution of land and for tribal population restructuring emancipator social, economic and political policies. But in the changing political economy, the corporate sector and the multinational players are grabbing land in the metro cities and towns. They make conspiracy to vacate lands owned by the poor and the latter are thrown to the debt trap of micro-finance from which they can hardly come out without surrendering the meager means of livelihood that they might possess. Another cause of concern is high rate of interest charged to members within the groups. The interest charged to individual member is quite higher then the bank rate of interest. Members taken a loan in time of crisis from its corpus are not able to repay the money with interest amount and ultimately surrendering whatever the meager assets to the groups to keep the group's rules and discipline. There are some major problems discussed below:

1. *Absenteeism:* There is 70 to 100 per cent attendance in the group meeting. The members and leader of the group shared that without the presence of all the members, it is quite difficult to pass the resolution in the meeting which further stops the activities of group. Therefore, the frequent motivation by the promoting agencies is required.

2. *Infrastructure:* Chimpu village about 6 kilometers away from Itanagar, the capital city of Arunachal Pradesh does not have much communication problems. But for the group, some infrastructure is required for venturing into income generating activities. There is no common facility centre for the group. They are holding the group meeting either in group leader house or in member's house.

3. *Bank credit:* This is one of the main problems in the study area. Out of five SHG, only two groups have availed the loan from bank. Other three are still waiting for the loan to be sanctioned by bank to increase the economic activities of group and its member. Many of the SHGs including five sample SHGs have shared that banker have lackadaisical attitude towards SHG loan even while opening saving bank accounts also. Only 1.16 per cent credit was realized against the target during 2006-07. There is also inadequate coordination between Banks and DRDA. As a result, DLCC meeting with banks is not held in time. Bankers are actually reluctant to extend loan to the SHGs in the fear of non repayment which would be directly reflected in their individual performance. Therefore, the sensitization training to change the attitude of bankers for financial inclusion of rural SHG needs to be focussed.

4. *Politics:* Election is the dangerous threat to the group. In the State, politics are taken very serious in the grassroots level. In this time many groups become defunct and break because of supporting various different political parties. Members are divided in two or three parties and hence the misunderstanding, disunity and dislike ness to each other occur. Women are used as channel for win by the candidates in the fray. As

usual they are never encouraged for leader but they are badly used in the campaign. They become star campaigners during the election time. The sad fact to note here is that in such a time women are against the women. Instead of listening and supporting the potential women leader they are listening to male folk. This may be the reason why women still stand lower than men and are subject to the discrimination.

SECTION - VI

Findings, Suggestions and Conclusion

Findings: Women of this state are getting habituated to savings and managing SHGs efficiently. Respondents are happy with functioning of SHGs because they inculcated a sense of belongingness, habit of thrift, and discipline among the members. The most important one is the solidarity amongst members in the world of male dominated society. The leader of Nit SHG has shared that once in a year they have a feast together in her house happily by celebrating the togetherness.

Suggestions: Development of the state is possible only when the rural area is developed. Despite massive development efforts undertaken by the central and State Governments in different schemes such as IRDP, DWCRA, ICDP and TRYSEM, the persistent problem of mass poverty, malignant growth of unemployed youth and large scale migration of people to urban areas from the rural areas prevails. Unless we improve the rural economy, we cannot lessen the burden of poverty nor can we solve the problems of unemployment. About 42 per cent of the rural population still lives below the poverty line in Arunachal. The problem of unemployment cannot be tackled by creating more jobs in the public sector and other various government departments. There must be avenues in micro and small enterprises for self-employment and expansion of job opportunities. The scope of job opportunities is very limited due to very limited presence of corporate sectors and it is impossible to absorb all unemployed persons in government sectors. Though the state government adopted two consecutive industrial policy, 1991 and 2001 to encourage the establishment of large and small scale industries in the state, the number of establishment of industries is so small in number that job opportunities in the private sector becomes very limited. Under these circumstances SHGs may play great role in establishment of micro enterprises and hence self employment of huge unemployed population as well.

However, with the above constraints, the Micro-finance for micro enterprises development through self-help group for poverty alleviation *vis-à-vis* socio-economic empowerment of women is considered as one of the effective and holistic approach under Swarnajayanti Gram Swarozgar Yojana. It has proved effective in many parts of the world including India. Rural scenarios are changing through the SHGs. Lives of women in Andhra Pradesh, Tamil Nadu, Kerala and many corners of the country have improved considerably through SHG revolution in India.

Time to Review and Amend Laws: Along with SHG movement for larger socio-economic and political empowerment of women, amendment and reviewing all laws and practices which discriminate against women is very urgent. A commissioner for women's rights to follow and monitor enforcement of legislation in this regard seems to be necessary. Experience has shown that though the national efforts for development have led to the all-round progress, their fruits have not reached all sections of the society, particularly the women who have constituted the single largest group of exploited citizens.

Economic Emancipation: In the context of India, now it is recognized that in the demographic features of female population, a far greater attention has to be paid for their economic emancipation. The low status of women in large segments of India's society cannot be raised without opening up of opportunities for independent employment and income for them. It has to be appreciated that since women will continue to be among the most vulnerable members of the family, their economic emancipation with necessary safeguards should constitute the family-centered poverty alleviation strategy in both urban and rural sectors. Things become much worse when our traditional attitudes prevent a correct appreciation of the meaningful role of women in the economic field. The same traditional perspective not only glosses over the unequal deal women get but finds nothing wrong with the arrangement by large segment of men and women. The genesis of discrimination and cruelty against women in general can be traced to the inexplicable attitude of social apathy on the part of the Indian populace. Though the Constitution provides for equality between the sexes with special protection for women and children, Indians in their family life have been governed by personal and religious laws which fail to give women their due place. These laws have relegated Indian women to an inferior legal as also social status.

It has been proved in the study area that there is a huge scope for the progress of SHGs and its activities in the study. Through the reviews of various research studies, it has been proved that SHG is playing tremendous role in socio-economic and political empowerment of rural poor and women. SHG is the best means to achieve the desired goals of the country that is to raise the 28 per cent BPL into APL till 2015. Moreover, with the growing unemployment pressure this is, one of the best means for creating self employment opportunities in the country as well as in the study area.

Education: Education is a milestone for women's empowerment because it enables them to respond to opportunities, to challenge their traditional roles and to change their lives. Similar ideas were supported by the

International Conference on women in 1994. It was said there that education is one of the most important means of empowering women with the knowledge, skills and self confidence which are necessary to participate fully in the development process. Educating woman benefits the whole society. It has a more significant impact on poverty and development than men's education.

Social change is possible only by empowering and educating women, *Jawaharlal Nehru* once said, "To awaken the people, it is women who is meant to be awakened; once she is in the move, the family moves, village moves and the nation moves". *Swami Vivekananda* also once said, "There is no chance for the welfare of the world unless the condition of women is improved. It is not possible for a bird to fly on one wing". Likewise no nation can flourish keeping half of its population in negligence and ignorance as women constitute half of its human capital. A modern society cannot achieve all round development without partnering the women in development efforts.

Keeping in view of the above, following are some suggestions that need specific care in the study area for economic empowerment which would automatically lead to social and political empowerment of women.

Capacity Building and Skill Training: The studied group are lacking in skill based activities. They need skill training in various skills oriented activities. The group are found to be in need of managerial and record keeping training also. Therefore, they should be trained in these aspects by DRDA and NGOs. It is to be mentioned here that out of total fund under SGSY, 10 per cent of total amount is only for training purpose. DRDA should assess the training needs of the SHGs and should provide training as per the requirement of the group. If the DRDA is not able to fulfill the training requirement of the group then the fund for training under SGSY i.e. 10 per cent should be transferred to training institute like SIRD. This 10 per cent should also enhance from 10 to 20 per cent keeping in view of the importance of the training. The training institute should be within the reach of women that means it should located within the cluster of village to suit the geographical condition of the state.

Federation of SHGs: To establish people's organization and achieve the desired goal, federation of SHG at various levels is required. This will take care of all the training needs based on the livelihood options that are available and can be created. Upgradation of traditional livelihood skills with appropriate technology is required in the study area.

Linkage with the Banks: Each VLF/SHG is required to open a savings bank account in its name. In case of absence of bank in an area, VLFs shall open accounts through BLF. In this case BLF shall function as a NBFC for their VLFs. SHGs and VLFs should prepare livelihood investment plan for each member and submit it to BLFs which will be further forwarded by BLFs to Banks for credit where the groups have its account. It is to be ensured that groups are getting loan in time. The project should be time bound ensuring sustainable self employment opportunities for BPL. This way there would be appreciable increase in standards of living of all the households. Revolving fund loan in the ratio of 1:4 that is 4 times of the group corpus should be at least provided to all the performing SHGs as per the SGSY and NABARD Guideline.

Marketing infrastructure to be created by State Government for SHGs Federations on need basis: Market infrastructure for each village level federation is in need. As mentioned earlier, SHGs doesn't have its own infrastructure till now. Some of the DRDA has created the market sheds for SHGs in the state but it is not under the management of SHGs. Therefore, once it is established and registered under suitable registration act, infrastructure whatever created from the any government fund sources should be handed over to federation for management ensuring that the performing SHGs are getting the stall to sell its products.

Investment Plans of SHGs: DRDA in collaboration with Federations should prepare Investment Plan of Each SHG on the basis of needs and availability of various livelihood options to rural poor. DRDA and Federation should undertake a systematic survey to assess livelihood options with due involvement of professional rural markets research organizations.

Conclusion: The success of these Self-Help Groups has not only improved the economic status of the women concerned, but there is also a drastic change in their social status. SHGs have developed human dignity among the poor women. Women were nobody earlier but somebody now. In the area of rural development SHGs certainly have a future role to play.

If proper watch and ward action is not taken, the main purpose of SHGs promotion will defeat. SHGs over time may see some set back due to internal rivalries, domination of self interested people, corrupt leadership etc. Everything is not going well with SHGs. It is true that quality of SHGs is diluting. Moneylenders' activities are done by SHGs dominating members. Therefore NABARD, Banks, NGOs and Voluntary Organizations have to be careful about these issues and mainly educate and guide the people to prevent such unhealthy practices.

REFERENCES

Arjun Y. Pangannavar (2009): "Rural Development: Women Self-Help Group", *Southern Economist,* March 1, Vol. 47, No. 21.

Anitha H.S. and Ashok D Revankar (2007): Micro-credit Through Self-help Groups for Rural Development, *Southern Economist,* August 15, Vol. 46, No. 8.

C.Gangaiah, B. Nagaraja, C. Vasudevulu Naidu — "Impact of Self-help Groups on Income and Employment: A Case Study, *Kurukshetra,* Vol. 54, No. 5.

Datta, Sankar (2009): "Consolidated the Growth of Micro-finance, *EPW,* Vol. XLIV, No. 30, July 25-31, Mumbai.

J.A. Ruby, James Devassia and Abraham George (2009): Women Empowerment: Meaning, Characteristics and Dimensions, *Southern Economist,* May 1, Vol. 47, No. 25.

Kalavati H. Kamble and Gangadhar B. Sonar (2006): The Role of SHGs in Women Empowerment: A Study on Selected SHGs Promoted by Voluntary Organization in Gulbarga District of Karnataka, J*ournal of Global Economy,* October.

Muniam, A. (2009): Micro-finance and Poverty Reduction: Analytical Issues, *Southern Economist,* May 1, Vol. 47, No. 25.

P. Loganathan & R Asokan (2006): Inter Regional Development of Self-help Groups in India, *Kurukshetra, Southern Economist,* September 15, Vol. 45, No. 10.

Ramesh. O. Olekar (2009): Opinion of SHG's Members on Women Empowerment, *Southern Economist,* March 15, Vol. 47, No. 22.

V.M. Rao (2002), Women Self-Help Groups Profiles from Andhra Pradesh & Karnataka, *Kurukshetra,* April.

Section–III
Women in Entrepreneurship

13

Women Entrepreneurship and Some Hurdles to Overcome

Dr. R. Ganapathi
Mr. S. Sannasi

"When women move forward, the family moves, the village moves and the Nation moves"

—Pandit Jawaharlal Nehru

"An enterprise owned and controlled by a women having a minimum financial interest of 51 per cent of the capital and giving at least 51 per cent of the employment generated by the enterprise to women"

—Government of India

Introduction

It is imperative to note the participation of women in economic activities as self-employed individuals. Many of the traditional occupations open to women were mainly based on caste and creed and the nature of self-employment was based on the standard of living. Presently, not only are women generating employment for themselves in the unorganized sector, they are also providing employment to others. The country needs to mobilize and utilize fully all its resources including human resources. The participation of women in economic activities is necessary not only from a human resource point of view but is essential even for the objective of raising the status of women in society. The economic status of women is now accepted as an indicator of a society's stage of development. Therefore, it becomes imperative for the Government to frame policies for the development of entrepreneurship among women. The long-term objectives of the development programmes for women should aim at raising their economic and social status in order to bring them into the mainstream of national life and development. For this, due recognition has to be accorded to the role and contribution of women in the various social, economic, policy and cultural activities.

Factors Influencing Women Entrepreneurs

The following are the major factors influencing women entrepreneurs:

- Economic independence
- Establishing their own creativity
- Establishing their own identity
- Achievement of excellence by building confidence
- Developing risk-taking ability
- Motivation
- Equal status in society
- Greater freedom and mobility

Women Entrepreneurs in India

The emergence of women entrepreneurs and women-owned firms and their significant contributions to the economy is visible in India. These businesses are ready for continued growth in the future.

The number of women entrepreneurs has increased, especially during the 1990's. The new generation of women-owned enterprises is actively seeking capital for their businesses, using modern technology to find and create a niche in both the domestic and export markets. While women-owned businesses possess the potential and are capable of contributing much more, it is essential to formulate strategies, invigorate, support, and sustain their efforts in the right direction.

Surveys demonstrate that women's primary entrepreneurial activity is focused on the small and medium enterprise (SME) sector. Approximately 60 per cent are small-scale entrepreneurs, 15 per cent are large-scale manufacturers, and the remainder consists of cottage and micro-entrepreneurs. They work in a wide range of sectors from trade and services, to tailoring, beauty parlours, and printing. However, the involvement of women entrepreneurs in the production sector is minimal and the development of this sector is rather slow.

Empirical evidence shows that women contribute significantly to the running of family businesses mostly in the form of unpaid efforts and skills.

Some Common Features of Women Entrepreneurs in India

- Women with small families are more likely to become entrepreneurs.
- A majority of women entrepreneurs are married.
- Unmarried women face difficulties in getting financial support to launch their enterprises.
- Many women entrepreneurs belong to the low-income group.
- A large number of women with little or no education enter into business without undergoing any training. Most of these practising women entrepreneurs lack vocational education.
- Working capital is limited and profit margins are low.
- Women from the low-income group exercise greater freedom in making the decision to start business as compared to middle-class women who suffer from cultural constraints.
- Many women become entrepreneurs out of economic necessity.
- Women's hard work is generally responsible for the launch and sustainability of the business.
- Support systems do not effectively handle their important need for vision and confidence building and also for developing better business orientation and skills.
- Gender discrimination is encountered at every stage of business development.
- Women entrepreneurs are more conscious of security than growth.
- Women prefer diversification to specialization.
- Women prefer stabilization of income and minimization of risk over maximization of income.
- Though the trend is changing, it is not uncommon to find enterprises owned by women but run by men.
- In the field of technology women have made a conscious decision to set up technology-based enterprises. Many have ventured into hi-tech areas such as manufacturing solar thermals, vacuum reactors, television boosters, air compressors, voltage stabilizers, and amplifiers as reflected in the data collected about women entrepreneurs. However, for most women, their businesses remain micro-enterprises.

Since the turn of the century, the status of women in India has been changing due to growing industrialization and urbanization, spatial mobility, and social legislation. Over the years, more and more of women are going in for higher education, technical and professional education. Their proportion in the labour force has also increased.

With the spread of education and awareness, women have shifted from the extended kitchen, handicrafts and traditional cottage industries to non-traditional higher levels of activities. During the 1970's, the decade of the International Women's Year, efforts to promote self-employment among women received greater attention from the government and private agencies. The new industrial policy of the Government of India has laid special emphasis on the need to conduct special entrepreneurial training programmes for women to enable them to start their own ventures.

Financial institutions and banks have also set up special cells to assist women entrepreneurs. The result has been the emergence of more women entrepreneurs on the economic scene in recent years, though the number is still quite low. Women's entrepreneurship, on the whole, still remains a much-neglected field.

While almost half the population of India comprises women, the business owned and operated by them constitutes less than 5 per cent. This is a reflection of social, cultural as well as economic distortions in the decades of development. However, women's contribution and participation in economic activity and production of goods and services is much greater than statistics reveal, since much of it takes place in the informal sector and also in households.

As education has spread and compulsions for earning have grown, more and more women have started to go out of the homes and opt for employment — for a wage, or for themselves or for an entrepreneurial career.

Challenges in the Path of Women Entrepreneurship

The problems and constraints experienced by women entrepreneurs have resulted in restricting the expansion of women entrepreneurship. The major barriers encountered by women entrepreneurs are as follows:

1. Lack of Confidence

Women generally lack confidence in their own capabilities. Having accepted a subordinate status for long, even at home, members of their family do not appear to have total confidence in their abilities and on their decision-making. Society in general, also lacks confidence in women's strength, traits and competence.

2. Problems of Finance and Working Capital

Another problem faced by women entrepreneurs is lack of access to funds because they do not possess any tangible security and credit in the market. Since it is felt that women do not enjoy right over property of any form, they have limited access over external sources of funds.

3. Socio-cultural Barriers

A woman has to perform her family duties irrespective of her career as a working woman or an entrepreneur. In our society, more importance is given to educating the male child as compared to the female child. This results in lack of schooling and vocational training for women, their lack of attaining technical skills and thereby lack of awareness of opportunities available.

4. Production Problems

Production in a manufacturing enterprise involves coordination of a number of activities. While some of these activities are in the control of the entrepreneur, there are others over which she has little control. Improper coordination and delay in execution of any activity cause production problems in industry. The inability of women entrepreneurs to keep pace with the latest advances in technology and lack of technical know-how results in high cost of technology acquisition and machinery utilization. These problems result in increasing the cost of production and adversely affect the profitability of the unit.

5. Inefficient Marketing Arrangements

Heavy competition in the market and their lack of mobility makes the women entrepreneurs dependent on middlemen. For marketing their products, women entrepreneurs are at the mercy of middleman who pockets a major chunk of profit. Further, women entrepreneurs also find it difficult to capture the market and make their products popular. They lack information on the changing market. In addition, women entrepreneurs, face difficulty in collection of payments.

Strategies for the Development of Women Entrepreneurs

- To overcome the resistance from husband and members of the family at the time of setting up of their venture, prospective women entrepreneurs are advised to maintain their cool and persistently convince them, without confronting them, regarding the benefits of setting up of an enterprise. The woman requires to have a strong will power under the circumstances. The inflow of money will eventually solve this problem.
- Shouldering the dual responsibilities of an entrepreneur and a homemaker can be effectively undertaken by a women entrepreneur through better time management. The members of the family can also be involved in the business which will help in sharing the burden of entrepreneurial work in addition to helping her in home making.
- A women can start her business when her children are grown up enough to take care of their own small needs. This gives the women enough time enough to manage her enterprise.

- For marketing her products, a women entrepreneur must establish her credibility in terms of quality and competitiveness of product or service. She should acquire relevant techniques and skills to win customer's loyalty. e-commerce businesses will also help greatly in this regard.
- Workshop and seminars should be organized frequently for the officials of financial and support agencies and for women entrepreneurs to make their relations more cordial.
- It has been observed, that there is a tendency to project a higher value of sales, production, and profits in project reports to impress the bankers. Such a project profile is not appropriate from a financial management point of view. So, women entrepreneurs need to undertake training in various aspects of financial management to understand its finer implications.
- Banks and financial institutions must maintain a minimum target of loan to be disbursed to women entrepreneurs. Collateral security should be dispensed with in the case of women entrepreneurs because many women hardly have any property or other assets in their name to keep as guarantee.
- Women entrepreneurs should acquire relevant training in technology and in details of their plant and machinery. They should be knowledgeable about the functioning of machines and processes. They should be more assertive with their employees.
- Group entrepreneurship is a viable option for the weaker sections of the society and it helps women to overcome their poverty.

Conclusion

In olden days, due to shyness and fear most of the women were not ready to come forward to undertake any work, job and business in the society. They concentrated only in family affairs. But nowadays women have more awareness about the society, problems and circumstances available before them. They are ready to take any risk to come forward economically as they have more responsibility to take care of their children and more interest in the development of their family. If there is an income to a woman in the family, surely it will be spent only for the development of the family not for themselves. Because there is a proverb i.e. "anything is possible with a help of women". But nowadays most of the women concentrate in developing the family both in the case of nuclear and joint family. So both the Government and men should encourage the women community to become entrepreneurs in all fields. They must be motivated to establish many business concerns in the society which will help to develop their family income and the standard of income of the particular region and a considerable contribution towards national income as whole from women side which in the long run will build our nation a super power in the world.

REFERENCES

Alberto Chilosi, *"Entrepreneurship and Transition"*, University of Pisa — Department of Economics.

Amir N. Licht, Jordan I. Siegel, Oxford Handbook of Entrepreneurship, *"The Social Dimensions of Entrepreneurship"*, Mark Casson and Bernard Yeung, eds., Oxford University Press, 2006.

Augustin Landier, *"Entrepreneurship and the Stigma of Failure"*, New York University, Department of Finance.

Bird, B. "Implementing Entrepreneurial Ideas: The Case for Intention", *Academy of Management Review*, 13 (3), 1988, 442-453.

Boyd & Vozikis, "The Influence of Self-efficiency on the Development of Entrepreneurial Intentions and Actions", *Entrepreneurship Theory and Practice*, Summer, 1994, 63-67.

Carland *et al.* "Who is an Entrepreneur? Is the Question Worth Asking?", *American Journal of Small Business*, 12, Spring, 1988, 33-39.

Laura Dunham, Patricia H. Werhane, *Darden Business School Working Paper No. 00-04*, "Moral Imagination: A Bridge Between Ethics and Entrepreneurship".

Nirankar Srivastav, Rickey A. J. Syngkon, "Emergence of Small Scale Industries and Entrepreneurship in the Rural Areas of Northeastern States of India: An Analytical Approach", *The Icfai University Journal of Entrepreneurship Development*, Vol. V, No. 2, pp. 6-22, June 2008.

Ramana Nanda and Jesper Sorensen, "Peer Effects and Entrepreneurship", *Harvard Business School Entrepreneurial Management Working Paper No. 08-051.*

Ravinder Rena, PNG University of Technology, "Entrepreneurship and Rural Development — A Case of Eritrea", *The Asian Economic Review*, Vol. 49, No. 2. pp. 165-178, August 2007.

Shantanu Bagchi and Debabrata Pal, *"Entrepreneurship and Indian Economy: Role of Government Policies in Entrepreneurship Development"*, www.papers.ssrn.com.

Tuzin Baycan Levent, Enno Masurel, Peter Nijkamp, "Diversity in Entrepreneurship: Ethnic and Female Roles in Urban Economic Life", *FEEM Working Paper No. 15*, 2003.

Women Entrepreneurs *Present Challenges and Future Prospects*

Dr. A. Sangamithra
Dr. Naagarajan

ABSTRACT

There are many promising predictions for women entrepreneurs in the near future. More coalitions will be formed among female associates, enabling the establishment of female business networks to flourish in the business world. In addition, the U.S. Census envisions that women entrepreneurs and female business networks will both remain dominant, comprising of over 50per cent of all business in the United States in the next several years. Many women entrepreneurs with home-based and service-related businesses will eventually shift to the information technology industry, making this once male-dominated commerce to be one of equal gender appeal. With progressive changes, the United States economy will refine itself to a financial system that will rely heavily on the internet and e-commerce for their business practices. Enterprises will also focus more on women-related issues and principles.

Women entrepreneurs have become a strong driving force in today's corporate world. Not only are they able to equalize their duties of both motherhood and entrepreneurship but they also comprise of almost half of all businesses owned today. Many women entrepreneurs have an average age of 40-60 years old because they have had previous careers in other areas. Their primary goal is not monetary reward but rather personal satisfaction and community involvement. Many of them are educated and assemble into groups in order to pool business ideas and resources together. Women entrepreneurs also have more access to business capital and seed funding than ever before. Yet despite the many opportunities, many prospective women entrepreneurs are intimidated to move forward. Overall, there are many promising forthcoming predictions for women business owners. They will continue to form female business networks, transition towards information technology, and rely strongly on e-Commerce as their form of trade.

As technology speeds up lives and the new millennium is now upon us, it is useful to take time to reflect on what will surely be one of the driving forces of the global economy of the 21st century. Women are an emerging economic force that policymakers cannot afford to ignore. In the global economy of the 21st century, international trade will be a key source of economic growth and development. Recent surveys conducted in several countries by the National Foundation of Women Business Owners (NFWBO) indicate that women-owned firms involved in the global marketplace have greater revenues, are more optimistic about their business prospects and are more focussed on business expansion than women-owned firms that are domestically oriented. Obviously, expanding into international trade can pay off for women-owned firms. However, it is not clear that smaller enterprises are benefiting from this potential as much as larger firms. Women's business associations can and should ensure that their members-large and small-are equipped to reap the rewards of expanding into the international arena.

Women must learn how to play the international trade game, and a global network of women's business associations can help them do that. Information technology can help identify markets, provide industry information and spotlight trends about what the role of women in national economies can be. More information about women-owned business enterprises is sorely needed to force policymakers to realize that women are an economic force to be reckoned with.

A recent United Nations report concluded that economic development is closely related to the advancement of women. In nations where women have advanced, economic growth has usually been steady. By contrast, in countries where women have been restricted, the economy has been stagnant. According to the 1995 UN survey, "two changes have occurred over the past 10 years in the enabling environment for women in the economy. One is the establishment of legal equality for women. The other is granting women equal access to education and training". Women entrepreneurs are significantly affecting the global economy.

Fact File

1. Women in advanced market economies own more than 25 per cent of all businesses.
2. In Japan — 23 per cent of private firms are established by women.
3. In Russia — women own 64 per cent of firms employing 10 people or more.
4. In China — women founded 25 per cent of the businesses since 1978.
5. In Germany — women have created one-third of the new businesses since 1990 representing more than one million jobs.
6. In Europe and Newly Independent States Transition Economies — women are 25 per cent of the business owners.
7. In Hungary — women started more than 40 per cent of all businesses since 1990
8. In Poland — women own 38 per cent of all businesses
9. In Mexico — 32 per cent of women-owned businesses were started less than 5 years ago.
10. In France — women head one in four firms.
11. In Swaziland — Women account for about 70 per cent of micro, small, and medium enterprises.
12. In USA — women own 38 per cent of all businesses (8 million firms), employ 27.5 million people (or 1 in 5 workers), and generate $3.6 trillion in annual sales.
13. In Great Britain — Women are one-fourth of the self-employed sector.
14. In the EU — one-third of new businesses are started by women.

Sources: Estes, 1999; NFWBO, 1998; Women in Business-Lesotho, 1998; Jalbert, 1999c; Carter & Cannon, 1992.

Suggestions to improve women Enterprenurial ability

1. Fostering an Entrepreneurial Culture for Women

(a) Foster awareness and a positive image of entrepreneurship among women: Efforts should be made to foster a greater awareness of the benefits of entrepreneurship among women. Governments should promote an entrepreneurial and risk-taking spirit, and eliminate the stigmas attached to failure. To this end, strong, positive female role models should be showcased to build self-confidence and encourage other women to consider becoming entrepreneurs.

(b) *Improve the conditions for women's entrepreneurship:* Governments and institutions should work to improve the status of women in business and remove gender-related obstacles to entrepreneurship. They should work to improve their access to support services and seek measures which can lighten the double burden of professional and household responsibilities for women, in order to allow them to undertake entrepreneurial activities under conditions more similar to those confronting men, e.g., as regards inheritance and ownership and as well as access to finance.

(c) *Encourage entrepreneurship through the educational system:* The educational system should be mobilized as a vehicle to introduce boys and girls to entrepreneurial challenges and offer them equal opportunities to learn and cultivate their skills from an early age. To this end, teachers should be trained in teaching entrepreneurial skills and sensitized to the gender issues involved in education. Opportunities to encourage entrepreneurship through cooperation between government, business and NGOs in the field of education should also be explored. This should include efforts to identify the appropriate and most effective platforms for discussion, dissemination and action for enterprise education programmes. Governments can also partner with private companies and educational institutions to provide infrastructure and other support to ensure better access for women to technical education and skill acquisition. In addition, it should be ensured that promotional and information material, programme content, timing and location is adapted to women's educational and skill levels, as well as time and mobility constraints.

(d) *Teach entrepreneurship to women:* Management and technical training for women entrepreneurs should be easily accessible, inexpensive, and available on flexible terms, maximizing the opportunities offered by e-Learning and new technologies for skill building. Public/private partnerships (i.e., government/universities/firms/NGOs, etc.) in this regard should be encouraged. Mentoring can also be an effective means of providing women entrepreneurs with one-on-one training, skills and guidance. In addition, good practices and female models of management should be shared and replicated where applicable.

(e) *Foster entrepreneurial networks:* Governments should improve the conditions and infrastructure for well-functioning business networks aimed at both men and women, including through cooperation with regional and international organizations. Governments should help women entrepreneurs to explore and take advantage of opportunities to join and actively participate in existing networks for business people, or create their own traditional or virtual networks, at the local, national and international levels.

2. Facilitating the availability of finance for women entrepreneurs

(a) *Disseminate financial information to women:* Governments should encourage women entrepreneurs to learn about the full range of financial instruments, through the education system, targeted informational campaigns, and well-functioning business networks. Government also should facilitate innovations to overcome the constraints to women's access to formal credit through simplified forms and procedures.

(b) *Encourage financial intermediaries to take a leading role:* Banks and other financial intermediaries should be encouraged to undertake research to learn more about the characteristics, financial needs and performance of women-owned businesses, and to share this information with other financial institutions. They should also be encouraged to work towards equitable treatment of women business clients, through comprehensive gender awareness training for staff at all levels, and better representation of women in high-level and decision-making positions. Networks for investors and entrepreneurs should also be encouraged to spread information about equity finance and bring investors and business owners together. Women should be integrated in these networks, where their participation remains limited, and may also want to form their own networks to share information and experiences.

(c) *Take women's needs into account in programme design:* When designing targeted programmes, governments should consider the following characteristics and carry out periodic evaluation to ensure that programmes remain pertinent: provision of finance on more flexible terms; mentoring/advisory services in conjunction with loans and monitoring of firm performance afterwards; assistance to entrepreneurs in establishing contacts with the business community and public authorities.

(d) Improve women's asset position: Governments should enforce or amend laws to ensure women's financial rights, particularly their rights to property, wages or inheritances, and work to improve basic social services for women and their families.

(e) *Promote micro- and equity finance:* Self-sustaining microfinance institutions should be promoted as an effective source of finance for women entrepreneurs with low capital requirements; best practices in this area should be shared, particularly between developing and developed countries, and replicated when appropriate. Governments should consider introducing legislation to create and regulate microfinance institutions.

3. Increasing the participation of women entrepreneurs in international trade and the global economy

(a) *Disseminate information on international trade opportunities:* Governments and business associations with significant female membership should assist women entrepreneurs in gaining a better understanding of the global, knowledge-based economy; work together to promote education and training programmes about the international trading system and the opportunities it offers; encourage participation in traditional and virtual trade missions and trade shows; and foster trade networks. Governments should also strengthen partnerships with relevant organizations to disseminate information and educate SMEs and women entrepreneurs about trade programmes, including trade finance initiatives.

(b) *Fostering public/private partnerships to globalize women-owned enterprises:* Government agencies should support efforts by the private sector to promote and develop trade capability, and strengthen women entrepreneurs' trade knowledge and networks. Governments can play a catalytic role in identifying and disseminating public and private sector trade best practices that are relevant for women entrepreneurs. Government agencies and large corporations should also work co-operatively to promote equal access to public and private sector procurement contracts for women-owned businesses, and to encourage their expanded participation in e-Commerce and the supply chain.

4. Improving awareness about Women's Entrepreneurship

(a) *Engender SME statistics:* Information about women entrepreneurs should be increased by gathering more SME-level statistics with a gender component.

(b) *Standardize SME research methodologies:* SME research coverage and methodologies should be standardized to increase national and international comparability. International cooperation should strive towards consensus and continuity concerning methodological issues and the timing of information-gathering efforts. Clarity and consistency in research should be encouraged regarding the definition of what constitutes a woman-owned business (e.g., percentages of ownership by women, management by women, or some combination of ownership and management).

Studies have shown that successful Women entrepreneurs start their businesses as a second or third profession. Many of them have experienced a considerable amount of dissatisfaction with their previous careers and in working for others. Often times, these innate desires to be their own boss are the driving forces that motivated them to pursue entrepreneurship.

As a business owner, these once unhappy individuals are now more satisfied and content with their personal and professional life. In addition, because of their previous careers, women entrepreneurs enter the business world later on in life, around 40-60 years old. Many of them have higher education degrees, a significant characteristic that many successful female entrepreneurs have in common. Women entrepreneurs also tend to offer better health care benefit packages, on the job training and education, more tuition reimbursement for students and continuing education employees, and provide more vacation and paid leave options to their staff.

From a large-scale perspective, female entrepreneurs encompass approximately 1/3 of all entrepreneurs worldwide. A recent international study found that women from low to middle income countries (such as Russia and the Philippines) were more likely to enter early stage entrepreneurship when compared to those of higher income countries (such as Belgium and Sweden). A significant factor that may play a role in this disparity can be contributed to the fact that women from low income countries often seek an additional means of income to support themselves and their families. As a result, many of them often resort to entrepreneurship in addition to their current jobs. However, women entrepreneurs from higher income countries were more successful at establishing their businesses and exuded more confidence than those of poorer nations, perhaps because of the availability of resources and financial backing from families and friends. In addition, women who had higher education experience were more likely to transform their existing businesses into successful ones, proving that learning and work familiarity is universal across all cultures and greatly contributes to the overall success of any business venture.

Recent studies also indicate that women entrepreneurs are assembling themselves into groups or confederacies. The reasons behind this trend have to do with the desire to establish solid women business networks, where members can collectively pool resources and expertise together. Women business networks have also been found to be more generous in their philanthropic contributions. At least seven out of ten women entrepreneurs of a new business volunteer their time at least once per month to community-related causes. In addition, 31 per cent of them contribute $5,000 or more to various charities annually.Even though many female entrepreneurs have home-based and service-related businesses, they are unafraid of technology and have recently entered many industries that were once male-dominated, such as construction, design, manufacturing, and architecture. In addition, the retail industry still makes up the largest share of women-owned firms.

One of the advantages of working in a women-owned new business is that the workforce is more diverse. Women entrepreneurs are more likely to employ a staff that is more gender-balanced, comprising of 52 per cent women and 48 per cent men on average. On the other hand, most male-owned businesses have a workforce that is often more than 65 per cent men. The fact that more women entrepreneurs have risen in the past few years has been made possible in part by the easy availability of business capital. Women entrepreneurs tend to fund their startups with different sources of funding, including 'bootstrap' finances (personal money from savings and credit cards) and commercial loans. Today, not only are there more grants and bank loans made available to women entrepreneurs, but there are also more diversity programmes that specialize in providing seed funding to female business owners.

However, despite the recent achievements, research shows that it still remains difficult for women of color to get access to seed funding. According to one recent study on women entrepreneurs, approximately 60 per cent of Caucasian women business owners were able to obtain bank credit, compared to 50 per cent of Hispanic, 45 per cent of Asian, 42 per cent of Native American, and 38 per cent of African-American women entrepreneurs. Much of a business woman's drive to pursue entrepreneurship is due to the immense passion she has for her work. Many women entrepreneurs are not afraid of taking risks and are two times more likely to make above average risks than their male equivalent, making monetary gain a less likely factor in their business pursuits. Instead, they possess very strong business ideas and seek any and all means to share their business ideas with others who may benefit from their discoveries. Another motivating factor behind women entrepreneurs is the desire for control. Many successful female business owners are provoked by the opportunity to be their own boss and run their own company, a prospect that would never occur if they had worked for someone else. Women entrepreneurs are also motivated by philanthropic commitment to society. Their new businesses will greatly stimulate economic development in their community and create new jobs for many people.

Another inspiring component that many successful women entrepreneurs share is the fact they have the tendency to balance family life and career. Many people may have had doubt in this ability when these women first entered the field because of the long work hours, but these reservations have often been proven wrong. It is no wonder that many successful women entrepreneurs have an amazing ability to multitask, properly balancing both personal and professional life with their goal-oriented approach.

Present Challenges

Even though female entrepreneurship and the formation of women business networks is steadily rising, there are still many prospective women entrepreneurs who do not follow through with their great business ideas. This is widely due to the fact that many challenges exist for them to overcome. First and foremost, many prospective women entrepreneurs may fear the debt associated with their startup. They may not have the resources available to make educated decisions about properly raising capital or may even have been discouraged by family and friends. As mentioned earlier, if an entrepreneur truly believes in their business ideas, then they will seek any means to move forward and commercialize their concepts.

A second challenge may be their lack of knowledge in information technology and business skills. Even though many successful business ventures are IT-related, there are many other thriving industries that do exist. Experience is always an advantage; however, one just has to conduct ample research on their industry, their consumer base and competitors, and speak to entrepreneurs who have already gone through the process. Entrepreneurship is a learning experience and even the most successful business owners have had to learn new things throughout the development of their company.

Another major challenge that many women entrepreneurs may face is the traditional gender-roles society may still have on women. Entrepreneurship is still a male-dominated field, and it may be difficult to surpass these conventional views. However, it is very important to be aware that despite the negativity that may exist, over 9 million women own their own businesses in the U.S. In fact, of all U.S. enterprises that exist, over 40 per cent comprise of women-owned businesses. The United States Census Bureau predicts that by the year 2025, the percentage of women entrepreneurship will increase to over 55 per cent. Many women feel a great deal of empowerment by the opportunity to own their own company and may now be motivated by such high statistics.

Future Prospects

There are many promising predictions for women entrepreneurs in the near future. More coalitions will be formed among female associates, enabling the establishment of female business networks to flourish in the business world. In addition, the U.S. Census envisions that women entrepreneurs and female business networks will both remain dominant, comprising of over 50 per cent of all business in the United States in the next several years. Many women entrepreneurs with home-based and service-related businesses will eventually shift to the information technology industry, making this once male-dominated commerce to be one of equal gender appeal. With progressive changes, the United States economy will refine itself to a financial system that will rely heavily on the internet and e-commerce for their business practices. Enterprises will also focus more on women-related issues and principles.

Conclusion

Women entrepreneurs have become a strong driving force in today's corporate world. Not only are they able to equalize their duties of both motherhood and entrepreneurship but they also comprise of almost half of all businesses owned today. Many women entrepreneurs have an average age of 40-60 years old because they have had previous careers in other areas. Their primary goal is not monetary reward but rather personal satisfaction and community involvement. Many of them are educated and assemble into groups in order to pool business ideas and resources together.

Women entrepreneurs also have more access to business capital and seed funding than ever before. Yet despite the many opportunities, many prospective women entrepreneurs are intimidated to move forward. Overall, there are many promising forthcoming predictions for women business owners. They will continue to form female business networks, transition towards information technology, and rely strongly on e-Commerce as their form of trade.

REFERENCES

Blanchflower, D., A. Oswal, and A. Stutzer (2001). 'Latent Entrepreneurship Across Nations'. *European Economic Review*, 45 (4-6): 680-91.

Das, D.J. (2000). 'Problems Faced by Women Entrepreneurs'. In K. Sasikumar (ed.), *Women Entrepreneurship*. New Delhi: Vikas Publishing House.

Denieuil, P.-N. (2001). 'Les Femmes Entrepreneurs en Tunisie Paroles et Portraits'. *Edition CREDIF*, 102.

Denieuil, P.-N. (2005). *Femmes et Entreprises en Tunisie*. Paris: Editions l 'Harmattan.

El Harbi, S., A. Anderson, and N. Mansour (2009). 'The Attractive of Entrepreneurship for Females and Males in a Developing Arab Muslim Country; Entrepreneurial Intentions in Tunisia'. *International Business Research*, 2 (3): 47-53.

Goheer, N.A. (2002). *Women Entrepreneurs in Pakistan: How to Improve Their Bargaining Power*. Geneva: ILO /SEED.

Hisrich, R., and S. A. Ozturk (1999). 'Women Entrepreneurs in a Developing Economy'. *The Journal of Management Development*, 18 (2): 114-25.

Hughes, K.D. (2006). 'Exploring Motivation and Success among Canadian Women Entrepreneurs'. *Journal of Small Business and Entrepreneurship*, 19 (2): 107-20.

15

Women Entrepreneurs in IT Sector
Emerging Opportunities for Developing Countries

Dr. A.Sangamithra
G.Vanithamani

ABSTRACT

India is one of the few developing countries to exploit the opportunities emerged from growth of global IT industry. Participation of women in IT is low in India, but gradually increasing as they constitute 21 per cent of total 650,000 IT workers in the country in 2007 when compared to 15 per cent in 2003. The enrollment of women in engineering is low and gradually increasing from 7.6 per cent in 1989-1990 to 16.2 per cent in 1999-2000. Percentage of women IT workers declines from low experience category (less than 3 years) 19 per cent, from to more experienced category (more than 10 years) 6 per cent. Moreover, women dominate in the low skilled segment of IT industry, i.e.IT-Enabled Services (ITES), constituting around 60 per cent of the total ITES workforce. women business owners are innovators, job creators, and providers of economic security. As owners of small and medium-sized enterprises (SMEs) women can also supply multinational companies with ideas, inventions, technology, raw materials, supplies, components, and business services. Ultimately, female business owners will be recognized for who they are, what they do, and how significantly they impact the global economy. Change is afoot in the global economy and it is bearing a woman's face. IT can offer significant opportunities for virtually all girls and women in developing countries, including poor women living in rural areas. However, their ability to take advantage of these opportunities is contingent upon conducive policies; an enabling environment in their countries to extend communications infrastructure to where women live, and increased educational levels. In other words, the ITC can be a viable sector through which the empowerment of larger women population could be envisaged. The empowerment process is one where women find time and space of their own, and had begun to re-examine their lives critically and collectively. They enable women to look at old problems in new ways, analyze their environment and situation, recognize their strength, alter their self-image, access new kinds of information and knowledge, acquire new skills and initiate action aimed at gaining greater control over resources of various kinds. In a way, the term empowerment is often used to describe a process whereby the powerless or dis-empowered people gain a greater share of control of resources and decision-making.

Introduction

India is one of the few developing countries to exploit the opportunities emerged from growth of global IT industry. Participation of women in IT is low in India, but gradually increasing as they constitute 21 per cent of total 650,000 IT workers in the country in 2007 when compared to 15 per cent in 2003. The enrollment of women in engineering is low and gradually increasing from 7.6 per cent in 1989-1990 to 16.2 per cent in 1999-2000. Percentage of women IT workers declines from low experience category (less than 3 years) 19 per cent, from to more experienced category (more than 10 years) 6 per cent. Moreover, women dominate in the low skilled segment of IT industry, i.e.IT-Enabled Services(ITES), constituting around 60 per cent of the total ITES workforce.

Today's world is changing at a startling pace. Political and economic transformations seem to be occurring everywhere as countries convert from command to demand economies, dictatorships move toward democracy, and monarchies build new civil institutions. These changes have created economic opportunities for women who want to own and operate businesses. Today, women in advanced market economies own more than 25 per cent of all businesses.In some regions of the world, transformation to a market economy threatens to sharpen gender inequality. Some of these changes are simply the legacy of a gender imbalance that existed prior to political and economic reforms. Other changes reflect a return to traditional norms and values that relegated women to a secondary status. As countries become more democratic, gender inequalities lessen; thus, offering a more productive atmosphere for both sexes.

Women's business associations play a vital role in identifying appropriate and/or emerging sectors where women entrepreneurs can succeed. The areas that are likely to take off quickly during a nation's market revitalization are public relations, transport, delivery, producing and marketing consumer goods, commercial banking, financial services, insurance, and other service-related industries. In this process, women business owners are innovators, job creators, and providers of economic security. As owners of small and medium-sized enterprises (SMEs) women can also supply multinational companies with ideas, inventions, technology, raw materials, supplies, components, and business services. Ultimately, female business owners will be recognized for who they are, what they do, and how significantly they impact the global economy. Change is afoot in the global economy and it is bearing a woman's face.

Female Business Ownership: A World Scenario

Worldwide, many women are entrepreneurs. Entrepreneurship emerges from an individual's creative spirit into long-term business ownership, job creation, and economic security. Women bring commitment and integrity because they care about economic empowerment, entrepreneurial development and innovation. Female entrepreneurs seek the professional and personal support that is found in business associations. Economic globalization has encouraged the expansion of female business ownership. "... The growing economic power and influence of women-owned businesses are changing the shape of the global economy," remarked Sakiko Fukuda-Parr, director of the UN Development Programme's Human Development Report. The global impact of women entrepreneurs is just beginning to gain intensity. Worldwide, the number of female business owners continues to increase steadily. For example, women produce more than 80 per cent of the food for Sub-Saharan Africa, 50-60 per cent for Asia, 26 per cent for the Caribbean, 34 per cent for North Africa and the Middle East, and more than 30 per cent for Latin America. Female entrepreneurs are active at all levels domestically, regionally, and globally.

In the business world, women entrepreneurs play a big role in business development . In Japan, 5 out of 6 new businesses are created by women, and they have at least five employees. The number of women-owned larger companies is not significant, but they start and manage the smaller companies. The information era has opened more opportunities for white-collar workers. The male was the prototypical industrial worker, while the information worker is typically a woman. Women are the Third World's powerhouse. They produce a staggering 60 per cent of all food, run 70 per cent of small-scale businesses and make up a third of the official labor force - in addition to caring for families and homes. Yet, their status rarely reflects this enormous and vital contribution. By any measure - income, education, health, land ownership, legal rights or political power - women get a raw deal. The poorest of the poor are usually women because discrimination cuts off their escape routes from poverty — education, health services, equal pay employment, access to land and finance. It is becoming increasingly clear, however, that there will only be sustainable development in the Third World when women play an equal part in decision making.

Women in developing countries are tremendous forces for change in their families, villages, cities and countries. Information Technology companies in India are increasingly becoming proactive towards promoting women workforce across all verticals by taking special efforts to recruit, retain and develop their talents. Rising number of women among their customers and lesser attrition rate of women employees are some of the factors which make the fairer sex more attractive to the IT giants. Kalpana Margabandhu, Director, Websphere Development, IBM, said maintaining women in almost all verticals has become a business imperative to understand the needs of a wider customer base that include a large number of women.

Women Entrepreneurs in IT Sector in India

The Indian work force participation rate is 37.7 per cent (2001 census). The rate for women is 25.7 per cent, which is less than half the rate of 51.6 per cent for men. The pattern of women's participation in the labour force varies across the country depending upon geographic region, caste, socio-economic class and formal and informal sectors. The rural female participation rate is 31.0 per cent, nearly thrice as much as the urban female participation rate of 11.6 per cent (Table 15.1).

Table 15.1: Work Participation Rates by Sex (1981-2001)

Census	Total/Rural/Urban	Females	Urban
1981	Total	19.7	52.6
	Rural	23.1	53.8
	Urban	8.3	49.1
1991	Total	22.3	51.6
	Rural	26.8	52.6
	Urban	9.2	48.9
2001	Total	25.7	51.9
	Rural	31.0	52.4
	Urban	11.6	50.0

Source: Census of India, 1991, Series 1 and Census of India, 2001, GOI, New Delhi.

The percentage of labourers employed as main workers is higher among men than among women. In the case of marginal workers, this proportion is larger among women than among men. The majority of the main workers (66.8%) are employed in agricultural and allied industrial sectors. The proportion of women employed in this sector is 80.7 per cent, compared to 62.7 per cent for men. In rural areas 89.5 per cent of the total female employed is engaged in the agricultural and allied industrial sector. In urban areas manufacturing, processing, servicing and repair, when it is in the household, absorbs larger proportions ofthe total female employment compared to men.

Women in developing countries are discovering new business opportunities through Information and Communications Technology (ICT). ICT enables creation of niche markets that require low capital investment where women can often establish or enter into businesses on their own. In the ICT field, women can provide a variety of services at multiple skill levels, from outsourced call or data entry centers to more training-intensive software engineering and geographic information system (GIS) jobs. ICTs help to empower women by improving their ability to access information, education, and services, such as market prices for crops, professional development opportunities, and tools to promote their and their families' health. ICTs also help empower women by improving the *availability* of information important to their lives. Through technology (alongside and in partnership with other development efforts), women can have a voice beyond their local community, allowing them to network with other women around the world and better advocate for greater government responsiveness and transparency, greater economic opportunity, greater equality, and greater recognition and protection of their legal and human rights.

Conclusion

IT can offer significant opportunities for virtually all girls and women in developing countries, including poor women living in rural areas. However, their ability to take advantage of these opportunities is contingent upon conducive policies; an enabling environment in their countries to extend communications infrastructure to where women live, and increased educational levels. In other words, the ITC can be a viable sector through which the empowerment of larger women population could be envisaged. The empowerment process is one where women find time and space of their own, and had begun to re-examine their lives critically and collectively. They enable women to look at old problems in new ways, analyze their environment and situation, recognize their strength, alter their self-image, access new kinds of information and knowledge, acquire new skills and initiate action aimed at gaining greater control over resources of various kinds. In a way, the term empowerment is often used to describe a process whereby the powerless or dis-empowered people gain a greater share of control of resources and decision-making. Equitable access to ICT technology and the autonomy to receive and produce the information relevant to their concerns and perspectives are therefore critical issues for women. Women should be empowered by enhancing their skills, knowledge and access to information technology. This will strengthen their ability to combat negative portrayals of women internationally and to challenge instances of abuse of power of an increasingly important industry. Women therefore need to be involved in decision making regarding the development of the new technologies in order to participate fully in their growth and impact. The priority themes like supporting electronic networks, promoting ,strategic use of information and communication technologies among partner communities, developing information content and tools, lobbying and advocacy etc. thus have to be given an emphasis.

REFERENCES

Abdul Kalam (2006), "Technology Empowers the Nation", *Productivity News,* Vol. 44. No. 3., May-June, 2006, p. 3.

Anil Kumar, *"Women Entrepreneurship in India"* First Edition, Regal Publication, New Delhi.

Arabi. U, (2005a), "Impact of 'IT" on Women's Work: Policy Implications on Employment in Developing World", *Sedme,* Vol. 32, No. 3, September, pp. 7-24.

Arabi.U, (2005b), "Empowerment of Women in Information and Communication Technology (ICT)-Enabled Services; Opportunities and Challenges", *The Asian Economic Review,* Vol. 47, December, 2005, pp. 465-485.

Enterprise and Industry, A Publication on, Best Project on *"Promoting Entrepreneurship Amongst Women"*, European Commission.

Helium, *What Makes a Good Woman Entrepreneur,* By Jennifer Moll 2002-2008 helium, inc.

Khanka, S.S., *"Entrepreneurial Deveopment"*, S.Chand & Company Ltd., New Delhi, 2003.

Manimekalai.M., and R.Ganesan, "Global Women Entrepreneurs Profile: An Analysis", *Southern Economist,* July 15, 2001.

Sunder, K.,J.Gupta, and Syzi! Ali, "Women Entrepreneurship in India", *Jagriti,* April 1, 2002.

The Hindu, Online Edition of India's National Newspaper Wednesday, December 14, 2005.

UNCTAD, (2002), e-Commerce and Development Report, United Nations, New York.

16

Constraints and Prospects of Women Entrepreneurs in IT Sector

Dr. A. Sangamithra
Miss. N. Savitha

ABSTRACT

In olden days due to shyness and fear most of the women were not ready to come forward to undertake any work, job and business in the society. They concentrated only in family affairs. But now-a-days women have more awareness about the society, problems and circumstances available before them. They are ready to take any risk to come forward economically as they have more responsibility to take care of their children and more interest in the development of their family. If there is an income to a woman in the family, surely it will be spent only for' the development of the family not for themselves. The enormous potential in IT have in bringing changes in the spheres of economy and society. IT sector has brought about changes in the organization of production and labour market situation. The case of India's IT growth is a success story. The gender differential impact of ITs on the labour market is difficult to comprehend as the change is yet to be accomplished and is transitional in nature. In the sphere of ITs production, women are mostly employed at the lower ends, which requires lesser skills. In India, the presence of home based telematic workers has created a lot of debate regarding their informalisation. Younger women who are employed in call centres and software industry, have an edge to acquire skills and prosper in their careers as they are more mobile in comparison to home-based IT workers. Men are more advantaged in terms of acquiring ITs skills as they have better access to general and technical education. The association of gender norms—masculinity and femininity with a particular discipline has added more problems. It has restricted the entry of women in those disciplines, which are considered to be masculine. Men, who enjoy better networks and socialization, have more information about jobs and career prospects. As we accept the increasing presence of women in the workplace, even in fields such as finance and technology, the focus is shifting from gender inclusive to gender neutral. Even the fast-paced and innovation-driven information technology sector has no numbers to fuel the 'weaker sex' debate. Not only do more women enter the IT industry each year, there are some who dare to branch out on their own.

Introduction

Women's number of population is about 498.7 million, according to the 2001 census India. This represents 48.2 per cent of the country's population of, 1027.01 million; hence we have almost fifty per cent of India's human resources and women constitute about 31.56 per cent of the workforce. In India, women entry into business is a recent phenomenon. It is traced out as extension of their kitchen activities to pickles, powder (masala) and Pepped manufacturing. At present, with growing awareness and spread of education over the years, women have started engrossing the modern activities like engineering. Electronic and energy in spite of the social, economic and psychological barriers. The entry of women in business is only a recent development in the orthodox traditional socio-cultural environment of our society, without belittling the traditional role of women in our society. In certain business, women entrepreneurs are doing exceedingly well and excelling their male counterparts. In India, women participation in the 9th plan is likely to raise up 20 per cent raising the number of women entrepreneurs to about 5,00,000. The selected viable economic activities for women are pottery workers, weaving, handicrafts, painting, printing press, workshop, electric repairs, typing, tailoring and jeweler work. Rural entrepreneurs are suitable for dairying, poultry, processing food products, vegetable vending, weaving and making of incense sticks. Women entrepreneurs are motivated by integral factors such as the family background, educational background and to do something independently. Therefore, this chapter examines constraints and prospects of women entrepreneurs.

Women constitute one half of the world population. Women either solely or largely support an increasing number of families. Projects aiming to improve the conditions of women can not be effective unless they participate in their formulation and implementation as contributors as well as beneficiaries. It is imperative to note the participation of women in economic activities as self-employed individuals. Many of the traditional occupations open to women were mainly based on caste and creed and the nature of the self-employment was based on the standard of living. Presently, not only are women generating employment to others. The country needs to mobilize and utilize fully all its resources. The participation of women in economic activities is necessary not only from a human resource point of view but it is essential even for the objective of raising the status of women in society.

Women and Economic Status

It is imperative to note the participation of women in economic activities as self-employed individuals. Many of the traditional occupations open to women were mainly based on caste and creed and the nature of self-employment was based on the standard of living. Presently, not only are women generating employment for themselves in the unorganized sector, they are also providing employment to others. The country needs to mobilize and utilize fully all its resources including human resources. The participation of women in economic activities is necessary not only from a human resource point of view but is essential even for the objective of raising the status of women in society. The economic status of women is now accepted as an indicator of a society's stage of development. Therefore, it becomes imperative for the Government to frame policies for the development of entrepreneurship among women. The long-term objectives of the development programmes for women should aim to raise their economic and social status in order to bring them into the mainstream of national life and development. For this, due recognition has to be accorded to the role and contribution of women in the various social, economic, policy and cultural activities. The following are the major factors influencing women entrepreneurs:

- Economic independence;
- Establishing their own creativity;
- Establishing their own identity;
- Achievement of excellence Building confidence;
- Developing risk-taking ability;
- Motivation;
- Equal status in society;
- Greater freedom and mobility.

Women Entrepreneurs in India

The emergence of women entrepreneurs and women owned firms and their significant contributions to the economy is visible in India. These businesses ready for continued growth in the future. The number of women entrepreneurs has increased, especially during the 1990s. The new generation of women owned enterprises is actively seeking capital for their businesses, using modem technology to find and create a niche in both the domestic and export markets. While women-owned businesses possess the potential and are capable of contributing much more, it is essential to formulate strategic invigorate, support, and sustain their efforts in the right direction.

Surveys demonstrate that women's primary entrepreneurial activity is focused on the small and medium enterprise (SME) sector. Approximately 60 per cent are small-scale entrepreneurs, 15 per cent are large-scale manufacturers, and the remainder consists of cottage and micro-entrepreneurs. They work in a wide range of sectors from trade and services, to tailoring, beauty parlours, and printing. However, the involvement of women entrepreneurs in the production sector is minimal and the development of this sector is rather slow. Empirical evidence shows that women contribute significantly to the running of family businesses mostly in the form of unpaid effort and skills. Some common features of women entrepreneurs in India are the following:

- Women with small families are more likely to become entrepreneurs;
- A majority of women entrepreneurs are married;
- Unmarried women face difficulties in getting financial support to launch their enterprises;
- Many women entrepreneurs belong to the low-income group;
- A large number of women with little or no education enter into business without undergoing any training. Most of these practicing women entrepreneurs lack vocational education;
- Working capital is limited and profit margins are low;
- Women from the low-income group exercise greater freedom in making the decision to start business as compared to middle-class women who suffer from cultural constraints;
- Many women become entrepreneurs out of economic necessity;
- Women's hard work is generally responsible for the launch and sustainability of the business;
- Support systems do not effectively handle their important need for vision and confidence;

- Building and also for developing better business orientation and skills;
- Gender discrimination is encountered at every stage of business development;
- Women entrepreneurs are security oriented rather than growth oriented;
- Women prefer diversification to specialization;
- Women prefer stabilization of income and minimization of risk over maximization of income;
- Though the trend is changing, it is not uncommon to find enterprises owned by women but run by men;
- In the field of technology women have made a conscious decision to set up technology-based enterprises. Many have ventured into hi-tech areas such as manufacturing solar thermals, vacuum reactors, television boosters, air compressors, voltage stabilizers, and amplifiers as reflected in the data collected about women entrepreneurs. However, for most women their businesses remain microenterprises. (*R.Ganapathy* and *C.Arjunan*, 2008)

Since the turn of the century, the status of women in India has been changing due to growing industrialization and urbanization, spatial mobility, and social legislation. Over the years, more and more of women are going in for higher education, technical and professional education. Their proportion in the labour force has also increased. With the spread of education and awareness, women have shifted from the extended kitchen, handicrafts and traditional cottage industries to non-traditional higher levels of activities. During the 1970s, the decade of the International Women's Year, efforts to promote self-employment among women received greater attention from the government and private agencies. The new industrial policy of the Government of India has laid special emphasis on the need to conduct special entrepreneurial training programmes for women to enable them to start their own ventures.

Financial institutions and banks have also set up special cells to assist women entrepreneurs. The result has been the emergence of more women entrepreneurs on the economic scene in recent years, though the number is still quite low. Women's entrepreneurship, on the whole, still remains a much-neglected field. While almost half the population of India comprises women, the business owned and operated by them constitute less than 5 per cent. This is a reflection of social, cultural as well as economic distortions in the decades of development. However, women's contribution and participation in economic activity and production of goods and services is much greater than statistics reveal, since much of it takes; place in the informal sector and also in households. As education has spread and compulsions for earning have grown, more and more women have started to go out of the homes and opt for employment-for a wage, or for themselves or for an entrepreneurial career.

Women and Information Technology Labour Market

The exact number or percentage of women at various levels in the Indian IT industry is not available due to the lack of gender disaggregated data in existing literature, including the National Association of Software and Service Companies (NASSCOM). It is estimated that women constitute 21 per cent of the total IT workforce, which is higher than their participation in the national economy as a whole, now at 13 per cent. Castells (2000) 18 anticipates a fundamental change in gender relations, family and sexuality due to the development of ICTs. If one sees the labour market, then one finds that most jobs in the IT sector is not skill-intensive and requires only maximum of a few months' training before they can be undertaken. On-the-job training for another 4-5 months may be required before a particular skill can be mastered fully. There is a great amount of pressure to learn and adopt quickly which brings about a high degree of insecurity for the professionals. They constantly face fear of being pushed out of the market due to redundant skill sets. Wage setting is linked to performance and hence, is highly individualized. This reminds one of the piece-rate system which is practiced in the traditional sectors to enhance efficiency through labour-intensive production. Most software professionals plan an individual career on the basis of short-term maximization. There are chances when professionals may burn out in the early years. Thus, one is required to learn management related skills, which is normally acquired in-house over time.

Majority of women in Indian software industry are women in the age group 20-30 years and very few are above 35 years of age. Single women are more advantaged compared to the married ones in terms of learning skills and moving up the career ladder, as they are more mobile. Men are given more preference in promotions and are hired at the senior level management positions. A serious problem for women in the manager and senior manager's levels is the lack of mentors. People who shift jobs faster rise faster and women, largely because of their domestic responsibilities, typically stay longer in each job as compared to men. Due to lower attrition rates, reaching the ranks of manager and learning new skills becomes difficult for women IT workers. However, the nature of job (such as flexi-time, teleworking and working from home), the tools (such as email and internet), and the individualization of capacities required by IT make women more capable to take decisions on their own and construct greater scope to enhance their agency. Indian companies like Novell Software or Wipro situated in Bangalore, now provide crèche to working women . However, since most of the women in software industry are married, they face the dual burden of family responsibilities and job pressures.

A study of the Indian software industry conducted by the ILO reveal that women are more concentrated in the middle-end firms, domestic low-end firms and IT enabled services compared to men. This is because of the fact that women are generally employed for monotonous type of work and are paid less. While addressing the problems of women IT workers. They are less mobile than their male counterparts. Most of the women have to balance household and office work, which leaves them with lesser time to concentrate on their careers. All these add up to opting of jobs by women, which are less paying and less competitive.

There is clearly a division of labour by gender in the IT industry. Women are mostly concentrated in call services, and they hardly reach the position of project manager. Even home based teleworking is becoming popular because women can then easily balance the demands of family and career.

Challenges in the Path of Women Entrepreneurship

The problems and constraints experienced by women entrepreneurs have resulted in restricting the expansion of women entrepreneurship. The major barriers encountered by women entrepreneurs are as follows:

Lack of Confidence: Women generally lack confidence in their own capabilities. Having accepted a subordinate status for long, even at home, members of their family do not appear to have total confidence in their abilities and on their decision-making. Society in general also lacks confidence in a women's strength, traits, and competence.

Problems of Finance and Working Capital: Another problem faced by women entrepreneurs is lack of access to funds because they do not possess any tangible security and credit in the market. Since women do not enjoy right over property of any form, they have limited access over external sources of funds.

Socio-cultural Barriers: A woman has to perform her family duties irrespective of her career as a working woman or an entrepreneur. In our society, more importance is given to educating the male child as compared to the female child. This results in lack of schooling and vocational training of women, their lack of attaining technical skills and thereby lack of awareness of opportunities available.

Production Problems: Production in a manufacturing enterprise involves coordination of a number of activities. While some of these activities are in the control of the entrepreneur, there are others over which she has little control. Impreper coordination and delay in execution of any activity cause production problems in industry. The inability of women entrepreneurs to keep pace with the latest advances in technology and lack of technical know-how results in high cost of technology acquisition and machinery utilization. These problems result in increasing the cost of production and adversely affecting the profitability of the unit.

Inefficient Marketing Arrangements: Heavy competition in the market and their lack of mobility makes the women entrepreneurs dependent on middlemen. For marketing their products, women entrepreneurs are at the mercy of middleman who pocket a major chunk of profit. Further, women entrepreneurs also find it difficult to capture the market and make their products popular. They lack information on the changing market. In addition, women entrepreneurs, face difficulty in collection of payments.

Conclusion

In olden days due to shyness and fear most of the women were not ready to come forward to undertake any work, job and business in the society. They concentrated only in family affairs. But nowadays women have more awareness about the society, problems and circumstances available before them. They are ready to take any risk to come forward economically as they have more responsibility to take care of their children and more interest in the development of their family. If there is an income to a woman in the family, surely it will be spent only for' the development of the family not for themselves. From the above literature, one can understand the enormous potential IT have in bringing changes in the spheres of economy and society. IT (or say ITs) has brought about changes in the organization of production and labour market situation. The case of India's IT growth is a success story. The gender differential impact of ITs on the labour market is difficult to comprehend as the change is yet to be accomplished and is transitional in nature. There is lack of gender disaggregated data at the macro level. However, there are empirical evidences from a few micro level surveys. In the sphere of ITs production, women are mostly employed at the lower ends, which requires lesser skills. In India, the presence of home based telematic workers has created a lot of debate regarding their informalisation. Younger women who are employed in call centers and software industry, have an edge to acquire skills and prosper in their careers as they are more mobile in comparison to home-based IT workers. Men are more advantaged in terms of acquiring ITs skills as they have better access to general and technical education. The association of gender norms—masculinity and femininity with a particular discipline has added more problems. It has restricted the entry of women in those disciplines, which are considered to be masculine. Men, who enjoy better networks and socialization, have more information about jobs and career prospects. As we accept the increasing presence of women in the workplace, even in fields such as finance and technology, the focus is shifting from gender inclusive to gender neutral. Even the fast-paced and innovation-driven information technology sector has no numbers to fuel the 'weaker sex' debate. Not only do more women enter the IT industry each year, there are some who dare to branch out on their own.

REFERENCES

Batliwala Srilatha, 1995: *"Education for Women's Empowerment"*, ASPBAE Position Paper for the Fourth World Conferences on Women, Beijing, September 1995, New Delhi, Asia-South Pacific Bureau of Adult Education.

Caldwell,C. John. 1979. Education As a Factor in Mortality Decline: An Examination of Nigerian Data. *Population Studies* 33(3): 395-413.

Crowell, A. Nancy Ana Burgess,(ed) 1996: *Understanding Violence Against Women*, National Research Council, 77-78.

Dey, A.S. 2002. Measurement of Women's Empowerment: Problems and Prospective, *Presented at the 25th Annual Conference of the Indian Association'* for the Study of Population International Institute for Population Sciences, Mumbai, India, [Unpublished].

Dey. D and S. Bhavsar 2002. Women's Empowerment and Its Relevance to Fertility and Child Mortality: An Analysis Based on NFHS-2, Gujarat Data, *Presented at the 25th Annual Conference of the Indian Association for the Study of Population,* International Institute for Population Sciences, Mumbai, India [Unpublished].

Dixon-Mueller, Ruth 1993: *Population Policies and Women's Rights*.Transforming Reproductive, Choice, Westport, Connecticut: Praeger.

Dyson Tim and Mick Moore. 1983. On Kinship Structure, Female, Autonomy and Demographic in India; *Population and Development Review*; Vol. 9 (I) pp. 35-60.

Ganapathy R. and Arjunan 2008, *"Women in the Indian Economy"* Ed. V.S.Ganesa Moorthy , New Century Publication, New Delhi.

Jeejebhoy.S.J and Zeba.A Sathar: 2001; Women's Autonomy in India and Pakistan: The Influence of Religion and Region; *Population Development and Review*; 27(4): 687-712.

Jeejebhoy.S.J, 1995. Women's Education, Autonomy and Reproductive Behaviour: Assessing What We Have Learnt, Programme on Population East-West Centre, p. 1.

Jeejebhoy.S.J, 1998.Wife Beating in Rural India: A Husband's Right; *Economic and Political Weekly*; Vol. 23, No. 15. pp. 855-862.

Jeejebhoy., S.J., 2002. Convergence and Divergence in Spouse's Perspective on Women's Autonomy. Rural India. *Studies in Family Planning* Vol. 33 (4) pp. 299-307.

Jeejebhoy.S.J, Shireen, 1998: 'Association Between Wife Beating and Fetal and Infant Death: Impressions from a Survey in Rural India', Studies in Family Planning, September 1998, 29(3), pp. 300-308.

Kasarda, J.D.J.O.Billy and K. West . 1986 Status Enhancement and Fertility: Reproductive Responses to Social Mobility and Educational Opportunity, Academic Press, New York.

Empowerment of Women Through Entrepreneurship

Dr. Pavan Mishra
Mrs. Swati Mathur

Introduction

The Confederation of Women Entrepreneurs is a NGO/social organization engaged in the social and economic "upliftment of women through entrepreneurship". The slogan "Gearing women power" stands for the democratic structure of COWE and stands for "Of the women, for the women and by the women".

Woman has remained backward owing to many factors though the scriptures laid down an-exalted status for them. In recent years, there has been an increasing awareness and reorganization of the fact women who formed half of the society cannot be ignored. An increasing roll of woman the unsung heroine of our country contribute her best to the welfare and progress of the society without any glare of publicity.

Entrepreneurship of woman will not only enable them to get better jobs and economically self sufficient or independent, but society will also gain. This education must be practically in relation to health nutrition and legal rights.

Need for Woman Entrepreneurship

"When woman move forward the family moves, the village moves and the nation moves". Employment gives economic status to woman. Economic status paves the way of social status. In the rural sector 56 percentages of the males and 33 per cent of the females are in the labour force. About 66 per cent of the female's population in the rural sector in idle and unutilized. This is mainly due to existing social customs. The young girls and woman are not allowed to work indecently.

But now the scenario is changing fast with modernization, urbanization nad development of education and business. Woman is seeking gainful employment in several fields in creasing numbers with the education and new awareness. Woman entrepreneurs are spreading their wings to higher level of 3Es namely engineering, Electronics and Energy. Today, no fooled is unapproachable to trained the taken off the ground and it is felt that the movement is still in a transition period.

Entrepreneurship for woman can be planned and developed and the need for providing appropriate awareness and environment to promote entrepreneurship is of vital importance.

Strategies for Woman Entrepreneurship

While taking about woman entrepreneurship the theme has been conceived with the following strategies in mind:

- Awareness generation initiatives;
- Promoting self-employment, through credit and training;
- Providing lean session wage employment;
- Providing saving habit among woman;

- Providing arrange of support service to meet gender needs
- Addressing minimum needs such as nutrition, health, sanitation, housing and education
- Direct involvement of moan who are likely to be effected by the development programmes
- The goals of poverty if poor woman could organize into groups for community participation as well as to assertion of their rights in various services related to their economic and social well-being

Requirements of Women Entrepreneurs

- Problems faced by the women entrepreneurs to build up courage and self-confidence.
- To fix priorities in family and business activities by allocation adequate time for both appropriately.
- They have urge to learn new things and to undergo training on various skills of entrepreneurship.
- Production-oriented must be changed to real marketing-oriented, to gain the maximum numbers of customers.
- They must involve in risk taking and effective decisions approximately.
- Unnecessary activities must be eliminated.
- A good relationship and working atmosphere for the employees must be built up.

Apart from the traits assumption that woman are frail and indecisive in their efforts to develop the enterprise the have established.

The main problems face by woman entrepreneurs in recent days are:

- Financial constrains
- Insufficient arrangement
- Over dependent on intermediaries
- Scarcity of raw materials
- Stiff competition
- High cost of production
- Low mobility
- Family responsibility
- Social status

- Low ability to bear risk
- Lack of education
- Low need for achievement
- Absence of ambition for the achievement

The above problems and scrubbing blocks, are most commonly mentioned by All woman entrepreneurs.

Woman have the potential and they will be establish and manage enterprise of their own. What they need in encouragement and support. Government and public enterprise should offer ancillary units to woman entrepreneurs. On priority basis with the assistance of family members and the government woman can join the main stream of national economy and thereby, contribute to the country's economic progress.

Remedies to Solve the Problems of Women Entrepreneurs

The following measures may be adopted to solve the problems faced by women entrepreneurs in India:

- Finance cell
- Marketing co-operatives
- Supply of raw materials
- Education and awareness
- Training facilities

Training Need for Women Entrepreneur

With the increasingly realization that entrepreneur are important, many state level and national level organization and institute are developing and administration training programmers aimed at specific requirements.

The essential components of effective training programmers for the women are listed below:

- Career which build up self-confidence
- Specific emphasis attitude change, giving preference to business
- Training on promotional management skills
- Effective trading to make efficient in quick decision-making at appropriate timings
- Training on assuming responsibilities for action
- Training on project formulation and implementation

Providing aptitude on increasing their knowledge on latest development

Entrepreneurship As a Tool

Entrepreneurship helps in solving problems like:

Natural production

Balance regional development

Harnessing youth vigour

Employment generation

- Chronologies
- Post-training support and follow-up services like promotional meetings, advertisement and publicity and so on.

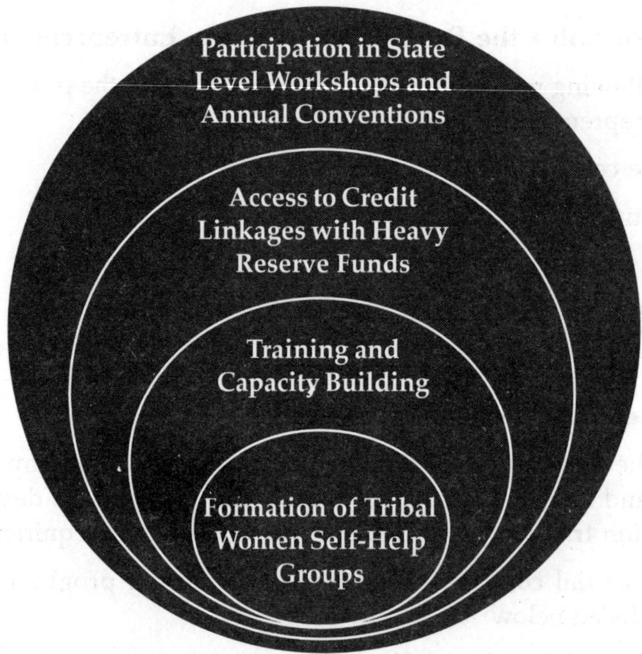

Steps in Entrepreneurial Process

- Decision to be self-employment
- Selection of the product
- Location of the enterprise
- Preparation of the project report
- Registration
- Finance (Term loan)

- Statutory licences/clearances
- Land and building procurement of machinery
- Finance
- Recruitment of personnel
- Installation of machinery
- Power connection/ water supply
- Procurement of raw materials
- Production
- Marketing
- Repayment of loans
- Profit generation
- Avoiding sickness
- Modernization and upgradation of technology

Scope of Entrepreneurship Among Women

Women are active in a variety of economic areas ranging from wage labour, subsistence farming and fishing to the informal sector. Women contribute to development not only through remunerated work, but also through a lot deal of unremunerated work. Women's contribution to the development is seriously under estimated and thus their social recognition is limited. Although, many women have advanced in economic structures even then majority still faces additional barriers and thus hindered their ability to achieve economic autonomy and to sustain livelihoods for themselves and their dependants. In many cases, employment creating strategies have not paid sufficient attention to occupations and sectors where women predominate: nor have they adequately promoted the access of women to those occupations and sectors that are traditionally male.

According to a study by Global Entrepreneurship Monitor which covers a wide range of 37 GEM countries.

The study of phenomenon related to women's entrepreneurship has been augmented by this tremendous growth in the formation and development of women-owned businesses. for women, the need for an effective and comprehensive approach for detecting and stimulating entrepreneurial potential I underlined by some other important issues like 'population pressure' and 'sluggish growth in developing nations' like India. Insignificant infrastructure and development also contributes to the reasons for poor entrepreneurship in women.

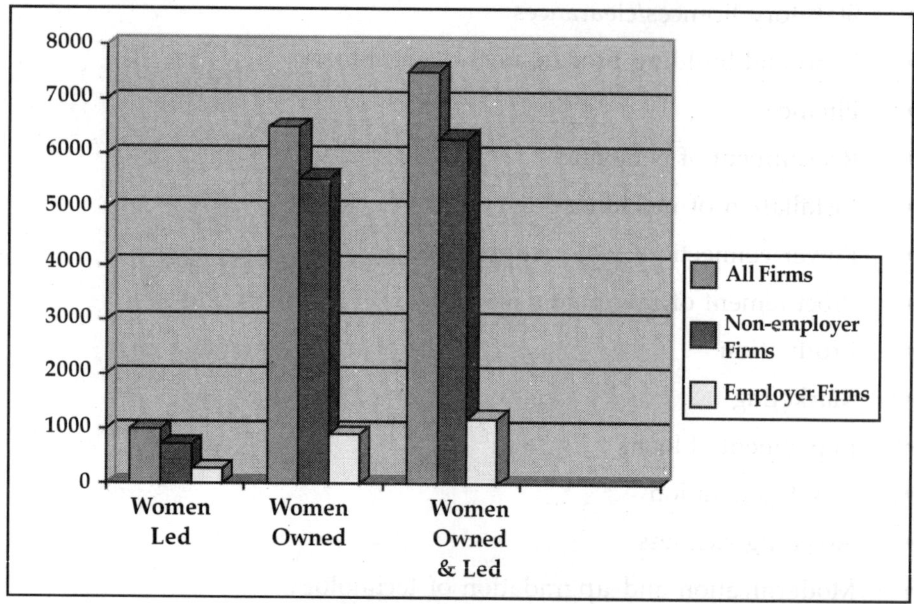

Distributions Women Business

Source: nwbc.gov

The proportion of educated and skilled women is increasing with reference to the total employment in India. The expansion of employment opportunities both to provide income and to harness the growth potential of educated unemployed women is very important The promotion of self-employment of educated women hands the additional advantage of creating more jobs for the aspiring educated women. Many studies have been conducted telling the status of women in terms of crucial demographic indicators such as sex-ratio, literacy rate, infant mortality Rate, and marriage and life expectancy in compared to national average has increased in some of cities like Kerela. Whereas the percentage of women in work participation as compared to national average. The reason for such a status is involvement of women in traditional agriculture and construction works only. The educated women tends to seek employment in offices or skilled jobs in the manufacturing and service sectors Entrepreneurship is an ideal tool where by women can be drawn into the mainstream of economic activity and there by improve their social status. When compared to the population and educational level, the number of women entrepreneurs is small. With growing awareness and education across our nation, the problem of educated unemployed women is on rise. This situation should change, but requires tremendous efforts by various agencies like the government, NGO's, training institutions etc.

Function and Role of Woman Entrepreneurs

A woman entrepreneur must perform some functions:

- Explore the prospects of standing new enterprises
- Undertaking of risk and the handling of economic uncertainties introduction of innovations
- Coordination, admission and control
- Routine supervision.

All these functions appear to be somewhat uneven in character. Moreover, these functions are not always of equal importance. For instant, risk taking and innovation are paramount of establishing or diversifying an enterprise. Coordination and supervision became increasingly important in improving the efficiency and assuming smooth, balance operation of the undertaking. In these functions, most likely she is also the owner of the enterprise.

Promotional Efforts Supporting Women Efforts in India

Women represents about 50 per cent of the world's population but receive only 10 per cent of the world income and less than 1 per cent of the industrial world's assets some encouraging efforts are also made by the government and non-government agencies all over the world to promote the women entrepreneurship for his many policies, programmes, procedures and institutions have been made to support the women entrepreneurship. Promotional measures includes:

1. Policy framework supporting women entrepreneurs
2. Programmes supporting women entrepreneurship
3. Institutional support to women entrepreneurship

Woman entrepreneurs can more easily undertake three types of industrial enterprises:

- Operation purely as a sub-contractor on raw material provided by the consumer;
- Manufacture an item to the large-scale unit;
- Manufacture the item for direct sale in the market.

Generally, the first two types of enterprises are known as ancillaries, woman entrepreneur produce both consumer goods and intermediate good, which are used in the production of the other articles.

Promotional Efforts

Policy framework	Programmes	Institutions
• National policy for empowerment of women	• Swa shakti project	• The federation of Indian women entrepreneurs
• Women components plans and gender focal points	• Rural women development and empowerment project	• International cooperation
• National commission for women	• Indira Mahila Yojna • Support to training and employment programme for women • Employment and income generation-cum-production unit • Rashtriya Mahila Kosh	

Conclusion

Women make a vital contribution to the industrial output throughout the world. The number of women owned firms has increased two and a half times faster than all businesses and employment in women owned firms has grown more than three times the rate for all firms. Women works not only sustain their families but also makes a major contribution to socio economic progress. The creativity of talent of all women is invaluable recourse and should be developed for their own self realization and for the benefits of the society as a whole. The number of women willing to take risk and starting their own business. Many policies and programme may continue to contribute to inequalities between women and men. On the basis of assumption that there is a latent, socio economic potential the interest in women interepreniours is increasing rapidly in relation to industrial policy, educational policy and research. The emergence of women interpreters their contributions and their number are quite visible in India. Women are capable of contributing much more what they already have but to harness their potential and for their continued growth and development it is necessary to formulate appropriate strategies in concurrence with field realities for stimulating supporting and sustaining their efforts. The woman force will get another dimension. If the entrepreneurial skill among effort in direction which would lead to a better human resource development and strengthen the nation's economic development. In the present global competitive business and industrial situation the tribal woman entrepreneurs can play a greater role and emerge themselves, in yet another new dimension to the entire universe.

REFERENCES

Tiwari Anshuja (2007), *Women Entrepreneurship and Economic Development*, Saurop & Sons, Delhi.

Carter Nancy M., *Female Entrepreneurship: Implications for Education*, Training and Policy.

2007, *Opportunities for Woman Entrepreneurship* (With Project Profiles), Niir Board—Business and Economics.

Everything *A Woman Needs to Know to Start, Run and Maintain Her Own Business* (Seal press to).

Dhameja S.K., *Woman Entrepreneurs*, Bacon (Unknown).

Alexender P.E. (1963), *"Real Estates in India"*, Asia Publishing House New Delhi.

Prime Minister's Rozgar Yojna Instructions Manual — DC (SSI) Ministry of Industry, Govt. of India.

Ganguly S, "What Motivates Small Entrepreneur *"Indian Management"*.

(2008. Accessed Oct 2009), *Employment Status of Women and Men in U.S.* Department of Labour.

U.S. Department of Labour, U.S. (Sept 2009), Bureau of Labour Statistics. *Women in the Labour Force: A Databook*. (Report 1018).

SBA Office of Advocacy (2007), *"Women in Business—2006. A Demographic Review of Women's Business Ownership"*.

Allen, I.E, Elam, A., Langowitz, N. and Dean, M. (2008), The Global Entrepreneurship Monitor 2007 *Report on Women and Entrepreneurship*. Ranking Calculated by NWBC, 2008.

U.S. Department of Labour. September 2009.

Women Impacting Public Policy (WIPP), WIPP Releases 2009 Member Survey "What Business Women Want" & Shares Results with Key Policymakers.

CWBR October (2009). *The Economic Impact of Women-owned Businesses in the United States*.

U.S. Census Bureau. Company Summary: 2002, *2002 Economic Census*, Survey of Business Owners, Company Statistics Series. September 2006.

National Association of Women Business Owners. NAWBO Survey Finds Women Business Owners Holding Their Own Amid Economic Downturn. Press Release: February 25, 2009.

CWBR (2007), Capturing the Impact: Women-owned Businesses in the United States.

NWBC. (2007) Voices from the Field: A Report from the National Women's Business Council Town Hall Meetings. September and Current Priorities and Challenges of Women Business Owners. Spring 2009.

Women Impacting Public Policy (WIPP). Economic Opportunity and the New Economy. Presentation for the May 2009 Regional Meeting. 2009b.

WIPP. 2009a.

NAWBO. Press Release: February 25, 2009.

National Association of Women Business Owners. NAWBO Policies and Positions. Accessed, September 2009.

CWBR (2007), Key Technology Facts from Women Business Owners.

CWBR(2007). Guide for Financing Business Growth Offers Actionable Advice for Women Business Owners. Press Release, April 4.

www.score.org

www.articlesb ase.com

www.chillibreeze.in

www.groundreport.com

www.indiaunheard.videovolunteers.org

www.dol.gov

Ibid. New Calculations by NWBC.

CWBR. 2008.

http://www.sba.gov/advo/research/rs280tot.pdf.

http://www.wipp.org/news/25252/WIPP-Releases-2009

http://nawbo.org/content_4970.cfm

www.bizwomen.com.

http://www.womensbusinessresearch.com/press/details.php

http://nawbo.org/section_104.cfm

18

Entrepreneurial Career Through Value Addition to Traditional Practices *A Success Story*

Dr. Mamoni Sharma

The occupations being pursued by the population of a community are integrated with their present as well as past socio-economic conditions. However, the demographers opine that for transforming the socio-economic order of an economy, certain distinct and predictable changes in occupational pattern are necessary. Such changes can be brought about by the present generation's innovative idea and entrepreneurial skill applied for adding value to their ancestral production practices. The tribal people in the North Eastern Region of India in general have their own life style with distinct production and consumption behaviour. They know how to live with nature and their practices bear high environmental value which was being mostly ignored till few years ago. However, now-a-days the environmental issues become the matter of concern for all over the world and hence the traditional practices have been regaining their weightage.

In the entire North East India, the tribal population constitutes close to 22 per cent of the region's total population. Further, in Assam 13 per cent of the total population is tribal, thereby, constituting 37 per cent of the entire region's tribal population (Goswami, 2006). Tinsukia, the district of rising sun in Assam is the abode of more than 600 tribes and sub tribes, namely, Tangsas, the Semas, the Singphoo, Tai Phake, Tai Khamyangs, Tai Khamti and many others. Among them Singphoo is one of the major tribes in the district with fascinating cultures and traditions. The district is located at the Northern fringe of the state, bordering the state of Arunachal Pradesh to the north (Lohit district) and east (Changlang and Tirap district), while the district of Dibrugarh in Assam bounds the western and southern borders. The international border of Indo-Myanmar (Nampang in Arunachal Pradesh) is a little more than 100 kms from the district head quarters of Tinsukia. Apart from being a very old commercial & industrial belt of Assam with many large industries viz, coal, tea, plywood & oil refinery, the district is the storehouse of rich biodiversity as well as cultural and ethnic diversity.

The tribal people of the district in general are very close to nature enjoying an eco friendly life and basically earn their livelihood from agriculture and allied activities. However in recent times they are occupationally diverse. As the district is endowed with rich forest resources and tribal people are residing close to the forest areas, the forest products like timbers are used to be a major source of income for most of the tribal families. Many tribal families used to support their living with activities relating to timber business. But the ban on felling of trees by Honourable Supreme Court of India during 1996, brought about a mighty blow for host of such families. Moreover, increasing number of tribal population, lack of job opportunities in their home states, sense of divergence from traditional economic life among the new generation, absence of adequate knowledge about available opportunities and above all, the absence of entrepreneurship zeal among the tribal youths in general are throwing a large number of such youths out of employment. Such a state is bound to destabilize the entire region in either way. Nevertheless, there are some tribal people who got themselves adapted to the changed situation and they are earning a good living through entrepreneurship with fruitful utilization of their available resources. But as compared to the increasing number of educated youths, the rate of placement in such ventures so far is not satisfactory. A study (Sharma,1980) made by the Small Industry Extension Training Institute (SIET), Hyderabad, on entrepreneurs in the North Eastern Region of India in 1976-78 shows that most of the entrepreneurs in the North Eastern Region are from upper caste Hindus and relatively few are from tribal and poorer sections. Though the finding is somewhat old (1976-78), the trend is still found to be unmistakable. It is therefore urgent need of the hour to motivate the tribal youths of the generation towards entrepreneurial career by unfolding their own unknown potentialities. Therefore this study makes an attempt to present the story of a tribal (Singphoo) entrepreneur who has become successful in reaching out to international platform through his entrepreneurial career built by adding value to their indigenous practices of tea processing.

Hand processed tea has been a part of the Singphoo culture. The ancestors of Singphoo community used to collect the tea leaves from nearby jungles and these leaves after heating in a metal pan were dried in sunlight.

The dried leaves were packed in green bamboo's hollow stems and then put in wood fire. These were to be kept in dry and warm places. Whenever they were to make their refreshing drink that is 'Phalap' (a cheerful drink) thin pieces were cut from the compressed and packed tea and steeped in hot water which gave them the cup of tea with nice flavour. A Singphoo enterprising youth has come to realize the uniqueness and medicinal value of this chemical free organic tea and he has succeeded in his sincere effort for commercialization and faster diffusion of their traditional hand processed tea. The present paper elaborates the profile of this successful tribal entrepreneur and his success story so as to set him as the role model for the prospective tribal entrepreneurs of the generation. The study is based entirely on primary data collected from direct personal interview with the selected successful entrepreneur.

Mr. Rajesh Singphoo, a young man of 40 years belonging to 'Singphoo' tribe, lives in his community village 'Inthem' about 22 km. from the sub divisional headquarter of Margherita of Tinsukia district in Assam. An undergraduate in Arts, Mr. Singphoo used to support his cultivator father in his paddy field, orchard (orange), citronella plantation and citronella oil processing unit while pursuing his studies at the college level. As the business expanded, he had to give up his studies in 1989 and devoted full attention to the family business. Given his full attention, the business started expanding fast. Eventually, as the market demand for citronella came down; he diversified his business to tea plantation during 1994 for selling green tea leaves to the factory owners. Meanwhile, he chalked out a plan to produce hand made organic tea in the same way in which his ancestors did during the early part of 19th. Century. It is said that Bisha Gum Singphoo, the then Singphoo chief offered the first cup of tea to the British explorer Mr. Robert Bruce during 1827. During that time, Singphoo used to produce tea on non commercial basis for their own consumption only. As Rajesh realized the importance of organic tea in the context of present day environmental degradation and health hazard, started processing hand made organic tea on commercial line during 2004 to give a boost to their ancestral heritage. In fact, processing of Singphoo organic tea on commercial basis had been started early back by one named Nirula Singphoo, but could not succeed much because of high cost of production involved. Moreover, environmental issue was not a matter of concern during that period.

Reaching Out to International Platform

Rajesh is fortunate to participate in the Coffee and Tea Expo, 2006 held in Canada on 25th September 2006 and make his presentation on "Traditional system, culture and Traditional Tea" therein. Rajesh was successful in drawing the attention of the representatives from various countries like USA, UK, Japan, Australia and New Zealand while attending a 'Tea Demonstration

Meet' in Comox valley, Canada as guest speaker during 2007. He came to know that people of the countries with cold climatic conditions are very much addicted to raw organic tea. Prior to these, during the year 2000 he participated in a community based seminar organized by the International Singphoo Community at Thailand. A discussion on organic tea was held in the said seminar in which Rajesh activity participated. In fact, in this seminar an international linkage was established following which few representatives from a Canada based NGO visited their village to see as to how they practice organic farming. Later, two research scholars from Canada also visited their village under an international research programme. During his same trip to Thailand, Rajesh visited Canada and China to have a market exposure on organic tea. In all his efforts towards popularizing organic tea, he was backed by his community and the Canada based NGO the 'Fertile Ground'.

In 2008 Rajesh got the opportunity to deliver his lecture on the usefulness of Singphoo organic tea at Bangkok in which he highlighted the medicinal benefits of Singphoo tea in curing hyper tension, diabetes and stomach disorders.

Supports Enjoyed

Rajesh had undergone a training on organic farming under the aegis of a Canada based NGO viz. World Community Development and Education Society (WCEDS) during 2002 and was supplied with safety instruments like hand gloves and masks for use of workers in practice of organic farming free of cost by the Canada based NGO viz. the 'Fertile Ground'. He also had undergone a training course under the PMRY scheme and enjoyed a loan of Rs. 1 lakh for tea plantation with a govt. subsidy of 25 per cent during the year 2000. Rajesh also enjoyed support and inspirations from his family, friends and the community.

Present Status

At present Rajesh is the proprietor of M/s Singphoo Agro Products located at Inthem village in Margherita sub division of Tinsukia district which produces and exports chemical free organic tea 'Phalap'. Its market prices are Rs. 2000 per kg for tea tablets/tea coins and Rs. 1000 per kg for loose tea. This business venture has created employment avenues for a large number of youths of his community. The Singphoo inhabitants of the village got the scope of earning their livelihood by engaging themselves in green tea leaf plucking and processing. Rajesh started exporting tea to Canada in the year 2006. In addition to the export market he reported to have a chunk of domestic consumers which has been increasing by 30 per cent every year.

Apart from this, Rajesh is the person behind opening of a community food outlet that was set up during 2003 beside the NH 38 at Margherita aiming at promoting eco tourism. The people of his community supply all the required inputs (organic) to the outlet for processing community food. The project is a glaring success and attracts visitors from far away places to taste delicious Singphoo dishes. Rajesh has gifted this project to his community. Accordingly, the whole income from the outlet goes to the community fund. Father of two infant daughters, Rajesh is happy with his small family.

Key to Success

Rajesh believes that he has "miles to go...". However; he attributes "work culture" as key to whatever he has achieved in life. He firmly believes hard work with sincerity of purpose and dedication pays in life.

Message to the Generation

Rajesh wants the youth of the generation to "Be Local, Go Global". He wants them to make their community self sustained through development of work culture in various fields of activities for which ample scopes are available.

Conclusion

Adaptation to the changed situation on the one hand and fruitful utilization of available resources as well as traditional knowledge on the other can bring about some desirable changes in occupational behaviour of a community. The tribal youths should realize the value of their cultures and should come forward to work for their preservation and popularization by upholding their traditional practices and bringing the cultural value into economic circuit.

REFERENCES

Goswami H. (2006), Tribal Demography in North East India, *Keynote Address of the National Seminar on Tribal Demography of North East India,* Conducted by the Department of Economics, Dibrugarh University, Assam on March 26, 2006. p. 3.

Sharma SVS (1980), 'Small Entrepreneurial Development — Indian Experience in North Eastern Region', in Sharma SVS and Akhouri MMP (Eds) *'Characteristics of Entrepreneurs, Developing Entrepreneurship, Issues and Problems'*, SIET Institute, Yousufguda, Hyderabad, India, p. 79.

19

Entrepreneurial Development
Where is It Heading For?

Dr. R. Ganapathi
Mr. S. Sannasi

ABSTRACT

In a capitalist economy, entrepreneurship is a basic feature and the entire economy depends on it. The entrepreneur is the key player in the development of the economy. He is the risk taker, innovator, facilitator, organizer, employment provider and in shorts the wealth creator. The success of a private economy depends on the blossoming of newer and newer entrepreneurs. In a socialist/ communist economy, the Government may act as an entrepreneur, but admittedly there is a total failure of Government entrepreneurship, as witnessed by the fall of iron curtain economies of former USSR and China. The integration of world economy through globalization has thrown open lot of challenges to entrepreneurs. Of course there are to be taken as opportunities. In this article, the writers have attempted to analyze the role problems and remedial measures for the successful entrepreneurship in India.

Introduction

The entrepreneurial role as a separate and important factor of production has been recognized since the days of industrial revolution. The entrepreneurship has been analyzed time and again by economists, sociologists, political scientists and social psychologists, each of them considering an entrepreneur from their own angle. Economists see him as an essential element in generating investment opportunities, sociologists as an energizer in modernization of societies, psychologist as an entrepreneurial man and try to decipher him as a character of economic development and political scientists consider him as a child of the political system. Over the years the entrepreneurship has developed both as art and science. An entrepreneur has to use his skills and originality for attaining the vision he has set for himself. He has to use his left brain and right brain attributes suitably to combine the resources and put them to optimum use for results.

An entrepreneur is a problem solver in his business opportunities and visualizes innovation and a potential of profit opportunity. The innovation may be in the form of new method of manufacturing, new products, new sources of raw material or new markets or combination of these. Instead of doing business in a routine way an entrepreneur does things in a new and better ways. Schumpeter has introduced a concept of innovation as the key factor in entrepreneurship in addition to assuming risks and organizing factors of production.

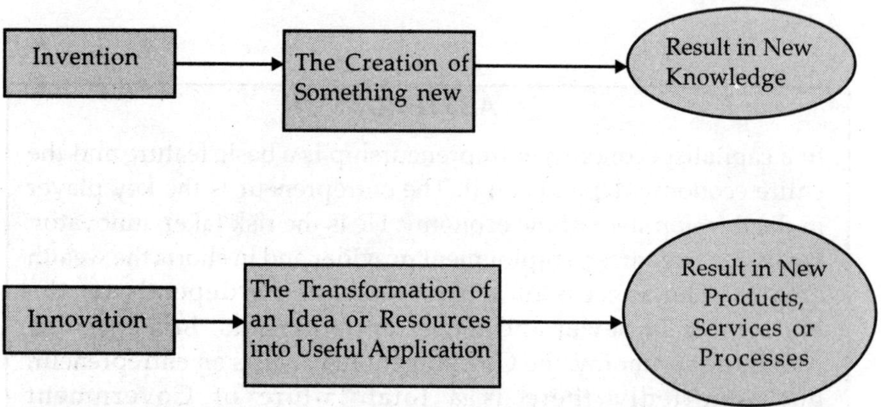

Wilken has added the concept of the changes that an entrepreneur brings:

1. Expansion of goods, products.
2. Productivity of factors of production such as finance, labour, material
3. Innovation in production such as, technology, process changes and increase in human resource productivity.
4. Innovation in marketing area such as the composition of the market, size of the market and new markets.

Entrepreneur refers to:

- A person

- Leader
- Planner
- Programmer
- Motivator
- Risk taker
- Communicator
- Creator
- Visualiser
- Innovator
- Technocrat
- Initiator
- Organizer
- Decision-maker
- Administrator

GROWTH OF ENTREPRENEURSHIP AFTER GLOBALIZATION IN INDIA

The globalization process started in India in July 1991 and has changed the face of industry. It has attracted new areas of development, foreign direct investments and new business areas which were unheard of prior to 1980's. For last two decades Indian economy is growing at an average steady. The exports and foreign trade are on the increase. Currently India is looking for 10 per cent GDP growth and industrial growth in double digits thanks to enhanced entrepreneurial activities and the consequent multiplier effect in the growth of economy. The growth of industry in India especially in the areas of Information Technology and Bio-Technology has been noticed by advanced countries and admired. Some of the important areas of growth of entrepreneurial activities are:

1. Small Scale Industries (SSI) Sector

This include small, tiny and cottage industries which are on the increase. The fastest growth is in service units. The SSI sector accounts for 40 per cent of manufacturing sector, employs 1.7 million and make up to 35 per cent of India's exports. Government of India and State Governments are developing schemes to help new entrepreneurs.

2. Special Sector

This is the area of Hi-Tech like Information Technology (IT), IT enabled services (ITES), Bio-Technology (BT) and Research and Development (R&D)

units. The area is fast growing one and needs less investment. Indian entrepreneurs have seized the opportunity and made a name for themselves in India and overseas in the field.

3. Service Sector

Indian entrepreneurs have been using growth opportunities in service sector. Accordingly investments and quality levels in service sectors have increased. The spectacular growth is observed in Business Process Outsourcing, transport, repair services, entertainment and hospitality sectors.

4. Rural Sector

The growth of entrepreneurial activities in rural India are in the areas of food processing, cold storage, export of food products like eggs, meat, fish, prawns and the like in processed and semi-processed condition. There are enterprises exporting agri-products like Basmati rice, wheat and wheat products, spices, cashew nuts, sugar and oil. SSI units in ready-to-eat and packed food sector are growing all over India.

5. Indians As Global Entrepreneurs

Industries and service providers are going global from India. Indian entrepreneurs in Pharma sector, IT sector, and steel sector have gone to many countries to start new ventures. Entrepreneurial activities are also seen in the areas of joint ventures, acquisitions and mergers and strategic partnership activities.

6. Women Entrepreneurs

Women entrepreneurs have taken up many new ventures and are able to manage two difficult role combinations namely as 'a home maker' and a business owner with active support of parents, it is only during last 20 years women in India have started becoming entrepreneurs and started industries. Women are yet to go a long way to be on par with men in the area of entrepreneurial activities.

ENTREPRENEURSHIP AND ECONOMIC DEVELOPMENT OF INDIA

An entrepreneur has a critical role in competitive market economy, especially in developing countries like India. An entrepreneur acts as a trigger head to give spark to economic activities by his entrepreneurial decisions. The economic development activities of an entrepreneur are detailed below:

1. Increasing Income Per Capita

Entrepreneur brings in new products and services and develops new markets for growth of economy thus increasing gross national product as well as per capita incomes of the people in the country.

2. Bringing Change in Structure of Business and Society

New enterprise and new products change the way we do the business. The entrepreneurial activity gives a new direction to the business and the way it is done. The classic example is that of India taking up in a big way Information Technology (IT), Information Technology Enabled services (ITES), Bio-Technology (BT) and Research and Development (R&D) services. Such avenues or services were not available 25 years ago. The new opportunities have been chosen by Indian entrepreneurs and thus bring changes in the structure of Indian business, economy and the way the society looks at them.

3. Wealth Creation and Distribution

Entrepreneurial activity leads to value addition and creation of wealth. The activity also generates more activities and gives a multiplier effect in the economy. The wealth also gets distributed to more people and geographic areas, thus giving benefit to larger section of society.

4. New Products, New Services and New Business

An entrepreneur brings new ideas for business, production techniques and services for horizontal i.e. varieties and vertical i.e., increase in volume and money growth of business.

5. Production Evolution Process

Entrepreneur understands and takes up product evolution process. This is a process where innovation develops and an entrepreneur commercializes the new products. Here an entrepreneur combines different technologies and fuses them in to products and services which turn into marketable items.

6. Knowledge and Social Need Filling

An entrepreneur does the job of iterative synthesis i.e. the combined role of social needs and product development process.

Innovation: Commercializations Technology

- Generation of technologies
- User of resources
- Act as social stimulant for growth
- A moral booster and
- Role model.

Challenges Faced by An Entrepreneur

An entrepreneur faces many difficult and challenging situations from initial concept stage to the management of the enterprise. Some of the commonly observed challenges are as follows:

1. Abnormal delays in getting factory shed, water and drainage connections, power supply, roads in industrial estates.
2. Buyers (mainly large size companies) delay in payment against bills of SSI units.
3. Lack of coordination between financial institutions and banks.
4. Lack of expertise with officials of SISI regarding guidance and training for entrepreneurs.
5. A first generation entrepreneur finds it difficult to follow and implement the rules pertaining to PF, Taxes, excise duty and labour laws.
6. Too many competitors in the market cut prices and the new entrepreneur will find it difficult to establish himself as a player.
7. Mobility of skilled workers from company to company hampers production rhythm and may upset quality standards and expectations.
8. Dependence on imported raw materials and export markets have their own limitations. These get adversely affected due to (a) political ups and downs and (b) currency conversion variations.
9. Global competition is another area which need to be watched carefully. Added to this dumping is a cause of concern.
10. In a male dominated society a woman entrepreneur finds it difficult to cope up with pressures and tensions of managing an organization.
11. Cash flow is a constant problem due to delays in realization of bills raised.
12. Constant necessity to update the technology, processes and product. In fact product improvement is a continuous exercise due to changes in consumer expectations.
13. Training and re-training employees to improve and update their skills needs constant attention.
14. Problems created by partners and other directors are to be solved for sustenance.

Measure to Solve the Problems of Women Entrepreneurs

1. *Financial Cells:* In various public financial institutions and banks, special cells may be opened for providing easy finance to women entrepreneurs. These cells should be managed by women officers and clerks.

2. *Marketing Co-operatives:* Encouragement and assistance should be provided to women entrepreneurs for setting up co-operatives. These co-operatives will pool the inputs of women enterprises and sell them at remunerative prices.
3. *Supply of Raw Materials:* Scarce and imported raw materials may be made available to women entrepreneurs on priority basis. A subsidy may also be given to the products manufactured by women entrepreneurs.
4. *Education Awareness:* It is necessary to change negative attitude towards women. Elders need to be made aware of the potential of girls and their dual role in society.
5. *Selection of Machinery and Technology:* The necessary workshop should be adopted by the government agencies or private industrialists to create awareness about the uses and benefits of machinery and technology that may be utilized to increase the production in order to blossom the industries run by the women entrepreneurs.
6. *Promotion Help:* Since, women entrepreneurs do not have capacity to invest a huge amount in promotional tools like sales promotion, advertising etc. adequate steps should be taken by Non-Governmental and Governmental agencies in order to propagate the product manufactured by the women entrepreneurs.
7. *Training Facilities:* Training and skills are essential for the development of entrepreneurship. Training schemes should be so designed that women can take full advantage.

Conclusion

Main objective of EDP is to create a viable enterprise. Hence the programme duration and course should include introduction to entrepreneurship, plant location, layout, selection of materials and machinery, marketing, project feasibility, motivation, support system required and monitoring of the progress. In short it covers guidance prior to and after choosing a product. The success of a training programme depends upon all the stake holders. The institutional head, faculty and trainees all should sincerely and seriously involve in their work. It is observed that many students do not take the EDP seriously and remain irregular to the classes. It will be very useful if executives of industries and professors of management institute are involved as guest faculty to improve the quality of input. This will improve trainee's attendance and attentiveness.

An entrepreneur faces many problems which are to be taken as challenges. The difficult situation also shows ways for advantages to organizations. Own family members try to dissuade entrepreneurs in favour of a well paid job. They may or may not support if the entrepreneur fails. In such situation entrepreneur should get guided by product and market related factors than emotional factors. Further there may be many natural and man made problems which may prove hurdles to progress of an enterprise. In such situation an entrepreneur's soundness is tested. One must withstand and overcome the problems.

Section–IV
Women in Education

20

Women's Education
A Tool for Rural Development

Dr. R. Ganapathi
Mr. S. Sannasi

ABSTRACT

Women are often subjected to the double burden of earning for the family and caring for the children and they are also often excluded from education. Literacy for women may impart knowledge and skills, which enable poor women to improve their earning potential and address their survival needs. It is, therefore, realized that women have to be provided with the vital educational inputs, if they are to become a powerful force in the process of rural development. Thus, literacy for poor women is a tool for rural development. The purpose of providing education to women is to make them play a positive role on their own in the development of the nation. It is evident from the empirical research that educational discrimination against women hinders the process of rural development. Expanding educational opportunities for women is desirable for increasing productivity on the farm, greater labour force participation, late marriage, lower fertility, child health and nutrition. Since females constitute a major proportion of the rural labour, it is essential that improved education and skill formation become crucial for better development process. It was the Tamil poet Subramania Bharati who declared early in the century that it is a crime to keep our women locked inside the house for reasons of safety and security. When we look back in the last two decades or so, it is amazing to see a paradigm shift by which women have entered hitherto unexplored fields. They have created the physical as well as metaphorical space necessary to assert their identities as capable professionals. There is the realization that education is a panacea for many of the ills of obscurantism, which plague the community. By keeping the above in mind as preliminary step the researchers tried to write an article on *"Women's Education – A Tool for Rural Development"*.

Introduction

Women are often subjected to the double burden of earning for the family and caring for the children and they are also often excluded from education. In India, most of the women living in rural areas are illiterate and trapped in a vicious cycle of poverty and deprivation. The proportion of women is high among the poor and illiterate persons, which is retarding the efforts to expedite rural development. A situational analysis of the status of women would indicate that they occupy a low position in society and the Indian educational gender gap is the greatest among the poorest countries. Recent studies have shown a strong link between education and development, particularly in the case of developing countries, as education is vital to rural development.

It was the Tamil poet Subramania Bharati who declared early in the century that it is a crime to keep our women locked inside the house for reasons of safety and security. When we look back in the last two decades or so, it is amazing to see a paradigm shift by which women have entered hitherto unexplored fields. They have created the physical as well as metaphorical space necessary to assert their identities as capable professionals. There is the realization that education is a panacea for many of the ills of obscurantism, which plague the community.

Women's Education

The purpose of providing education to women is to make them play a positive role on their own in the development of the nation. It is evident from the empirical research that educational discrimination against women hinders the process of rural development. Expanding educational opportunities for women is desirable for increasing productivity on the farm, greater labour force participation, late marriage, lower fertility, child health and nutrition. Since females constitute a major proportion of the rural labour, it is essential that improved education and skill formation become crucial for better development process.

Women's Education as Basis for Rural Development

The greatest hindrance to the progress of India and eradication of many social evils of her people is illiteracy of the masses. For example, while lack of education is one of the prominent causes of poverty, the poverty of the people is one of the most common causes of illiteracy. It seems plain that efforts for the rural development must go together with educational progress especially or particularly in women education. Efforts have been made to link women's education to larger social and economic development that impinges upon their education. It is against this background of the general neglect of educating illiterate women that we need to examine salient issues pertaining to gender equity in literacy in India.

Literacy for poor women is a tool for empowerment in a wider struggle against inequality and injustice in society. Literacy for women can impart knowledge and skills, which enable poor women to improve their earning potential and address their survival needs.

Literacy Rate

Particularly after independence, literacy has been viewed as the essential component of the overall architecture of development planning in India. The Government has recognized the role of women in the process of rural development.

Major Reasons for Low Literacy

The major reasons for low literacy rate among women are listed below:

- Early marriage and dowry.
- Reluctance to send girls out of the house after puberty.
- High intensity of poverty and parent's inability to bear educational expenses.
- Lack of access to schools.
- Shortage of women teachers.
- Lack of infrastructure facilities which lead to low enrolment and large dropouts.
- Need for girls to help in the farms or family occupation or household chores or responsibility of looking after younger siblings.

The following are some suggestions to remove gender bias and to improve literacy rate among women.

- Special support services that reduce costs to parents and create incentives for them to enroll their daughters.

- Appointment of women teachers.
- Involving women's group like Self Help Groups in promoting women's literacy.
- Appointing more girl child promoters at the village level.
- Providing free and compulsory education for all girls up to 20 years.
- Establishment of more number of primary schools to meet the demand
- Effective implementation of mid-day meals programme.
- Removing misconceptions about girls' education and bringing changes in the attitudes of parents and society.
- Involving academic institutions and NGOs in implementing literacy programmers.
- Effective implementation of follow-up programmes including vocational training and skill development courses especially for girls in school curriculum.

Conclusion

In recent years, momentum has been gathering all over the world, demanding gender equality and push for equal representation of women in all spheres of activity. Literacy for women may impart knowledge and skills, which enable poor women to improve their earning potential and address their survival needs. It is therefore, realized that women have to be provided with the vital educational inputs, if they are to become a powerful force in the process of rural development. Thus literacy for poor women is a tool for rural development.

21

The Role of Education in Women Entrepreneurship

Dr. A. Sangamithra
Miss. S.C. Karpagavalle

ABSTRACT

Women entrepreneurs have become a strong driving force in today's corporate world. Not only are they able to equalize their duties of both motherhood and entrepreneurship but they also comprise of almost half of all businesses owned today. Many women entrepreneurs have an average age of 40-60 years old because they have had previous careers in other areas. Their primary goal is not monetary reward but rather personal satisfaction and community involvement. Many of them are educated and assemble into groups in order to pool business ideas and resources together. Women entrepreneurs also have more access to business capital and seed funding than ever before. Yet despite the many opportunities, many prospective women entrepreneurs are intimidated to move forward. Overall, there are many promising forthcoming predictions for women business owners. They will continue to form female business networks, transition towards information technology, and rely strongly on e-commerce as their form of trade. If we want to realize women empowerment, Firstly we will try to minimize the literacy gap between men and women and give priority to educate a woman. So that education plays a crucial role in accelerating the women empowerment. Thus education is seen as "Unique investment" in present and future in reference to Women Empowerment. Access and equality are the two most important components to empower women and to facilitate the delivery of social justice to them. If we want to achieve and sustain a high growth rate must have educate women without any discrimination. Since woman has a prolonged role in procreation, emergency obstetric help must be rendered to all women who experience complications during their pregnancies. At the same time men must be encouraged towards responsible sexual and reproductive behaviour. They must be encouraged to participate more actively in family planning programmes. "Education is one of the most important means of empowering women with the knowledge, skill and self confidence necessary to participate fully in the development process" says the International Conference on Population and Development (ICPD) Programme of Action. Educated women can recognize the importance of health care and know how to seek help for themselves and their children. Education helps girls and women to know their rights and develop confidence to claim them.

Introduction

Women entrepreneurs have become a strong driving force in today's corporate world. Not only are they able to equalize their duties of both motherhood and entrepreneurship but they also comprise of almost half of all businesses owned today. Many women entrepreneurs have an average age of 40-60 years old because they have had previous careers in other areas. Their primary goal is not monetary reward but rather personal satisfaction and community involvement. Many of them are educated and assemble into groups in order to pool business ideas and resources together. Women entrepreneurs also have more access to business capital and seed funding than ever before. Yet despite the many opportunities, many prospective women entrepreneurs are intimidated to move forward. Overall, there are many promising forthcoming predictions for women business owners. They will continue to form female business networks, transition towards information technology, and rely strongly on e-Commerce as their form of trade.

Gender Equality and Fundamental Rights

The principle of gender equality is enshrined in the Indian Constitution in its preamble, fundamental rights, fundamental duties and directive principles.The Constitution not only grants equality to women but also empowers the state to adopt measures, a position; indiscrimination in favour of women. Within the framework of democratic polity, our laws, developmental policies, plans and programmes are aimed at women's advancement in different spheres. India has also ratified various international conventions to secure rights of women. Women today are trying to understand their position in the society. Women have become increasingly aware of sexual inequalities in every sphere of life and are seeking ways to fight them. Free India has, besides her woman prime minister, women ambassadors, women cabinet ministers, women legislators, women governors, women scientists, engineers-doctors-space researchers-giant IT specialists, women Generals, women public officers, judiciary officers and in many more responsible positions. No distinction is now made in matters of education between boys and girls. Their voice is now as forceful and important as that of men. They are becoming equal partners in making or dismissing of a government.

Empowering may be understood as enabling people, especially women to acquire and possess power resources, in order to make decision on their own or resist decisions that are made by others that affect them. The National Policy on Education (1986) suggested certain strategies to empower women. Accordingly, women become empowered through collective reflections and decision making enable them to become agency of social change. Keeping this in view the year 2001 was celebrated as "The Women's Empowerment Year". Human resource development and empowerment of women unlock the door for modernization of society. Instated of remaining as passive beneficiaries, women must become active partner.

Empowerment of Women Through Education

The concept of 'Empowerment' is a global issue .Education is milestone of women empowerment because it enables them to responds to the challenges, to confront their traditional role and change their life. Empowerment is an active and multidimensional process which enables women to realize their full identity and powers in all sphere of life. Education is milestone of women empowerment because it enables them to responds to the challenges, to confront their traditional role and change their life. So that we cannott neglect the importance of education in reference to women empowerment. Education is the first step towards empowerment and the most crucial factor in over all development of the individual as well as nation. Literacy sets one free from ignorance, exploitation and poverty .It liberates the minds, opening up new horizon, new hope/opportunities and self-confidence further equipping them with the knowledge, skills, self respect and freedom to participate sustain and excel in their life .Illiteracy on the other hand, breeds ignorance, which, leads to exploitation, poverty, neglect crimes and number of social evils. Literacy deprives women from all opportunities and further prospects of leading a meaningful life and enjoying good standard of living. Education is an effective instrument for social and economic development and national integration. Education enables women to understand their social and legal rights, become economically independent,, acquire a voice in the affairs of the family and the community. Education is a gateway to information, opportunities and empowerment.

More than two thirds of the world's 960 million illiterates are women. In India, literacy rates are 39 per cent among women and 64 per cent among men A recent literature review by the International Center for Research on Women (ICRW), entitled 'Impact of Investments in Female Education on Gender Equality', shows that education is a necessary but not sufficient investment to achieve gender equality. Education is significant for girls and women because it is an entry point to other opportunities and the educational achievements of women can have ripple effects not only within the family but for many generations to come. Educated women recognize the importance of health care and know how to take care of themselves and their families. Education helps to know their rights and they get the confidence to claim them. An educated mother plays a greater role in household negotiations and she secures more resources for her children. An educated mother can pay more attention to her children. The Indian scenario has provided enough role models that stand out as icons of gender equality. Maharani Lakshmi Bai, Rajia Sultan, Indira Gandhi, Kiran Bedi, Medha Patkar, Sania Mirza, Sonia Gandhi, Kalpana Chawla and Sunita Williams are but a few names which highlight the heights women can achieve.

Women Empowerment—Still an Illusion or Reality?

Notwithstanding the remarkable changes in the position of women in free India, there is still a great divergence between the constitutional position and stark reality of deprivation and degradation. Whatever whiff of emancipation has blown in Indian society, has been inhaled and enjoyed by the urban women, their population belonging to the rural areas are still totally untouched by the wind of changes. They still have been living in miserable conditions, steeped in poverty, ignorance, superstition and slavery. There still exists a wide gulf between the goals enunciated in the Constitution, legislations, policies, plans, programmes and related mechanisms on the one hand and the situational reality on the status of women in India, on the other.

Although, gender discrimination has been banned by the Constitution and omen have been guaranteed political equality with men, yet there is a difference between the constitutional rights and the rights enjoyed in reality by women. Even after half a century of independence, barring a few exceptions, women have mostly remained outside the domain of power and political authority. Although they constitute about half of the citizen and over the years their participation by way of voting has increased, yet their participation and representation in law making and law implementing bodies are not very satisfactory. No doubt the 73rd and 74th constitutional amendment acts have provided access to women in the decision making process at the grass-root level but their representation in the Parliament and state legislatures is woefully poor. Insecurity does not allow the women leaders to identify leadership at the grassroot level. In these days of scam-ridden politics, the increasing role of money and mafia in elections keeps most of the women away from politics. Increasing violence and vulgarity against them intimates women and consequently they prefer to stay out of politics.

Steps to be Taken

There cannot be any dramatic movement in the system just by including women members in Gram Panchayat. At the same time, it is also essential to shed certain stereotyped prevailing notions about role and importance of women in socio-economic development. Women should be encouraged to play a more active part. The male representatives have to establish a rapport with female representatives and give due respect and attention to their views. In the process of development and decision-making women have to operate along with men. The women of India must oppose this sex determination of foetus, eve-teasing, bride burning, child marriage, exploitation in the offices, lower wages for labour etc. women from all walks of life must unite and must give priority to their education, growth and the prosperity of their families. Police should accept more female officers and constables so that they are able to deal with the female victims of our society. Female infanticide, female torture, Sati and dowry must be banned in the country.

Women must become literate, as education is beneficial for them as well as their families. The family web is woven around the women. She has to be up to the mark and educated so that she could fend for herself and her family during the hour of crisis. The status of women would improve only if they educate themselves and grab every opportunity to become stronger and more powerful than before. The discussion brings a major conclusion to light—the status of women could be improved by women themselves and nobody else. It is the modern era of satellites, achievements and technology-based gadget. Why should women be left behind? There should be a better and fuller understanding of the problems peculiar to woman, to make a solution of those problems possible. As these problems centre round the basic problem of inequality, steps should be taken to promote equality of treatment and full integration of woman in the total development effort of the country.

The main stress should be on equal work and elimination of discrimination in employment. One of the basic policy objectives should be universal education of woman, the lack of which tends to perpetuate the unequal status quo. The popular UNESCO slogan should come in handy:

educate a man and you educate an individual; educate a woman and you educate a family. Women will have to empower themselves from below in order to compel the government to empower them from above. Further, there is a need for a change of values and behaviour in the society, a need for positive socio-cultural and economic empowerment and above all the will power and strong determination of women to join politics. Education can play a vital role in bringing about the desirable behavioural changes among the women and make them well equipped in terms of knowledge, competence and capacity to deal with different political problems.

Social Empowerment of Women

Education

Equal access to education for women and girls will be ensured. Special measures will be taken to eliminate discrimination, universalize education, eradicate illiteracy, create a gender-sensitive educational system, increase enrolment and retention rates of girls and improve the quality of education to facilitate life-long learning as well as development of occupation/vocation/technical skills by women. Reducing the gender gap in secondary and higher education would be a focus area. Sectoral time targets in existing policies will be achieved, with a special focus on girls and women, particularly those belonging to weaker sections including the Scheduled Castes/Scheduled Tribes/Other Backward Classes/Minorities. Gender sensitive curricula would be developed at all levels of educational system in order to address sex stereotyping as one of the causes of gender discrimination.

Health

A holistic approach to women's health which includes both nutrition and health services will be adopted and special attention will be given to the needs of women and the girl at all stages of the life cycle. The reduction of infant mortality and maternal mortality, which are sensitive indicators of human development, is a priority concern. This policy reiterates the national demographic goals for Infant Mortality Rate (IMR), Maternal Mortality Rate (MMR) set out in the National Population Policy 2000. Women should have access to comprehensive, affordable and quality health care. Measures will be adopted that take into account the reproductive rights of women to enable them to exercise informed choices, their vulnerability to sexual and health problems together with endemic, infectious and communicable diseases such as malaria, TB, and water borne diseases as well as hypertension and cardio -pulmonary diseases. The social, developmental and health consequences of HIV/AIDS and other sexually transmitted diseases will be tackled from a gender perspective.

Nutrition

In view of the high risk of malnutrition and disease that women face at all the three critical stages viz., infancy and childhood, adolescent and reproductive phase, focussed attention would be paid to meeting the nutritional needs of women at all stages of the life cycle. This is also important in view of the critical link between the health of adolescent girls, pregnant and lactating women with the health of infant and young children. Special efforts will be made to tackle the problem of macro and micro nutrient deficiencies especially amongst pregnant and lactating women as it leads to various diseases and disabilities.

Drinking Water and Sanitation

Special attention must be given to the needs of women in the provision of safe drinking water, sewage disposal, toilet facilities and sanitation within accessible reach of households, especially in rural areas and urban slums. Women's participation will be ensured in the planning, delivery and maintenance of such services.

Housing and Shelter

Women's perspectives will be included in housing policies, planning of housing colonies and provision of shelter both in rural and urban areas. Special attention will be given for providing adequate and safe housing and accommodation for women including single women, heads of households, working women, students, apprentices and trainees.

Environment

Women will be involved and their perspectives reflected in the policies and programmes for environment, conservation and restoration. Considering the impact of environmental factors on their livelihoods, women's participation will be ensured in the conservation of the environment and control of environmental degradation. The vast majority of rural women still depend on the locally available non-commercial sources of energy such as animal dung, crop waste and fuel wood. In order to ensure the efficient use of these energy resources in an environmental friendly manner, the Policy will aim at promoting the programmes of non-conventional energy resources. Women will be involved in spreading the use of solar energy, biogas, smokeless chulahs and other rural application so as to have a visible impact of these measures in influencing eco system and in changing the life styles of rural women.

Science and Technology

Programmes will be strengthened to bring about a greater involvement of women in science and technology. These will include measures to motivate girls to take up science and technology for higher education and also ensure that development projects with scientific and technical inputs involve women fully. Efforts to develop a scientific temper and awareness will also be stepped up. Special measures would be taken for their training in areas where they have special skills like communication and information technology. Efforts to develop appropriate technologies suited to women's needs as well as to reduce their drudgery will be given a special focus too.

Conclusion

Education plays a crucial role in accelerating the women empowerment .Thus education is seen as 'Unique investment' in present and future in reference to Women Empowerment. Access and equality are the two most important components to empower women and to facilitate the delivery of social justice to them. If we want to achieve and sustain a high growth rate must have educate women without any discrimination. Since woman has a prolonged role in procreation, emergency obstetric help must be rendered to all women who experience complications during their pregnancies. At the same time men must be encouraged towards responsible sexual and reproductive behaviour. They must be encouraged to participate more actively in family planning programmes. "Education is one of the most important means of empowering women with the knowledge, skill and self confidence necessary to participate fully in the development process" says the International Conference on Population and Development (ICPD) Programme of Action. Educated women can recognize the importance of health care and know how to seek help for themselves and their children. Education helps girls and women to know their rights and develop confidence to claim them.

REFERENCES

Akthar Najma., *"Higher Education in Future"*, Manak Publication Pvt. Ltd, New Delhi, 2000.

Competitiveness Report — 2005 World Economic Forum. In Press.

Das Suranjan., *"The Higher Education in India and the Challenges of Globalization"*.

Social Science Vol. 35, No 3-4, March-April, 2007.

Janaki.D., *"Empowerment of Women Through Education: 150 Years of University Education in India"*, University News, vol. 44 (480, November 27 – December 3, 2006, pp. 82-84.

Sarkar, C.R. (2004). *Poverty, Education and Economic Development.*

Wixard Kausar and Arya Vrat Vijay., *"Women in Higher Education in the Work Force"*.

Need to Bridge the Gender Gap, *University News*, Vol. 45(3), December10-16, 2007.

22

Status of Ethics and Values in Educational Institutions

Dr. R. Ganapathi
Mr. S. Sannasi

ABSTRACT

According to Vivekananda, "Education is the manifestation of the perfection already in man". Knowledge is inherent in man, no knowledge comes from outside, it is all inside. He also said "we want that education by which character is formed, strength of mind is increased, the intellect is expanded and by which one can stand on one's own feet. The end of all education, all training should be man making. The end and aim of all training is to make the man grow". But the situation prevailing now in almost all educational institutions except few is in a pathetic condition. The number of educational institutions in all disciplines has considerably increased in accordance with the growth in population. Due to the introduction of new education policy, the curriculum for all disciplines was changed in a way that it will help the students to understand easily and the examination pattern was also changed to their convenience. This led to the students scoring high marks in all the examinations. Further, due to the entry of private sector in higher education, considerable number of professionals and talented candidates are produced every year by majority of the educational institutions. Nobody can deny this fact. But almost in all institutions, human values are gradually decreasing. We cannot expect good culture from all students. Some students do not give respect to their parents, teachers and elders. Sometimes senior citizens and even handicapped persons are ill treated by the students' particularly in public places and in buses. Eve teasing is another problem that we are facing frequently in public places. In urban areas, this problem occurs even in the campus of the educational institutions. Some students become addicted to drugs. Surprisingly, even some students who study well and get good grades indulge in certain unwanted habits. Keeping all the above views in mind the researchers tried to write an article on ***"Status of Ethics and Values in Educational Institutions"***.

Introduction

In olden days, the educational institutions were considered as a place for acquiring knowledge, human values, ethics and culture. In Gurukulam schools, students were taught more about the ethics and cultural values more than the knowledge of subjects in various disciplines. Further, the educational institutions were established by the reputed persons and by those who were interested in providing social service. The educational institutions were purely coming under service sector and were meant for rendering service at a maximum by imparting knowledge and inculcating the values and ethics in mankind to bring out desirable changes in the behaviour of the students. The students also were anxious to develop their knowledge, ethics and cultural values when they learn. The relationship between the students and teachers was good. The teachers were considered Gurus and acharyas by all the students. The teachers rendered their service with a sense of satisfaction without expecting monetary benefit. Money was only considered a secondary factor. Service was the primary factor in all educational institutions. The quality of education got improved simultaneously with the development of human values in mankind.

But the situation prevailing now in almost all educational institutions except some is in a pathetic condition. The number of educational institutions in all disciplines has considerably increased in accordance with the growth in population. Due to the introduction of new education policy the curriculum for all discipline was changed in a way that it will help the students to understand easily and the examination pattern was also changed to their convenience. This led to score high marks in all the examinations. Further, due to the entry of private sectors in higher education, considerable number of professionals and talented candidates were produced every year by majority of the educational institutions. Nobody can deny the fact. But almost in all institutions the human values are gradually decreasing. We can not expect good culture from all students. Some students do not give respect to their parents, teachers and elders. Sometimes senior citizens and even handicapped are ill treated by the students' particularly in public places and in buses. Eve teasing is another problem that we are facing frequently in public places. In urban areas this problems occur even in the campus of the educational institutions. Many students become addicted to drugs. Surprisingly, some students who are studying well and get rank also indulge in certain unwanted habits.

What is Education?

Education is an important social activity planned and shared by the parents and the society. Education is a process of learning to live the life of the community. Education has been defined by different people in different ways. The meaning of education has been changing according to people, places and times. Some took education to mean the process, others the results, still others the methodology. Since the concept has changed, the definitions have also changed. Yet, there are certain definitions, which are 'all time popular' and also acceptable. *Aristotle* has defined education as "Creation of a sound mind in a sound body". By this, we can understand that education should pay attention to our physical needs and also to the mental needs. *Mahatma Gandhi* wrote "By education, I mean an all round drawing out of the best in child and man's body, mind and spirit". By this we can very well understand that Mahatma wanted a harmonious development of the various faculties of human beings.

The Aims of Education—Recommendations of Vivekananda

- Education should create faith in one's own self.
- Education must create self confidence and self reliance through Shradha (Concentration- Self regarding Sentiment).
- Education must develop moral character.
- It should develop the practical side of life.
- Education must promote universal brotherhood.
- Mere book learning is no education.
- It should develop the spirit of renunciation.
- It should develop immense faith in man.

Role of Educational प्देजपजनजपवns

The contributions made by educational institutions have considerable impact on the economic development of a nation. In India, we have developed well due to the growth of literacy rate since the time of independence.

Regarding human values, the educational institutions and ashrams are considered as the right places for teaching ethics and values. But, the reality is not so. Almost all institutions concentrate more and more to cover the syllabus, to make the students well versed in subjects and to secure more marks in the annual examinations. All institutions conduct various programmes like cultural events, sports day, seminars, etc. Various coaching classes are conducted by them to help their students in getting seats in the professional colleges in the case of schools and getting placements in reputed business concerns at the college level. Further, every year some colleges in the urban areas invite a popular film star as a chief guest on college day functions. Lakhs of rupees are spent for such programmes. How many of them try to impart values and ethics to the students? Some two decades back almost in all State board schools, an hour a week was allotted for moral science, where the staff concerned narrated some stories related to ethics and values. We could find some moral behaviour and values among majority of the students. But today's teachers rush to cover the syllabus within the time specified by the heads of the institution. Fashion shows are being conducted frequently by the educational institutions. Cultural programmes are also conducted particularly in English medium schools. Large amount is said to be collected from the students for the costumes and dance practices for the annual day celebrations.

Role of the Teachers

Lack of sincerity in some teachers is a major problem to these teachers have a secure job, they do not seem to bother about the future of the students and their character. In the case of self-financing institutions, due to the problems of the salary and the instructions from the head, teachers give much importance to cover the syllabus only. Due importance is not given by the staff to shape the behaviour and character of the students. At the school level, most of the teachers conduct private tuitions at their home. Due to this reason, they show partiality among the students. There is no personal grievance or motive to blame the teachers. But there is an amount of reality in our statement. Teaching profession is the only profession which gives full mental satisfaction to the teacher. Hence, teaching is called noble profession. But, nowadays, the profession has lost its sanctity. There are many teachers, who render various services to the society apart from teaching. With the help of NSS and other extension activities, teachers involve themselves in the social activities. It is the right time to mention the valuable services rendered by the NSS students and volunteers from the educational institutions at the time of Tsunami. Without any discrimination all the students were involved in rescuing the affected people. It is a minority of insincere teachers that fetches a bad name for the entire noble community. In general the sincerity of the teachers when discharging their duty is gradually reduced.

Role of the Parents

The parents contribute much for the development of culture, values and behaviour of the all students, because most of the time the students are with their parents. In olden days, there was joint family system in almost all parts of the country. The children were brought up under the care of all the family members along with the parents. The elders in the family i.e., grandfather and grandmother normally used to tell some stories with morals and ethics. But nowadays, due to nuclear family system, the children are brought up and cared by parents only. If the parents are employed or engaged in some business activities, nobody is there in the family to look after the children up to schooling. In many families, children are brought up and cared with the help of aayas or servant maid, where we cannot expect teaching of human values or good culture to the children. Parental love is also missing. Some children are put in hostel due to the problems and misunderstanding between father and mothers, which creates depression in the minds of the children.

Role of the Government

It is the duty of the government to provide all infrastructure facilities and other amenities to the society. In education also, the government plays vital role. The curriculum is framed as per the instructions from the government authorities. The modern curriculum pattern should have provisions for teaching values and ethics to the students at all levels of education. Government is the apex body to maintain law and order within the domestic area of the nation. The officials and executives of the government are the representatives, who should take necessary action to maintain law and order.

Role of Press and Media

Press and media are considered to be the fourth pillar of a nation. They have to publish genuine and quality information in their dailies, weeklies, monthlies etc. In earlier days, we could see the quality in all information disseminated by the press. But nowadays commercialization has leads a decrease in the quality of information carried by the press and media. The press and media must be impartial and should partake the responsibility of creating a sense of social awareness among the reading — public.

Role of Film Industry

The film industry is playing important role in influencing the behaviour of the students. All students and public are easily attracted by the incidents and events exhibited in the cinema. The students are heavily attracted by the styles and costumes followed by the film stars. This powerful media along with the television programmes, if rightly used can bring about the desired changes in the youth.

Problems that Influence the Students

- Curriculum does not have any measures or syllabi for teaching values and ethics to the students.
- The family background of the students lead to influence the behaviour and character of the students.
- Managements are keenly interested only in improving the reputation of the institution.
- Parents have limited time to look after the children as they are employed or engaged in some other activities.
- To Glamour and extravaganza displayed in films, to some extent, have a negative impact among the students.
- Some students get their admissions because of money play or power play shattering the value of education. This has a considerable impact on the behaviour and values of the students.
- Teachers are concerned only with covering the syllabus and condition the students to secure high marks. So, teaching of values and ethics to the students has become a rare commodity in educational institutions.
- Media do not take enough initiatives to convey the values and ethics to the society as a whole.
- Due to nuclear family system the possibility of teaching values and ethics to the children in the family, has become remote.

Suggestions for Improving the Ethics and Values in Educational Institutions

- Curriculum should be framed separately for teaching moral values among the students. The government should take necessary steps regarding this issue as early as possible.
- Media should also focus on ethics and values of human beings.
- Film industries should try to minimize the use of terror in the film and should produce films to inculcate the social culture and values.
- Separate hours should be allotted for moral classes and teaching of ethics to the students.
- The parents should have proper watch over their children's activities and frequently they have to visit the school or college where there are studying.
- Teachers are the role model of students at all levels of education. So much care should be taken by the teachers to improve the values and spirituality among the students.

- Joint family system can be given importance by the parents so that children learn values and ethics from elders in the family.
- The management in educational institutions should try to provide reasonable pay scale to all the staff members so that the teachers themselves voluntarily come forward to shape the students with desirable change in their behaviour.
- NGO's and Government should jointly arrange programmes for teaching the values and ethics in the villages as well as in the towns like the Adult Education and Aids Awareness Programme.
- Students should learn and have the capacity to differentiate the events and incidents which are experienced by them in their schooling or collegiate education and adopt the best out of them in their career and in future.

Conclusion

About the aims of education Vivekananda has summed up his ideas in one sentence. "The end of all education, all training should be man- making". It is necessary to create a good man to face problems and lead a peaceful life in the competitive and complex world today. To lead a peaceful life, every man should have values of mankind and ethics. Teaching of ethics and values is nowadays almost missing in many educational institutions, so the community as a whole should be taught with good moral values and behaviour. It is possible only through the educational system. So the management, teachers, parents and government should give a hand of support to teach moral values to the children from the beginning to their college life which will help them to lead a better and prosperous life in their future and will be useful to minimize terror and immoral behaviour among the citizens of the nation.

23

Empowerment of Women Through Education and Some Selected Opinions

Dr. Ram Krishna Mandal

ABSTRACT

The status of women in India has been subject to many great changes over the past few millennia. From equal status with men in ancient times through the low points of the medieval period, to the promotion of equal rights by many reformers, the history of women in India has been eventful. The Indian woman's position in the society further deteriorated during the mediaeval period when Sati among some communities, child marriages and a ban on widow remarriages became part of social life among some communities in India. Still women are fighting hard to get their political justice with limited success in Panchayati Raj Institution where the seats are reserved for 33 per cent of the women. The Women reservation bill is yet to be passed in our parliament which seeks to equalize the advantage of women participation in politics at the national level. Therefore, this made Gandhiji's thinking more relevant as we are still struggling to match his wishes to place women on an equal footing in our male dominated society.

Introduction

Another debated topic in which Government of India as well as the non-government organizations and inter-governmental organizations including UN is taking interest is 'women empowerment'. But it is true that the real development of society is neither possible nor desirable by leaving half of the population in dark and depression. Realizing this virtue Gandhi advocated for the "women empowerment". By supporting women empowerment he writes, "of all the evils for which man has made himself responsible, none is so degrading, so shocking or so brutal as his abuse of the better half of humanity to me, the female sex, not the weaker sex. It is the nobler of the two, for it is even today the embodiment of sacrifice, silent suffering, humility, faith and knowledge. Therefore, he was in favour of educating women and giving them all freedom which men enjoy. He writes, man should learn to give place to woman in the country or community where women are not honoured. He even encouraged the women to join politics hand by hand with man but also warned them to be independent in their thinking without simply carry the wishes of their parents or husbands. When the country was still struggling to escape from the clutches of foreign ruler Gandhiji was thinking about to rescue the women folk from the clutches of parochial caste ridden thinking of Indian male bastion. But this progressive thinking of Gandhiji is yet to be realized even after 64 years of independence of the country. Still women are fighting hard to get their political justice with limited success in Panchayati Raj Institution where the seats are reserved for 33 per cent of the women. The Women reservation bill is yet to be passed in our parliament which seeks to equalize the advantage of women participation in politics at the national level. Therefore, this made Gandhiji's thinking more relevant as we are still struggling to match his wishes to place women on an equal footing in our male dominated society.

Women's empowerment and their full participating on the basis of equality in all spheres of society are fundamental for the achievement of equality, development and peace (IV World Conference on Women, Beijing, 1995). From time immemorial, women have faced the challenges of coping with a male chauvinistic milieu. Even after several years of planned development of India, the status of women in our country is low and their socio-economic conditions are much more depressed than that of men.Empowerment by means of education, literacy or modest income-generating projects is clearly insufficient to ameliorate the prospects for a higher quality of life for women. The process of empowerment is taking place at so many levels that it is quite difficult to gauge the actual nature and extent of empowerment in improving status of women. Certainly the process is entangled in the struggles of civil society against the state, and under the weight of historical practice and on going debates over the appropriate role of ideologies. Women constitute 48 per cent of the Indian population, but when we often sermonize human rights, we often forget that women as human beings are also entitled to fundamental human rights. We have denied and continue to deny them basic human rights. Even after 61 years of independence these women continue to live in a state of neglect and exploitation. The concept of women empowerment was introduced at the International Women's Conference at Nairobi in 1985. The term empowerment was defined as "a distribution of social power and control of resources in favour of women". Empowerment is not something which could be made available in the form of a capsule to those whom we think is in need of it. It is not just a concept that could be defined with the help of some universally accepted parameters. Empowerment is a process and includes the following components:

- Equal access to opportunities for using society's resources.
- Prohibition of gender discrimination in thought and practice.
- Freedom from violence.
- Economic independence.
- Participation in all decision-making bodies.
- Freedom of choice in matters relating to one's life.

The national policy of empowerment of women has set certain clear cut goals and objectives: The goal of this policy is to bring about the advancement, development and empowerment of women. The policy will be widely disseminated so as to encourage active participation of all stakeholders for achieving its goals. Specifically, the objectives of this policy include:

(i) Creating an environment through positive economic and social policies for full development of women to enable them to realize their full potential.

(ii) The enjoyment of all human rights and fundamental freedom by women on equal basis with men in all spheres- political, economic, social, cultural and civil.

(iii) Equal access to participation and decision making of women in social, political and economic life of the nation.

(iv) Equal access to women to healthcare, quality education at all levels, career and vocational guidance, employment, equal remuneration, occupational, safety, social security and public office, etc.

(v) Strengthening legal systems aimed at elimination of all forms of discrimination against women.

(vi) Changing societal attitudes and community practices by active participation and involvement of both men and women.

(vii) Mainstreaming a gender perspective in the development process.

(viii) Elimination of discrimination and all forms of violence against women and the girl child.

(ix) Building and strengthening partnerships with civil society, particularly women's organizations.

Education is central to the process of sustainable development. The role of education in empowerment is not only learning of three 'R's (reading, writing and arithmetic) but includes:

- Raising awareness;
- Critical analysis of various structures; and
- Acquiring knowledge for empowerment at all levels.

Education should include not only formal education but also skill training and functional literacy. First and foremost of all is to demystify the myth that girls are not sent to school because they are girls and in view of their primary role as mothers and housewives. Girls and women are not only housewives and mothers but they are also 'workers' in the economic sense. They should be educated to perform an indispensable role in the home and in the household economy, as well as for bringing enlightenment and emancipation. Empowerment of women through education will develop:

- Self-esteem and self-confidence of women;
- A positive image of women by recognizing their contribution to the society, polity and economy;
- Ability to think critically;
- Decision-making abilities and action through collective process;
- Choices in areas like education, employment and health;
- Equal participation in development process;
- Knowledge and skill for economic independence; and
- Access to legal literacy and information relating to their rights.

Women of today certainly play a vital role in the development of the society. Man's natural tendency is to remain happy. For attaining peace, happiness and full fledged satisfaction, we require certain basic steps. One such step is 'Women Empowerment'. Women Empowerment through education is considered as the only effective instrument of their capacity building. There is always a high degree of correlation between the attainment of education and the level of economic development. This notion is true both at the macro and micro level. If education plays a pivotal role in designing the course of development, it is the women folk that form the primary element of the development process. The pre-requisite in the development process is their empowerment and the initiatives for empowerment should, obviously, begin with education. The deprivations of women are significantly visible in various macro indicators like education, health, employment etc. In different spheres of life they are also subject to a lot of hurdles, which are necessarily gender specific. Sincere effort is urgently required for the emancipation of women from all distress. The significance of women empowerment has gathered momentum over the years. It is also reflected in the recent Union Budgets of the Government of India. The 7th Five Year Plan had adopted the Women's Component Plan (WCP) to initiate a mechanism for identifying and monitoring the schemes, directly benefiting women. In the 9th Plan, provision was made for allocating unconditional minimum quantum of funds for the women welfare related schemes run by the different Ministries/ Departments. The WCP was the precursor of Gender Budgeting. The 10th Plan went a step further when it decided to launch Gender Budgeting. In 2004-05, the Ministry of Women and Child development, Government of India had adopted "Budgeting for Gender Equity" as a Mission Statement. Finally based on the recommendations of the Ashok Lahiri Committee on "Classification of Budgetary Transactions", the Government of India has introduced a statement on Gender budgeting in Union Budget 2005-06. It included 10 demands for grants. The Gender Budgeting is, now, well institutionalized in India. The Draft Approach Paper to the 11th Five Year Plan aimed "Towards Faster and More Inclusive Growth" (Planning Commission, June 14, 2006). Its objective is to include the excluded and it gives stress on 'Gender Balancing'. All the steps echo the concern of the nation for women, for their overall development, and thus empowerment. The Government has recognized that education is the primary step towards women's empowerment. The policy of the Government gives stress on the removal of illiteracy among women and all the hurdles towards their access to education.

In India, at present, there are as many as 1578 women's colleges. Along with this, there are five universities exclusively for women. Today the importance of education in capacity building and empowerment is no longer any unfamiliar notion. If basic education forms the preliminary step of women's progress, the higher education is, perhaps, the best medium to ensure social, economic and political empowerment of women in India. When any one talks about women empowerment, the topic involves a large number of issues like economic opportunity, social equality, political representation, participation in governance, property right. The agenda is always to remove the gender-based asymmetry in all events. All the gender-asymmetrical issues in all events against the women can be removed through enlightening of education.

For centuries, under an artificial dispensation, women's intrinsic qualities had been suppressed, and they were forced to live a wretched life. Not being counted as human beings, women did not even have voting rights.

The statement recalled that it was on March 8, 1857, in New York City that the Suffragette movement had brought a new awakening. Making it clear that women were no less capable then men, a sustained movement for women's rights had been launched.

Accordingly, the United Nations General Assembly had declared March 8 as International Women's Day, the statement noted, adding that this day is an occasion to examine how far the goals of equality among the sexes, peace and development have been achieved.

It is only when men and women work hand in hand that the economic and political problems facing Arunachal Pradesh can be successfully resolved (*The Assam Tribune,* 12th March 2007).

A manual, developed after a year long intensive research by the Gender Training Institute (GTI) of the Delhi-based Center for Social Research, deals with crimes related to dowry, illegal trafficking and domestic violence.

"The law is the same for both men and women. However, if those who implement it (policemen) lack sensitivity towards women's problems, that gets reflected in their behaviour," say Sucharita of the Purogami Mahila Sangathan, a national women's organization that has been active for close to two decades.

However, Kiran Bedi, India's best known policewoman feels that on its own, the manual will struggle to solve problems related to the way the police treat women. Welcoming it as a significant step, she says, "The manual is a very clear roadmap which tells the trainer exactly what path he should take. However, the problem may lie not with the trainer, or the training method, but with the trainee", she says (*The Telegraph,* 12th July 2006).

Former Human Resource Development Minister Arjun Singh said, it is civil society to understand that a nation can only progress if the women are literate, since the child learns his words from her. The country can only be proud when the rate of literacy among all sections of society is high.

Women's empowerment and their full participating on the basis of equality in all spheres of society are fundamental for the achievement of equality, development and peace (IV World Conference on Women, Beijing, 1995).

From time immemorial, women have faced the challenges of coping with a male chauvinistic milieu. Even after several years of planned development in India, the status of women in our country is low and their socio-economic conditions are much more depressed than that of men.

Former M.P. Murlidhar Bhandare said it was necessary for the Govt. to take programmes of the female literacy on a war-footing and ensure that adequate funds are put at the disposal of the implementing agencies and non-Govt. organizations for the purpose (*The Arunachal Times*, 4th September, 2005).

The resolution on the National Policy on Education (1968) stressed the importance of women education in these words, "The education of girls should receive emphasis not only on grounds of social justice but also because it accelerates social transformation".

The United Nations Declaration on the Elimination of Discrimination against Women (1967) took note of the great contribution made by women to social, political, economic and cultural life and the part they play in the family and particularly in the rearing of children and recommended the following in Article 9 of the Declaration: "All appropriate measures shall be taken to ensure to girls and women, married or unmarried, equal rights with men in education at all levels and in particular".

(a) Equal conditions of access to and study in educational institutions of all types, including universities and vocational, technical and professional schools;

(b) The same choice of curricula, the same examinations, teaching staff with qualifications of the same standards and school premises and equipment of the same quality, whether the institutions are co-educational or not;

(c) Equal opportunities to benefit from scholarships and other study grants;

(d) Equal opportunities for access to programmes of continuing education, including adult literacy programmes; and

(e) Access to educational information to help in ensuring the health and well-being of families.

Phenomenal Progress Since Independence

Education is a vital channel to prepare people for the kind of effective role mentioned above, to achieve a sound democratic system, with full knowledge of the citizens' duties and rights. The benefits of education are many. Education is the best investment that a country could make, of lasting benefit.

Importance of education of women has been recognized since the achievement of independence. Accordingly strenuous efforts have been made in this area. The following figures in Table-1 reveal that literacy among women has increased proportionately as compared with men. Yet much more is needed to bring it at pat with men.

Table 23.1: Sex wise Literacy Rate 1951-2001 in India

Year	% Literate	Male	Female
1951	18.33	27.16	8.86
1961	28.31	40.46	15.34
1971	34.45	45.95	21.97
1981	43.56 (41.42)	56.37 (53.45)	29.75 (28.46)
1991	52.11	63.86	39.42
2001	55.30	64.13	45.84

Source: Census of India, Various Issues.

Notes: (i) Literacy rate for 1951, 1961 and 1971 related to population aged five years and above. The rates for the years 1981 and 1991 relate to the population aged seven years and above. The literacy rates for the population aged five years and above in 1981 have been shown in brackets.

(ii) The 1981 rates exclude Assam where the 1981 Census could not be conducted. The 1991 Census rates exclude Jammu and Kashmir where the 1991 Census was not conducted.

The number of women per hundred men since 1950 to 2000 is depicted in following Table 23.2 in India. From the very beginning the women were much lagging behind the men but in the later part they are getting much progress in the field of higher education.

Table 23.2: Number of Women per Men in Higher Education Since 1950-51

Year	Number of Women per Hundred Men
1950-1951	14
1960-1961	17
1965-1966	24
1981-1982	38
1982-1983	39
1983-1984	40
1985-1986	42
1987-1988	46
1988-1989	46
1989-1990	47
1990-1991	47
1999-2000	55

Source: Ministry of Human Resource Development, Department of Education.

Causes of Slow Progress of Women Education

(a) Economic backwardness of the rural community.

(b) Lack of proper social attitudes in the rural areas for the education of girls.

(c) Lack of educational facilities in rural areas.

(d) Lack of women teachers.

(e) Lack of proper supervision an guidance due to inadequate women personnel in the Inspectorate.

(f) Lack of proper incentives to parents and children.

(g) Lack of adequate incentives.

(h) Lack of suitable curriculum.

Some Selected Opinions

Former President Dr. A.P.J. Abdul Kalam, said, "Empowering women is a prerequisite for creating a good nation, When women are empowered, society with stability is assured. Empowerment of women is essential as their thoughts and their value systems lead the development of a good family, good society and ultimately a good nation".

Jawaharlal Nehru once said, "To awaken the people, it is women who is meant to be awakened, once she is on the move, the family moves, village moves and the nation moves".

Again, Jawaharlal Nehru stated once, "Truly no argument is required in defense of women's education. For my part, I have always been strongly of the opinion that while it may be possible to neglect men's education it is not possible to neglect women's education. The reasons are obvious. If you educate the women, probably men will be affected thereby, and in any event children will be affected".

M.K. Gandhi in his *True Education* said clearly, "As for women's education I am not sure whether it should be different from men's and when it should begin. But I am strongly of the opinion that women should have the same facilities as men and even special facilities where necessary.The question of the education of children cannot be solved unless efforts are made simultaneously to solve the women's education. And I have no hesitation in saying that as long as we do not have real mother teachers who can successfully impart true education to our children they will remain uneducated even though they may be going to schools. She must have special knowledge of the management of the home, care of children, their education, etc."

Again, Mohandas K. Gandhi stated, "There is no occasion for women to consider them subordinate or interior to men".

Dr. Radhakrishnan has very emphatically stated, "Women are human beings and have as much right to full development as men have. The position of women in any society is a true index of its cultural and spiritual level".

Netaji Subhash Chandra Bose said, "The best means of conquering lust are to visualize the mother image in all women, to invest women with the hello and to worship God in the mother form, such as Durga and Kali. When man contemplates God or Guru in the form of the Mother, we learn to see divinity in all women. ..."

Swami Vivekananda also once said, "There is no chance for the welfare of the world unless the condition of women is improved. It is not possible for a bird to fly on one wing". Likewise no nation can flourish keeping half of its population in negligence and ignorance, as women constitute half of its human capital. A modern society cannot bring all round development without utilizing the talent of its women.

If you do not raise the women who are living embodiment of the Divine Mother, don't think that you have any other way to rise. All nations have attained greatness, by paying proper respects to the women. That country and that nation which does not respect the women have never become great, not will ever be in future. You will find in the Vedic and Upanishadic age Maitreyi, Gargi and other ladies of revered memory have taken the place of Rishis. In an assembly of a thousand Brahmanas who were all erudite in the Vedas Gargi boldly challenged Yajnavalkya in a discussion about Brahman. —Swami Vivekananda (1863-1902) (*The complete Works of Swami Vivekananda, Vol. VII*).

The union of man and women will represent a perfect co-operation in the building up of human history on equal terms in every department of life. [Rabindranath Tagore (1861-1941)]

According to Vedas, women should have opportunity to attain knowledge of Vedas from all the four corners. —Atharved: 14.1.64.

In Vedas, woman has been called updeshtri of knowledge and this indicates women as teachers. —Rigved: 1.3.11.

From the point of view of reverence due, a teacher is tenfold superior to mere lecturer, a father a hundredfold to teacher and mother a thousandfold to father. —Mnusmriti: 2.145.

Where women are respected, there the gods delight, and where they are not there all work and efforts come to naught. There is no hope of rise for that family or country where they live in sadness. —Manusmriti.

Atreyi's reply was that 'In this region several savant sages like Agastya, etc., reside. I am coming from the ashram of Valmiki to study Vedas from them'. Clearly indicates women's educational pursuits in ancient India. – Uttar Ramcharitmanas: 2.3.

Indeed, if the education is to have its maximum result, it must begin even before birth. The part of education which the mother has to go through is to see that her thoughts are always beautiful and pure, her feelings always noble and fine, her material surroundings as harmonious as possible and full of a great simplicity. —Aurobindo [(1987-1950)].

"Several forms of gender discrimination emerged from a contradiction in the Indian Constitution. It ensures equality for all before law and prohibits discrimination on grounds of religion, race, caste, sex, or place of birth but it also guarantees freedom of religion — the right freely to profess, practice, and propagate religion. This provision of religious freedom takes away much of the freedom and equality extended to women by the Constitution".

Prof. S.C.Dube, Sociologist
(Indian Society, NBT, 1990)

"If the Indian civilization has survived for the past several thousand years, while others there have vanished, it is because of our strong sense of culture and morality which is rooted in our families. Central to this is the role of women. Whether the woman is a wife or mother, she has always played a crucial role. Can we afford to vulgarize her"?

Promod Navalkar,
Maharashra Minister of Transport and Culture
(Replies to S. Balakrishnah's question)
The Sunday Times of India, August 6, 1995.

"Education must be illuminated and re-illuminated in the light of the soul.... The new community of girls and women in India must be a community of Light. And Light knows no distinction or creed or community".

Sadhu T.L.Vasvani

"Despite my thirty years of research into the feminine soul, I have not been able to answer... the great question that has never been answered what does a woman want"?

Sigmund Freud

"The history of woman is the history of the continued and universal oppression of one sex by the other. The emancipation of woman is her restoration to equal rights and privileges with men".

Tennesse Claflin

"The history of men's opposition to women's emancipation is more interesting perhaps than the story of that emancipation itself'.

Virginia Woolf

"Why are women ... so much more interesting to men than men are to women"?

Virginia Woolf
(*The Times of India*, 8th March 2007)

Conclusion

Education is a milestone for women empowerment because it enables them to respond to opportunities, to challenge their traditional roles and to change their lives. Similar ideas were supported in International Conference-1994. It was said that Education is one of the most important means of empowering women with the knowledge, skills and self-confidence necessary to participate fully in the development process. Educating woman benefits the whole society. It has a more significant impact on poverty and development than men's education. It is also one of the most influential factors in improving child health and reducing infant mortality. At least 60 million girls lack access to primary education and the gender gap in literacy persists till date. Although literacy and school enrolment among both girls and boys have increased dramatically, yet much remains to be done. More and more girls should be enrolled in school, and should complete their schooling. This will become true as the level of education increases. There are signs of progress, as enrolment of boys and girls in primary schools edges closer and closer to parity.

Every year, even at the university level, women are catching up and even surpassing male enrolment in some countries. In Kuwait, Bahrain, the Philippines and Cuba, more women are now enrolling in university than men. Although girls and women's access to education is improving, but they are often channeled into traditionally 'female' fields of study that reinforce their traditional roles in society.

The greater demands for more gender equality and women's empowerment that are being made both socially and politically are certainly not the result of public policy promoting gender equality, but rather emerge from past and present gender oppression and discrimination against women.

REFERENCES

Aggarwal, J.C. (2004): *"Development and Planning of Modern Education"*, Vikas Publishing House Pvt. Ltd. Ed'-8, pp. 273-79.

Ruhela, Sarya (1999): "*Understanding the Indian Women Today: Problems and Challenges*" Indian Publishers' Distributors, Delhi, pp. 164-66.

The Times of India, Thursday, March 8, 2007.

The Arunachal Times, September 4, 2005, Vol. 17 No. 89.

The Assam Tribune, Guwahati, Monday, March 12, 2007.

The Telegraph, Calcutta, Wednesday, July 12, 2006.

Index